LIFE IN THE PAST LANE

MICHAEL O'BRIEN

Life In The Past Lane

First published in Australia by Michael O'Brien 2020

Copyright © Michael O'Brien 2020
All Rights Reserved

 A catalogue record for this book is available from the National Library of Australia

ISBN: 978-0-646-82157-3 (pbk)

Typesetting and design by Publicious Book Publishing
Published in collaboration with Publicious Book Publishing
www.publicious.com.au

No part of this book may be reproduced in any form, by photocopying or by any electronic or mechanical means, including information storage or retrieval systems, without permission in writing from both the copyright owner and the publisher of this book.

Dedicated to the memory
of John and Jean O'Brien

I am the family face;
Flesh perishes, I live on,
Projecting trait and trace
Through time to times anon,
And leaping from place to place
Over oblivion.

Thomas Hardy
Heredity, 1917

Life in the Past Lane

IN THE BEGINNING...[1]

At some stage in our life, we become curious about where we came from. We are told numerous myths by our parents that involve birds and bees and storks and cabbage patches until eventually, we find that we are an end-product of the union between our father and our mother. They were the end-products of unions between their own parents and so on and so on and so on. One day, generally later in your life than earlier, you decide to trace all these unions and discover your heritage. And that's when you start to realise that if you had started the project a wee bit earlier in your life, it might not have been so bloody hard.

I had decided to trim the weeds around my family tree not long after my father passed away, when I found an old letter that had been written to his sister by a distant cousin. The letter was like the blurb on the back of a Dan Brown novel, promising mystery and intrigue if you went further. Then a chance discovery of two rusted biscuit tins full of tiny black and white photographs of my mother's family piqued my interest further. Who were these people and what did they do? A myriad of questions leapt into my head after I had found these family relics – but there was only my mother left to ask questions of, and she was quite ill. It appeared at present, I was running out of future to uncover the past.

Sadly, I did not have the opportunity to meet two of my grandparents as they had passed away well before I was born. However, when I was younger, my father's mother and my mother's father had been alive and kicking. They used to visit our house regularly and I would regard these two people with awe. God, they were old. Really, really, old. My grandmother had shrunk with age - I was convinced that I could wrap her up and put her in my school bag. At Christmas time, she would always give me a pair of socks or a packet of hankies and there would be a scrunched-up five-dollar note for my birthday – a good old-fashioned paper note, not like the money made out of the hardened cling-wrap that we use now. I would have to let my parents purchase my return present - I wasn't sufficiently mature enough to walk into a shop and buy elderly people's smalls.

On the other side of the family, my grandfather, for one reason or another that had not been explained to junior me, lived with us for some time. He wore pale blue cardigans, crisp Fletcher Jones trousers, dark brown Grosby slippers and slicked his hair back with fistfuls of Brylcreem until it looked like each strand had been glued on. He went to the local Senior Citizens Centre and made bowls out of paddle-pop sticks and discarded bathroom tiles. I didn't show any interest in these creations – I was too busy playing cricket, kicking footballs, riding bikes or watching Marty and Emu on an enormous piece of furniture that we called a television. There was no doubt in my Sunnyboy-and-Redskins-addled mind that I was going to become a famous footballer or a cricketer or an astronaut or something. I simply didn't have time for these old people.

And isn't that a shame?

My grandfather died in 1979, my grandmother in 1994 and I still hadn't learned to appreciate them. All I had learned in those years was that I wasn't going to be a famous footballer or a cricketer or an astronaut, but I had discovered the existence and the delights of girls and alcohol. My previous experiences with these things had been unremarkable and uninspiring. Girls couldn't play cricket, couldn't kick a football, they had long hair, they smelled funny, they played silly games and their willies had broken off. As for alcohol, I had watched my father drink fluid from gold-coloured cans that were labelled "KB" and the more of them he drank, the more he laughed, the more lop-sided he became and the more he thought he was Al Martino. I remember thinking that when I am older, I'll drink this KB thing and I too can be a grown-up.

You must remember I was only young.

So, basically cricket and football and the moon and girls and beer in a gold can had stood in the way of me developing a substantial relationship with my grandparents. All I have left of their legacy are some yellowing hankies and a broken paddle-pop stick bowl. I could have asked them about their lives and their families and their experiences. For instance, my grandmother was born in 1895. 1895? Australia, as we know it now, did not exist. It was only a handful of colonies that would not become a federation for another six years. There was no Prime Minister. Queen Victoria was on the throne of the United Kingdom; Orville and Wilbur Wright were still on the ground and not destined to change that status for a while; x-rays had only just been discovered; Ethiopia and Italy were at war; a bloke called Grover Cleveland was President of the United States; the first modern Olympics were a year away; Oscar Wilde went to jail for his non-heterosexual activities and George Selden patented the first gasoline-driven car. Bushranger, Ned Kelly, had been dead for only fifteen years. Elsewhere in the world, some people only had seventeen more years to live before a giant ship called the *Titanic* took them to the bottom of the ocean. My grandmother had lived a long life. In her time, she had seen six different British monarchs, nine Catholic popes and twenty-four different Australian Prime Ministers – not to mention two world wars. My grandmother had been living history.

Now that I am older and have developed a keen interest in my family tree, I have a thousand questions. But there is no one left to answer them. As I walk along the path in the forest, my feet are brushing the fallen leaves and I find I am disturbing what is underneath. The path is not clear and there is a mist circulating around me. I could have had guides to help me through the forest but I am on my own now. It is up to me to find my way to the end … which is really the beginning.

In my quest to discover the family tree, I admit I was hoping to find some skeletons in the closet – not only did I find them, they were swigging rum and dancing a wild tango when I got there. The secrets from the past slowly emerged. I didn't know whether these secrets had been hushed up by the family elders, as they sipped tea and whispered quietly, seated in comfortable recliner rockers in beige-coloured living rooms or if the winds of time had blown them out of their memories. It didn't matter; my job was to uncover the secrets, not pass judgement upon them.

This book tells the tales of many journeys. It tells of people who left their homeland and everything they knew and came to an unknown country in search of a new and better life. Some of them had no choice but to leave -the authorities had decreed it was that or face an appointment with the hangman's noose. Some of my ancestors found a better life in Australia and some did not. But all of them did what they did for one reason – a reason that has kept humans going for centuries. Survival. For some people, the unknown is better than the known.

It is also an insight into historical times and what my family experienced within that chronology. To know what year your ancestor was born is interesting; to know what living in that year was like is fascinating. It puts perspective into your family history; it puts life into their lives.

This is their story, my story and history.

1. Roots

By all accounts, Brian Boru was a very powerful man. He was born in Ireland in the tenth century, when life was simpler – that's if you could avoid being robbed, pillaged and hacked to pieces by your neighbours or having a bunch of smelly and unpleasant Norse invaders kick down your door – if you had one – wanting a piece of the action, and you, as well. Brian was the son of Cennétig mac Loráin, the King of Thomond in Munster. After his father and brother, Mathgamain, died, Brian found himself as the new king. But apparently Munster was not enough for him, so he bumped off the King of Limerick and took control of the lands known as Leinster. Soon he had control of the southern half of Ireland and had grand designs on the rest of it. When he wasn't snapping up real estate, he was marrying various chief's daughters and siring numerous children. In time, he became High King of Ireland and developed into the historical figure that people feared and admired and minstrels wrote songs about. Historian, James Lydon, noted that Brian was described as 'a great warrior, shrewd politician and statesmanlike in his dealings with churchmen, kings and foreigners'.[1] But no matter how great you are, when a Viking sword removes vital parts of your body, your number is up. Brian Boru left this world in 1014, a little less intact then when he was born.

However, Brian's name lives on. His offspring were known as Ui Briain (meaning 'descendant of Brian' in old Irish) and over the centuries, this name was changed to O'Brien and several other deviations – much to the chagrin of the English. As far back as the 14th century, they had decided that the Irish had become too

---

1. James Lydon, *The Making of Ireland, Routledge,* London, 1998, pg 32

independent so they banned the use of Irish names and spelling. The Irish would revert to traditional names when the overlords from across the sea weren't around. But whatever way you spell it, my family tree is done. I'm descended from Irish royalty. Yep, just me, and the millions of other people who share that surname. And if that's not bad enough, the job of High King of Ireland seems to have been made redundant. Further research showed that even if the position were to become valid again, I would still miss out. It seems, at the time of writing, there is a man who has more of a claim due to his good self being recognised as chief of the O'Brien clan. His name is Sir Conor Myles John O'Brien and his official title is: The O'Brien, Prince of Thomond, Chief of the Name, the 18th Baron Inchiquin, the 10th Baronet of Leamaneh. And if that title is a bit hard to shout across a crowded pub at closing time, his mates call him – 'The Great Condor'. So that was making me feel like I was somewhat down the pecking order. My dreams of golden palaces, guards of honour, horse-drawn carriages, buxom serving wenches and coins bearing my profile will have to be shelved, along with the Christmas Day message I had been writing. There is no throne for me.

Okay. I'll have another go. My mother's maiden name was Kingdom. In 1799, Sophia Kingdom (a daughter of my great-great-great-great-great-great grandfather's brother – yeah, I know it's tenuous) married Marc Isambard Brunel and one of their children was the great English engineer, Isambard Kingdom Brunel. So I'm extremely-vaguely related to a genius.

Sad, aren't I?

Oh well. To escape my disappointment, I would return to my study of Ireland but make a leap through time and leave the Dark Ages behind. I would leave the people of that period to their days of fighting, land-grabbing, treachery and civil unrest and I would move forward eight hundred years to where I would find … er … fighting, land-grabbing, treachery and civil unrest. The year is 1839 and we're in County Limerick, on the western side of Ireland. The threat of rampaging Vikings has gone as the raiders had integrated themselves into the community. But there is another threat – poverty. The common folk are doing it tough. During the previous fifty years, the population of Ireland had increased dramatically. The wars with Napoleon's forces were over – wars that had kept the Irish busy for over twenty years, whether as soldiers or providing the catering. The soldiers returned home to find that the rich landowners had decided to raise cattle instead of crops. There is less land for the people to live on and less employment. A German travel writer, Johann Kohl, visited Ireland and wrote –

> 'Until one has seen the west of Ireland, he has no idea that human beings can live in a state of greater misery than in the fertile environs of Dublin.'[2]

The government had introduced the Poor Relief Act, making wealthier people responsible for the care of the poor in their area. This was a band-aid solution and the politicians had to come up with a better plan. They had too many people and not enough land. The Irish situation was similar across the sea in England, but the English were overcrowded with criminals as well as the poor. The prisons were stuffed to the brim and they couldn't hang everyone – someone would eventually complain. So they had decided to put their prisoners on ships and sail them off to the newly-found colonies. Sweep them under the carpet and that takes care of that. There was plenty of room in Australia – in the bits they had seen, anyway – so maybe the Irish problem could be solved in the same way. The Government called for expressions of interest from the Irish population – anyone care for a spot of emigration? The response was overwhelming.

One of the first ships out of Cork harbour was the *Aliquis*. There were nearly three hundred people on board – people who had made a momentous life-changing decision. They had a choice between staying in Ireland and living a life of quiet desperation while they slowly starved to death – or they could pack up their stuff, sail thousands of miles across oceans in a rat-infested ship with no guarantees that they would actually survive the voyage, to finally arrive in an unknown land that England used for a prison.

What would you have chosen?

---

2. Johann Georg Kohl, *The British Isles and Their Inhabitants,* Chapman & Hall, London, 1844

On the *Aliquis,* there was a family of eight from the village of Loughill in Limerick. The father was a stonemason named Mathew O'Brien, aged 50, and he was married to Catherine, a 45-year old dressmaker. They were joined by their six children: Mary aged 24, Sarah 22, Ellen 18, Catherine 13, John 11 and Thomas who was 5. The more perceptive amongst you would see that I am leading into something here and you are right; they were my ancestors. Mathew was my great-great-great grandfather; John, my great-great grandfather. I'm sure many Australian dynasties started from the passengers on this ship and there are many stories that could be told – but we will just deal with this one.

The emigrants were allowed only one chest to store their worldly belongings in – which appears to be the precursor of carry-on baggage limits. The journey took a little over three months which was quick for those days and only seven people died on the trip - also close to a record. This was no P&O cruise. There was no swimming pool, no deckchairs, no cocktails, and no fun.

"I spy with my little eye, something beginning with 'W'."

"Ah … water."

"Very good … your turn."

"I spy with my little eye, something starting with 'W'."

"Is it … water?"

To assist passing the time, the people would make their beds (which was more like a hammock), sleep, make their beds again, unpack their chest, pack their chest, sing some songs, dance a little jig, then attend a divine service to repent all their sins. And then do it again. For ninety-nine days. On the 16th March 1839, the *Aliquis* finally sailed through the domineering and frightening rocky heads of Port Jackson and passed a triangular-shaped protrusion called Pinchgut Island. The island probably displayed the rotting and bird-pecked body of an executed criminal swinging from a gibbet – a marketing feature that NSW Tourism have not used for a while. The O'Brien's would then have their first glance of Sydney Cove.

Can you imagine what those people felt as they leaned on the ship's rail, looking with wide-eyed awe at this new landscape? No green and pleasant lands here. Were their first impressions one like – "Oh Sweet Mother of God, this is exciting and it marks the beginning of a new life!" or was it more like – "Oh Sweet Mother of God, what the feck have we done?" And what were the sights that greeted these emigrants? Charles Darwin had arrived in Sydney only three years earlier and this is what he thought:

> "Having entered the harbour, it appeared fine and spacious; but the level country, showing on the cliff-formed shores bare and horizontal strata of sandstone, was covered by woods of thin scrubby trees that bespoke useless sterility … In the distance stone houses, two and three storeys high, and windmills, standing on the edge of a bank, pointed out to us the neighbourhood of the capital of Australia."[3]

So far, so good – however, the weather was very warm and the colony was suffering from drought. The people on board, who must have been itching to put their feet on dry land, had to stay on board while they were checked by the quarantine people to see if they were itching from something else. Then they had to wait for the emigration people to check all the paperwork. Please, the passengers might have prayed - let us stand on this shore under the blue, welcoming sky and let us embrace our new home.

While they waited, a bloody big ship called the *Prince Regent* crashed into the *Aliquis*. According to the *Sydney Gazette* and *New South Wales Advertiser,* the pilot of the *Prince Regent* attempted to steer across the bows of the *Aliquis,* failing to allow for a strong tide and a lack of sail. The *Prince Regent* was the fourth different ship the pilot had brought into the harbour and only one of them had escaped undamaged. The passengers of the *Aliquis* managed to eventually disembark and the ship itself stayed in the harbour for another month. It set sail for Calcutta on April 21st and twenty-four days later, sank in the Torres Strait.

Back to the family. They would have stood on the shore of Sydney Cove and stared at this strange world. While sailors scurried amongst the emigrants, unloading precious cargoes, the O'Brien's could see the sandstone outcrop to the west, behind the area known as Dawes

---

3. Charles Darwin, *The Voyage of The Beagle,* London, 1839

Point. It was littered with a rag-taggle collection of houses with rivulets of human waste pouring down through cracks in roughly-hewn stairs. People were lurching drunkenly up and down the dirt-covered roads. That area is now known as the Rocks and for one of the O'Brien's, it would become both heaven and hell. Over to the east was Bennelong Point and a basic version of the Botanical Gardens we know today. Behind the gardens they would have seen the mansions of Woolloomooloo, Government House, a church, an infirmary, and a prison. In front of the O'Brien's was the colony's original water supply and sewerage outflow, the Tank Stream, which dripped water, rotting garbage and dead animals into the harbour. A thoroughfare called George-street ran southwards and the early shops fought for customers while stray dogs fought for scraps. The O'Brien's, having taken all this in, would have been marshalled towards Philip-street and the Emigration barracks. Here, they would be offered work and their new life would begin.

Mathew O'Brien, being a stonemason and able to read and write, found work quickly and the family settled in Druitt-street. However, some of them didn't settle there for long. Daughters, Mary and Sarah, apparently must have found their own form of entertainment on the voyage as both were married within five months of arriving in Australia. The O'Brien girls wed two unrelated O'Brien boys – Mary to Daniel and Sarah to Patrick. As both the lads were from Limerick, it is entirely possible they knew the girls before embarkation. Sadly, Mary was destined for only six more years on earth; she died in 1845 with two young children and a husband left behind. As she died before the introduction of compulsory death certification in 1856, there are very few details on her demise. Was the different environment and climate too much for her? Her parents, Mathew and Catherine, had brought the family halfway around the world; there must have been some days when they asked themselves – Have we done the right thing?

2. Taking Leaves off our Census

It was 1841 and time to leave our adventurous Irish folks for a while. We will head back to the United Kingdom and make our way to the west of England. It is census time and the government wanted to know who you are, what you were doing and who you were doing it with.

We will focus on Knowstone, a town in north Devon. George Kingdom, who in various documents is also known as Kingdon, was an agricultural labourer. George's baptismal date was 27th December 1813 but the census of 1841 has him aged 25. During my research, I found several inconsistencies with ages and there maybe a couple of reasons for this. Firstly, the census takers of yesteryear were somewhat liberal with their recording – the rounding-up or down of ages to the nearest five was very popular. Also the education level of the lower classes wasn't high; George was illiterate and seemingly remained that way for the whole of his life. It is extremely possible that, as the years went by, George simply had no idea of how old he was. But one thing is certain; he was from a big family. One Kingdom family researcher has him listed as one of seventeen children and these children seemed to pop out annually, like the flowers in the back garden. However, judging by the repetition of several names on the list, some of the flowers didn't last long. If a child died in those days, it was common to name the next-born child of that sex with the same name as the deceased one. On the 1841 census, there are only seven Kingdoms listed at the one address; death, marriage and being sent out to work had reduced the family.

It did seem unusual to me that George was in his 20s and still living at home with his middle-aged (and probably exhausted) parents and his younger siblings. Further investigation and input from Kingdom family expert, Peter Holden, pointed out a reason why. George had been a bit naughty – when he wasn't labouring with agriculture, he was labouring in prison. In March of 1836, he had been convicted of larceny and sentenced to six month's imprisonment. June of 1840 saw him in front of the judge again on the same charge and he received the same punishment. George was released from the lock-up just in time for the census.

Across the county border, in Somerset there is a town called South Petherton. It is only 78 kilometres from Knowstone and if the people of those days had what we now have, the trip would have taken just over an hour. But the 1840s were simple times and there was no such thing as the A361 motorway (WARNING: SPEED CAMERAS), the A358, the Taunton Deane Service Area (ROAD CHEF) or the Southfields Roundabout which adorn the route today. At the end of the trip, however, is the Tything of Over Stratton. In 1841, one dwelling there housed the Coller family and they had a fifteen-year old lad living with them named John Elliott. The orphaned John was like George Kingdom; he too was an agricultural labourer – but then so was every working male on that page of the census. Not far away in the same town, was a family named Edmonds. They also had a herd of agricultural labourers in the family apart from a daughter, who made gloves. Her name was Susan and she was nineteen years old.

It's possible that John and Susan were aware of each other in 1841 but if they weren't, it wouldn't be for long. They might have conversed at agricultural labourer's work functions. No doubt the Christmas parties at Over Stratton were riveting affairs with many a story about crops, bracken and soil entertaining the throng. But jokes aside, John, Susan and George lived in hard times. A report by the Parliamentary Commission of Enquiry into the state of the poor revealed some 2,300,000 people of the working classes were living in a state of utter destitution. Like Ireland, unemployment was high and food was scarce. The basic recommendation of the Commission was to ship out the poor to North America and Australia because it was cheaper than keeping them at home. The only way the country could look after its people was by sending them to another one. The ironic aspect of the emigrant matter is that on the fifth of July 1841, a man named Thomas Cook opened the first ever travel agency. I'm sure his clients weren't travelling abroad just so they could find their next meal.

Back in Australia, the O'Brien's were splitting up. Son-in-law, Patrick, a carpenter, strangely hadn't been able to find work in Sydney so he had taken his wife, Sarah, to Melbourne in 1840. It would have been a momentous decision; the southern settlement had only been in existence for five years and the major problem was getting there. The country was still in drought, fresh food on the journey was hard to find and there was the danger of attacks from natives and/or bushrangers. As there was no XPT or Jetstar, the transport was by horse and cart or by foot – and that is a long walk. Patrick appeared to have made a good decision, though; within sixteen years he had become a respected businessman, a member of the Legislative Assembly of Victoria and an owner of a mansion and considerable parcels of land within the state.

On the 18th October 1841, the third eldest O'Brien daughter, Ellen, married a chap called John Kennedy and they had a son named Robert in 1842. Only fifteen-year old Catherine, fourteen-year old John and eight-year old Thomas were left at home now. John followed his father into the stonemasonry business and they would have been kept busy as the town of Sydney grew. A look through the pages of the *Sydney Gazette and New South Wales Advertiser* found an article, first published in England by the *Morning Chronicle* :

> 'It is quite evident that Sydney has become a busy, bustling, important, gossiping, visiting and in fact, Londonish, kind of place. There are two theatres, four newspapers, a concert room, police offices, fancy dress balls, races, floral and horticultural shows, sales by auction, law courts, meetings of the legislative council and public companies. There are shops stocked to the ceiling with goods of every description, fashionable tailors, hatters, dressmakers, milliners, linendrapers [sic] and haircutters.'[1]

There was also an enormous amount of pubs. In the list of publican's licences granted in May 1841, I counted 33 in George-street,

---

1. *Sydney Gazette and New South Wales Advertiser,* 3rd August 1841

15 in Pitt-street, 10 in Castlereagh-street, 14 in Sussex-street, 7 in Kent-street and 10 in York-street – not to mention numerous others and the illegal sly home stills that were present in the town. However, the thirsty O'Brien's would have had to walk further to the pub than most because there weren't any in Druitt-street. This may have something to do with the presence of the police office on the corner of Druitt- and George-streets. The coppers were busy back then; over two nights in May, the Police Court dealt with 143 cases of drunkenness. If you did go for a drink, you could be scoffing down glasses of Batson's Ale, Taylor's Porter, Teneriffe Wine, Mondella Brandy, St Julian claret and Jamaican Superior rum. After a pub crawl in Sydney, you could wake up and find yourself dead – or at least wishing you were. And if you did wake up alive, you might find yourself in the lockup.

Then maybe the O'Brien's didn't drink. They may have found other ways to pass the time. They may have strolled down to Harper's Wharf on the corner of Sussex- and Druitt-streets. There they could have donned their Gentlemen's Steam Boat Travelling Caps that they bought from Uther's Hat Manufactory in Pitt-street and boarded the steamer, *William IV*. It would have transported them to East Gosford where they could sample what the newspaper advertisement described as the 'most beautiful scenery, the rural amusements and the intellectual pleasures which are so peculiarly identified with the Brisbane Water District'. (I have lived on the Central Coast for twenty years now – I don't know about the intellectual pleasures, but the peculiar is still here.)

Upon returning from their trip, they could have gone to see John Curr in Pitt-street and picked up some Jew's Eye Tobacco and Screws Scotch Snuff. They could have arranged some finance with the Australian Society for Deposits and Loans, who were offering loans of £20 at the rate of 15% pa. They could have gone to Samuel Lyon's Auction House, which had a bigger range than eBay. One of Lyon's auction lots in April consisted of a ton of glue and various pieces of a shipwreck – but the obvious attraction on the day was the selling of 'two splendid asses'. And if the O'Brien's were a bit more cashed-up, they could have purchased forty acres of land in Camperdown – the land was part of the estate of the former Governor and *Bounty* mutiny survivor, Admiral William Bligh.

But it wasn't all shop to you drop and drink till you drop again. There were unpleasant aspects of life in Sydney, too, as described in an October issue of the newspaper:

> 'Now that the sultry weather is setting in and scarlet fever so prevalent, it is hoped that slaughter-houses, distilleries, butchers shambles [sic] and the marketplace, will be scrupulously attended to by the police, and that the intolerable nuisance of meeting dead dogs, cats, rats and other offensive putridity, in our daily rambles through the town, will be abated.'[2]

The poor old police must have been run off their feet; not only did they have to get the pissheads off the street, they had to worry about the putridity, too.

Still, the idea of a life in Australia beckoned and temptation's luring fingers kept reaching out to Britain. In Knowstone, George Kingdom had been tempted by something else, however – a lady. On the 22nd September 1842, George married twenty-two-year old Charlotte Voysey, in the Knowstone Parish church. His sister, Maria, was a witness and everybody signed the register with their mark, an 'X'. The marriage to Charlotte should have settled him down and kept him on the straight and narrow.

You will notice I said – 'should have'.

---

2. *Sydney Gazette and New South Wales Advertiser,* 5th October 1841

Michael O'Brien

3. Two Funerals and a Wedding

In 1844, Queen Victoria gave birth to her fourth child, Alfred; Charles Dickens gave birth to the novel *Martin Chuzzlewit* and in the late Somerset spring, Susan Edmonds gave birth to a child named George. The father was John Elliott.

George Elliott came into a difficult world. If he lived for another six years – and that was a big if – he would be old enough to go out and work. The Government's Factory Act had recently imposed a maximum 12 hour working day for women and as for children aged 6-13, they could work no more than six hours a day. An organisation called the Ragged Schools Union had been set up so destitute children in industrial areas could receive an education. But there was some good news from the Government - if you found yourself broke, you couldn't be sent to debtor's prison anymore. Ironically, you probably would have got some sort of meal in the prison; outside, with no money, you were a big chance of starving to death.

Elsewhere in the world, Oscar I was King of Sweden and Norway; James Polk was President of the other original English colony, America, and Sir George Gipps was Governor of New South Wales. In Sydney, the people had started to branch out – Paddington had a population of 289, Surry Hills 209 and Botany had 256 people living there. In the CBD, Mathew O'Brien and his family were settling in and trying to make the best of things. They may have even been happy – until tragedy struck in 1845.

Mathew and Catherine's eldest daughter, Mary, passed away. She was thirty-two years old. After a funeral at St Mary's Cathedral on the 25th

February 1845, her parents, brothers and sisters, her husband, Daniel, and her two young children, Catherine and John, would have led the procession to the burial ground. As Sydney's living population was growing, so was its dead one. In 1819, the Sandhills (or Devonshire-street Cemetery) had been established to take the place of the Old Burying Ground, which is now where Sydney's Town Hall is situated. Devonshire-street became the new Old Burying Ground and that is where Mary had been taken to rest in peace.

As one life ended, another two joined together. In South Petherton, Somerset, John Elliott married Susan Edmonds. While times might not have been easy in England, at least the Elliott's weren't living in Ireland, as the potato famine began. The potato was a food that most of the population lived off and the famine, started by diseased potatoes, caused the death of over a million people. A similar number fled the country, in fear of their lives. Those who could afford the fare sailed to America or Australia and they would never see their homeland again.

But 1845 wasn't all doom and gloom as the Industrial Revolution rolled along with its brilliant inventions and creative minds. It was one stunning innovation after another – Henry Jones patented self-raising flour, Stephen Perry invented the rubber band and the work of another genius was rewarded with a patent granted for a product which we now know as the Band-Aid. The proliferation of inventions continued into 1846 as a chap named Mr Sax invented the saxophone. Another two gentlemen both claimed they had discovered a new planet in the night skies and fought quite bitterly about who had seen it first. The planet was Neptune. While they arm-wrestled over celestial bodies, the two royal bodies, Queen Victoria and Prince Albert, were at it again and this time, Princess Helena was the result of the union. How Victoria ever found time to run the empire is beyond me.

Moving on to 1847 and before the couple at Buckingham Palace could pop out another heir destined to be disappointed by the future, John and Susan Elliott popped out another heir, destined to be disappointed by the present. Mary Elliott was born in the same year as Thomas Edison, while Charlotte Bronte published *Jane Eyre,* the opera *Die Fledermaus* premiered and somebody invented the doughnut. In one of the Empire's former colonies, a town in California named Yerba Buena received a new name – San Francisco. This, no doubt, made life easier for future songwriters. In Scotland, a man named Alexander Graham Bell was born and he went on to claim that he invented the telephone – this invention led to many flow-on projects, such as Indian call centres. However, the Indians of that time couldn't take your call, even though it was important to them, as they were busy fighting a war against the British. Across the ocean, the United States had declared war on Mexico.

In Australia, there was to be more sadness for the O'Brien's. Eight years after bringing his family across the globe and hoping that he had brought fresh hope to their existence, Mathew O'Brien died at the age of fifty-seven – although the burial records state that he was sixty-seven. This is probably a typographical error, but he may have lied about his age on the shipping records; he would not have secured a passage to Australia under the Government scheme if he was over 50. His burial certificate is a piece of paper that has little information written on it (and what is written is mostly spelled incorrectly) and pays no tribute to the strength of character and the family loyalty showed by the man. Mathew's remains were taken to the Devonshire-street Cemetery also; he may have been placed near his daughter, Mary, but we will never know.

In 1901, the cemetery had been closed for many years. It was full, it was covered in weeds and overgrown bushes and it was a disgrace. The government had decided to exhume all the bodies and re-inter them at other cemeteries around Sydney i.e. Bunnerong (at the present day Botany cemetery), Rookwood, Camperdown, Gore Hill, South Head and Waverley. Descendants, if they could be found, were advised of the decision and had to apply for the relocation of remains and monuments. If no application was received and the remains could not be identified by a headstone, the government would just dig'em up and plant'em at Rookwood. This appears to be the fate of the O'Brien's. Once the massive undertaking by the undertakers was completed, the block of land at Devonshire Street became the site of Central Railway Station. And ever since the disturbance of the dead from their resting place, the trains have never run on time.

Back to 1847 and in Devon, George Kingdom was in a spot of bother again. He had nicked a chicken from a Mr Benjamin Elston and then George had been nicked. George had quite a record. Less than three months after his marriage to Charlotte back in 1842, it looked as if he had his own little gang, if the following excerpt from *Trewman's Exeter Flying Post* reveals:

> 'Thursday, December 15, 1842. Five poachers, named Richard Joslin, his son, Richard Joslin, aged 24, William Harris (a returned transport), George Kingdon and John Davies, all residents of Southmolton [sic], were detected on the grounds of the Right Hon. Earl Fortescue on the night of the 6th inst., and on the following day were taken before the Rev. William Karslake, by whom they had been committed. One of the keepers received a very severe blow in the arm [sic], it is supposed with a stone-breaking hammer, as one was found on one of the men. His Lordship's preserves, it appears, have been lately much infested by these nocturnal visitors and a large force is nightly employed to detect them.'

The subsequent court case in Devon on the 29th March 1843 resulted in George being put away for eighteen months. Now, back in court again in 1847 on the chicken stealing charge and it seemed that the judge had lost his patience with George. On the 23rd February 1847, George Kingdom was found guilty of larceny and sentenced to seven year's transportation to Australia.

Three weeks later, Charlotte Kingdom, while probably fearing that she would never see her husband again, gave birth to a son. Twenty-two days after George's trial, Charlotte took the little boy, Henry, to the Knowstone Parish church for his baptism. The following day, baby Henry, having never lain eyes on his father, died of unknown causes.

What are those blue remembered hills?
What spires, what farms are those?
That is the land of lost content,
I see it shining plain,
The happy highways where I went
And cannot come again.

A.E. Housman, 1896

4. Something Wicked This Way Comes

By 1848, John and Ellen Kennedy had brought four children into the world; Robert, John, Sarah Anne and William. However, John senior appears to vanish sometime after this year and according to family folklore, he sailed to California in search of gold. Whether he went with wifely permission or if he took off like a rat up a drainpipe is unknown but he left a young brood behind and life for them would have been a struggle.

Sydney appeared to be in the midst of a crime wave. The following shocking classified appeared in the newspaper:

> 'MISSING: A LARGE SILVER GRAVY SPOON WITH A STRAINER IN ITS CENTRE. Mr Lyons, having some months ago lent a spoon of the above description to some person who has not yet returned it, will thank the borrower to do so without delay.'

Days later, while Mr Lyons endured life without gravy, a woman appeared at the Police Court, having been charged by an Inspector of Nuisances (great title, isn't it?) for keeping a pig at an illegal distance from the street. Then a Margaret Faris was sentenced to be confined in Sydney Gaol for stealing a bucket and a saucepan, while an aged female named Catherine Mitchell, 'a notorious drunkard', was found by the police in the George-street burial ground, 'in a state more dead than alive' – but then I thought that was the whole idea. In December of 1848, a Mr Cummins of Lower George-street appeared before the court, having been accused by a Mr Taylor of stealing a valuable parrot. According to the report, 'the bird's flow of language caused the case to last twice as long as it otherwise would have done'.[1] I'm picturing the parrot, perched on the witness box, pointing a wing at Cummins and saying – "RAARKK … he did it".

Considering the colony was only sixty years old and having started with next to nothing, it was amazing that the people of the 1840s could buy just about everything they wanted. Everyday items like a dozen eggs could be bought for a sixpence while a ton of potatoes would set you back six pounds. B. S. Lloyd, of 489 George-street could sell you pill machines, ointment jars, enemas, breast pumps, night floats and turkey sponges. If you were feeling unwell, Holloway's Medicine (available from J. K. Heydon at 78 King-street and other selected stockists) could be used with 'the greatest confidence' for the treatment of blotches on the skin, dysentery, constipation, headaches, sore throats, weakness, piles, dropsy, rheumatism and 'the turn of life'. And once you were over your various maladies, you could pop into the Fancy Ware Depot in Hunter-street for some Chinese vermillion, fencing foils, boxing gloves, billiard balls, cricket bats, fireworks or artificial eyes for birds and beasts. The store was run by a Mr Henry Parkes – a man soon destined for a life away from retail.

While the Australians found new ways to spend money, the British were relying on the old ways. The bill for stationery used in the houses of Parliament came to £295,518 which equates to around twenty-six million dollars today. The cost of rural police in England and Wales was over 196,000 pounds (that's around 17 million dollars and means they spent more money on paper and quills than they did on police), and the 4,972 lawyers in London cost a staggering £16,210,165 (over one and a half billion dollars). The prisons were full again, bursting at the seams with common criminals. The British government had ceased convict transportation in 1840 but the foreign secretary, Earl Grey, was keen to start it up again. He was that keen that he appears to have started the ball rolling without official approval. In a session of British parliament in 1849, a proposal was put forward to open a new penal colony. Earl Grey put down his cup of tea, harrumphed behind his silk handkerchief

---

1. *Sydney Morning Herald*, 25th December 1848

and told parliament that a plan to revive transportation to New South Wales was currently being considered.

In fact, a ship of convicts had set sail for Australia three months earlier.

That's not to say some Australians didn't know it was coming. A committee headed by William Charles Wentworth loved the idea of transportation, as there was a shortage of labourers in New South Wales. Not only that, but a convict labourer's salary was cheaper than one of a free settler, who demanded a higher payment for his work. But while the committee thought renewed transportation was tickety-boo, a large selection of the colony didn't. On the ninth of June, 1849, a ship named the *Hashemy* sailed into Port Jackson. It had left Portsmouth some four months previous, having been delayed by a cholera outbreak. Six convicts died on board before the ship put up its first sail and eleven had to be left behind. After stopping at the Cape of Good Hope and Port Phillip, it finally arrived with 212 convicts on board. The Colonial Secretary of NSW had been instructed by Earl Grey to issue tickets-of-leave (a sort of get-out-of-jail card that allowed convicts to live and work in a designated area until their sentence expired or they were pardoned), to the transported men that had behaved well during the voyage. The ship's arrival didn't please some, as Ian Hoskins tells us:

> 'A great protest meeting of 5000 people gathered at the waterfront. The protestors wanted free immigration and greater commerce. Governor Charles Fitzroy doubled the guard on the gate of Government House… Robert Lowe said, "The waterway is again polluted with the presence of that floating hell – a convict ship". The passengers of the *Hashemy* were condemned as "the moral filth of Great Britain" despite the penal origins of many in the crowd.'[2]

One of the loudest demonstrators was Henry Parkes, who had obviously put down the glass eyes for the day to come and protest. He would, in later years, become Premier of New South Wales, embark the

---

2. *Sydney Harbour- A History,* Ian Hoskins, University of New South Wales Press, 2009, pg 193

country on a path of federation of the colonies and suggest the title of 'Commonwealth of Australia'. But for now, he was just another person shouting.

The protests fell on deaf ears as eventually the convicts were off-loaded and hired by the landowners. On the twenty-fifth of June, twenty-five of the ticket-of-leave holders from the *Hashemy* reached Morpeth by steamer. They had been engaged by a Mr Henry Dangar for two years and they would be paid between twelve and fourteen pounds ($1068-$1246) a year. They would work on his property, a massive pastoral holding in New England. The property was known as Gostwyck. According to John Ferry:

> 'This was sheep country, as magnificent as any in the world. Arguably the best of these central New England runs as Gostwyck, sweeping in an arc from the gorges and waterfalls of the eastern escarpment to the ponds and watercourses south of Uralla. The run took in Kelly's Plains, Gibbons Plains and Wisemans Plains. It was dotted with permanent lagoons and was threaded by Salisbury Waters and Samuarez Creek. In good seasons upwards of 20,000 sheep grazed in flocks of close to 1,000 animals.'[3]

One of those twenty-five ticket-of-leave holders, one of the 'moral filth', was George Kingdom.

Elsewhere in the world, 1849 was a good year for the Elliott's as Susan gave birth to a daughter named Ann, and Queen Victoria was recovering after another birth in the previous year, this time to Princess Louise. But it wasn't a good year in London as a cholera epidemic killed 14,000 people and it wasn't a good year for writers. Edgar Allan Poe had been found in a delirious state, lying in a gutter and Fyodor Dostoevsky was sentenced to death for anti-government activities in Russia. The sentence was later commuted to being sent to a gulag, which for many was the same as a death sentence, only the execution took longer.

1849 also saw the birth of a new player on our stage – a girl named Ellen Cunningham. Some family historians would tell you that she was

---

3. *Colonial Armidale,* John Ferry

born in Ireland and emigrated here when she was seventeen years old, however most birth and death certificates indicate that she was born in Sydney, at Glebe. Neither birthplace can be substantiated and even the year is a work of mathematics, but a birth in Sydney looks the most likely. It was the first mystery concerning Ellen but it certainly wouldn't be the last. As far as the story goes, it's probably not important where she was born but it is important that she existed – she was my great-great-grandmother and we will be returning to her in later years.

The population of the United States in 1850 was over twenty-three million people and one of them, a man named Levi Strauss, had created the first pair of jeans to clothe the rest of them. The population of Great Britain was also increasing, thanks to Queen Victoria and Prince Albert as yet another heir, Prince Arthur, came into the world. And in the January of 1850, the population of Parramatta increased by 78 as forty men and thirty-eight women, who had been diagnosed as lunatics, arrived at their new home at the Parramatta Lunatic Asylum. They would be housed in the complex formerly known as the Female Factory, a holding place for female convicts and children. There were already some three hundred people there, watched and guarded by twelve law enforcement officers. The Asylum was pleased with its cleanliness and its record of health – they stated that at the end of 1849 that only six per cent of patients had died during the year.

So how did you get to be called a lunatic in 1850? Would you parade up and down George-street with no clothes on, telling passers-by that you were Napoleon's dog? Would you have to make an assassination attempt on Governor Fitzroy with a sharpened eucalyptus twig? Or was there a simpler way to be called simple? Sadly, there was - it was the worsening problem of alcohol addiction. Many people had developed a dependency on booze, whether it was spirits, imported and colonial ales or the rotgut sold in dirty backyard illegal distilleries. When a Robert Oram died in 1850, Mr Cartwright, a surgeon, declared at the inquest that the deceased had passed away from exhaustion, induced by previous excessive intemperance – or as Monty Python would say, he was permanently pissed. Mr Cartwright went on to say that from his experience of medical practice in Sydney, he was of the opinion that drinking colonial ale to excess had a more ruinous effect on the person than the use of spirits and liquors. He concluded that the ale had a powerful narcotic effect. David Clark, writing in *Nineteenth Century Sydney*, mentions one brewery made beer from water out of a reservoir that drained through Devonshire-street cemetery. God only knows what these people were drinking.

The newspapers of the time are full of stories of intoxicated people staggering down the streets and of drunkards suffering from delirium tremens, a violent reaction to chronic alcoholism. Some were so caught up with the horrors that they threw themselves into the harbour or cut their own throat with a razor. The ones who were saved from committing suicide or from running amok in the town – with the help of a certification by two doctors – were off for a stay in the Lunatic Asylum. Some never left there – well, not walking, that is.

In the Sydney area in 1851, there were 318 publican's licences applied for. If you were taking a stroll down George-street and you were feeling thirsty, you only had to pop into the Harbour View Hotel. Or the Commercial Hotel. Or the King's Head, the King's Arms, the Observer Tavern, the Marine, the New York, the Fortune Of War, the Patent Slip, the Land We Live In, the Australian, the American, the Rose Of Australia, the Blue Posts, the Glasgow Arms, the Liverpool Arms, the Vine Tavern, the Crooked Billet, the St John's Tavern, the Castle Tavern, the City Wine Vaults, the Forth And Clyde, the General Washington, the Skinners, the Star, the Golden Fleece, the Black Boy, the White Horse, the Royal, the Farriers Arms, the Crown And Anchor, the White Horse Cellar, the Bull's Head, the London Tavern, the Swan With Two Necks, the Emu Inn, the Friendship Inn, the Currency Lass, the Dublin Tavern, the St John's Tavern (yes, another one), the Crown, the Jew's Harp, the Britannia Arms, the Fountain Of Friendship, the Square And Compass, the Golden Fleece (another one of those, too), the Woolpack, the Peacock, the Omnibus Inn, the Steam Engine, the Odd Fellow's Hall, the Black Swan, the Dog And Duck, the Farmer's Home, the Wellington Inn or the Rising Sun.

And if none of those were to your liking, you could always try the pubs in Pitt-street.

It's interesting to note that Mr Oram's inquest, like every inquest at the time, was held in a pub. It's also interesting to note that on the same day of Mr Oram's inquest, Mr E. Day, Superintendent of the Sydney Police, was removed from his office. It seems there had been an inquiry into the circumstances of Mr Day being intoxicated at the Mayor's Fancy Ball. Was anyone safe from the demon drink?

Parramatta had more than just an asylum, of course, and had become quite popular as a place to live, start a farm or even just spend a pleasant spring day at. The Commissioner of Roads was quick to notice this so he announced that as of the 1st of January 1851, there would be a gate on the road between Sydney and Parramatta and travellers would need to pay a toll. Judging by the charges, the toll collectors would need to be reasonably good at their sums. For every sheep, lamb, pig or goat that passed through, a farthing would be charged. Every ox or head of cattle would cost a penny and every horse was worth twopence. Carts with two wheels would cost threepence, with that fee increasing depending on how many horses were pulling the cart. Wagons started at eight-pence and coaches were nine-pence and both were also subject to the increased costs of extra horses. No doubt, if old MacDonald moved his farm from Surry Hills to Parramatta, the toll collector would have run and hid behind a tree.

1851 arrived and Edward Hargraves arrived at Bathurst and found gold, which led to many people arriving in New South Wales so they could find their fortune. Most found nothing but heartache and starvation and they moved onto try their fossicking luck in Victoria, which had just become a separate colony. But there was still 197,000 people living in New South Wales, compared to the mother kingdom of Britain which had 21,000,000 souls. Queen Victoria had a year off from baby-making but John and Susan Elliott didn't, as Emily Elliott was born in South Petherton. We will keep an eye on Emily as she is an unusual element to our story.

In England, the Great Exhibition of Works of Industry of All Nations opened at the newly built Crystal Palace. People came from everywhere to see the exhibition and the building it was housed in. The Crystal Palace was a remarkable feat of engineering for the time. Its outer shell consisted of over a million square feet of glass, which might have excited the government revenue collectors if a recently abolished tax had still been gathered. The Window Tax, which had been levied since the late 1600's, was charged on all dwellings in the United Kingdom. At census times, the amount of people inside a house was recorded as was the amount of windows the house had. The owner of the house would then pay tax on each window. The government's logic was simple: the more money a person had, the bigger the house they would have, the more windows the house would have, the more tax they could afford and would have to pay. So when you undergo your next tour of historic buildings of Great Britain and discover all the rooms are dark due to boarded-up windows, you will know why.

England had the Great Exhibition for entertainment but Sydney had its own amusements. On the 5th of February, the Royal Australian Circus performed at Malcolm's Adelphi Hotel in York-street. The show included such highlights as the Trained Mare - Black Bess; Mr Clark's Wondrous Feats on the Slack Rope - Surrounded by Fireworks; the Jiggling Jumper of China and the Extravaganza entitled 'Billy Button's Journey to Brentford'. Howard's Ethiopian Serenaders were playing at the saloon of the Royal Hotel. The Royal Victoria Theatre featured Albert Smith's celebrated 'Esmeralda', followed by Mr Reading appearing as a 'real Virginian Nigger', singing 'Jenny Get Your Hoe Cake Done'.

The fun didn't stop there. The Sydney Museum was pleased to announce that they were displaying a four-horned, shaggy-coated mountain goat from Sierra Nevada. Or people could have taken a day trip in May to the Berrima Annual Races. In that year, the Town Plate race was won by Calendar. It was literally a two-horse race as the only other runner was Tros. The time was slow due to the heavy state of the track and 'the bad condition of Tros'. Meanwhile, applications for Publican's Booths were being accepted for the Homebush Races. There was a stern warning that 'no parties will be allowed to sell ginger beer or lemon syrup' if they didn't have one of those booths. Or perhaps you favoured a quiet night at home with a warm dinner smothered with Roby's Celebrated Warwickshire Sauce. The Rev. Dr. Joseph Wolff even gave the sauce a testimonial: 'Sir, I consider your sauce to be far better than any sauce used at the court of any Eastern Monarch or even at the table of the luxurious Umeer Naper Oollah or his Vixier at Bakhara'. Wow, it must have been good.

And what about my family? At some stage between 1847 and 1851, Catherine O'Brien packed up her home in Druitt-street and took her three youngest children to Victoria. There they lived with Patrick and Sarah. Patrick had given away his occupation as a carpenter and was now a wine and spirit merchant – he could see where the money was to be made. In 1851, Catherine junior married Eugene Sorahan with John and their sister Sarah as witnesses and the happy couple settled in Kilmore. Mr Sorahan has caused some chaos in genealogy searches. On his marriage certificate he is known as Eugene but on a later birth certificate for one of his children he is listed as Owen; if you have a good look at the marriage certificate, in the space where the priest has written the groom's name, he has printed an 'O' then crossed it out and written 'Eugene'. And as for looking up his surname on official sites – there are many ways his surname was spelt – suffice it to say that I found one birth certificate under 'Jogohan' and on his shipping record to Australia, he is listed as 'Soryan'. I have decided to stick with 'Sorahan' as that is how he signed his name on his marriage certificate. Tip No. 1 for researching your family tree: think outside the square.

With no name problems and living in Gostwyck, George Kingdom was tending sheep and trying to stay out of trouble. In Somerset, England, John and Susan Elliott raised their four young children and dreamed of a better life. And what about poor old Charlotte? Her husband – who had spent most of their marriage in gaol – sailed off to seven year's transportation to Australia in 1849. She must have had a sinking feeling that she would never see him again – and it appears that feeling was correct. A recent genealogical find shows that she reverted back to her maiden name and married another gentleman – four months after George arrived in Australia.

If we do not find anything pleasant, at least we shall find something new.

Voltaire, 1759

5. WHEN WORLDS COLLIDE

Not only were the British considered the masters of the Industrial Revolution, they were also avid explorers. They had spent decades traversing the globe in search of new things to stick their nose into – but they weren't always the first to get there. Robert Scott, of Antarctic fame, came a very poor second in the race to the South Pole and depending on which expert you listen to, Australia had been visited by every man and his dog before James Cook sailed into Botany Bay. But in 1852, the English were quick to spot a mountain in Nepal was the highest mountain in the world. The mountain was known by the locals as Chomolungma or Goddess Mother of the World. The English gave it a less romantic name – Peak XV. It would take another thirteen years for the mountain to be named after a man who probably never even saw the peak, let alone climb it. His name was Colonel George Everest.

On a lesser high note, the first public toilet for men opened in London on the second of February. Nine days later, the first women's toilet opened – I hope they had been able to hang on for that long. In America, the men were definitely wearing the pants as an Emma Snodgrass was arrested in Boston for wearing a pair of trousers. In Australia, and particularly Victoria, the gold rush was running hot. In Melbourne, it appeared that most of the shopkeepers and merchants had adjusted their retail marketing strategy for the influx of miners. Mr Thomas Ham was selling maps of the route to Ballarat for five shillings and the Gold Diggers Emporium on Queen-street was selling clothing, bedding and American buckets. F. Gamson, Chemist, was flogging Persian Sherbet Powder, 'invaluable for persons at the gold mines to allay thirst'; W. H. Cropper had given up auctioneering and had commenced business as a gold broker and, after you had finished with the digging, the *Helene* could sail you and your gold to Europe.

Not everyone was catering to the prospectors, though. In April, a Mr Hurrey held a massive auction which consisted of pawnbroker's unredeemed pledges. And if you are wondering what they pawned back then in search of some quick cash, the auction offered telescopes, French slippers, Britannia metal spoons, handsaws, dog collars, whips, dish covers, bottled fruit and rather worryingly, girls shoes. But if you were after something a little less second-hand, Francis & Cohen, auctioneers in Collins-street, Melbourne, was probably the place to go. Their auction provided variety as the following items were put up for sale: 122 land allotments in Flemington, buildings in Swanston- and LaTrobe-streets, 39 casks of Carolina rice, 140 tins of red herrings, a case of Paris hats, 12 cases of Perks patent folding iron bedsteads, 30 tons of Adelaide Fine Flour, 240 bags of Derwent potatoes, 7 cases of raspberry vinegar, 2 cases of shooting coats and 509 assorted cedar boards.

So, you were not short of a place to buy a wedding present or a gift for a christening, and you might have needed one on the 28th of March and the 21st of April. In March Eugene Sorahan and Catherine had a little girl, Rosanna, while in April, in the St Francis Church of Melbourne, John O'Brien, Mathew and Catherine's eldest son, married Mary O'Sullivan. The witnesses were William Copeland and Ellen O'Sullivan, who married the following year. Mary was the daughter of Thomas O'Sullivan, merchant, and Maria Coghill and was born in Castlereagh, Roscommon, Ireland between 1830 and 1834. One O'Brien family researcher, the late Gillian O'Brien, thought that Mary came to Australia with her father, who was a former soldier and escort of convicts to Tasmania. Indeed, Mary's brother was baptised in the Hobart Catholic Church. But apart from the fact she was a Catholic, as was her groom, there is no further information about Johnny and Mary on the certificate.

While the wedding bells were ringing in the south, up in northern New South Wales Henry Dangar and his brother, William, still needed labourers for their extensive properties. The supply of convicts had dried up so the Dangar entrepreneurs resorted to employing agents in Britain to find potential emigrants. The emigrants could bring their entire family to Australia and part of the fare would be paid by Henry and William, providing the emigrant worked for them for at least twelve months. It is not known exactly when one of the agents made his way to South Petherton in Somerset, but it would have been around late 1852 or early 1853. He must have been a good salesman or perhaps life was just so miserable in South Petherton, as he signed up quite a few families. One of those signed was the Elliott family.

In 1853, Vincent van Gogh was born as was Prince Leopold, the seventh child of Victoria and Albert. In the month before the royal birth, a ship sailed from Plymouth Harbour, bound for Australia. It was called the *Malvina Vidal* and had 25 single men, 99 single women, 166 married couples and 130 children aged fourteen or younger on board. Included in those figures were John and Susan Elliott and their four children along with Susan's brother, William Edmonds, his wife Sarah and their four children. Sarah's brother, William Monckton, and his wife and six children were there as well. There were five deaths and three births on the journey, which lasted 95 days. The ship's surgeon, Dr Williams, reported favourably on the conduct of the emigrants.

The *Malvina Vidal* arrived in Port Jackson on the 21st of June 1853 and anchored off Dawes Point, at the usual inspection and hiring point. The meteorological report indicates there was a full moon on the twenty-first and the people of the town were obviously affected. A John Denning had been engaged in a quarrel with a man named Hemmings. Denning had bitten off Hemmings's thumb which unsurprisingly didn't please Hemmings so he retaliated by 'chomping off a considerable portion of Denning's nose'. A Roderick Logon was committed to stand trial for striking a Patrick Tracy on the head with a spade and a Samuel Brown was nabbed stealing a saucepan from the doorway of Hoolan's Ironmongery Shop. Ironically, after a big day of flying implements and body parts, that night the Ethiopian Serenaders were back in town performing at the Royal Hotel and their concert started with a chorus of 'We're The Boys For Pleasure'.

Back on board the ship, the men without a position were offered to prospective employers. There were labourers, carpenters, sawyers, masons, bricklayers, plasterers, smiths, gardeners, office keepers, tailors, wheelwrights, bakers and a shopman. If you wanted to hire one of the unmarried females, you would have had to go to Hyde

Park Barracks for your perusal during the following week. And if you were a male prospective employer, you had to bring along a letter from your local minister, that indicated that you were a respectable gentleman and you weren't just shopping for a bit of skirt. Even if the whole process had the markings of a glorified slave market, it still had moral standards.

The Elliott and Edmonds families were no doubt bemused by the change in their environment. Gone were the green and fertile plains of England, replaced by a brown and dusty landscape, dotted with trees and thick shrubs that were alien to them. Gone were the chirping sparrows and the burrowing badgers, replaced by birds that seemed to be laughing at the new arrivals and tall rat-like creatures that bounced on their back legs. Gone were the hard times and the unbalanced English economy, replaced by hope and a colony that was raking in the cash. In 1853, the NSW bean-counters tallied up the money that had been raised from land sales, import duties, gold licences, fines and all the other fees that had been charged. It amounted to £815,859, close enough to 75 million dollars today – not bad for a place that had only been going for sixty-five years. Ship upon ship was arriving with more goodies and the people were salivating for them. £298,000 worth of apparel was imported that year along with 79 thousand pounds worth of furniture, 88 thousand pounds in stationery and books and dare I say it … £703,372 (about 65 million dollars) worth of wine and spirits. The stores and the auction houses were bursting at the seams; at Mr Mort's rooms in Pitt-street, Mr Rishworth was selling ten cases of French plums, nine cases of olives, a mahogany grand pianoforte and a ton of arsenic. Terms – cash only.

In the same year that the Elliott's arrived in Sydney, John and Mary O'Brien brought a new life into the world – a daughter named Mary. The baby could have been named in honour of two people: her mother, obviously, and her aunt, John's sister, who had passed away eight years ago. We don't know Mary's exact birthday due to the lack of compulsory birth registration – a thorn in the side of many a genealogist. Across town, one of John's other sisters, Sarah, was giving Queen Victoria a run in the children production department while her husband, Patrick, was making a name for himself. In 1853, there was an election for the Legislative Council of Victoria and Patrick stood for the seat of Kilmore, Kyneton and Seymour. He won convincingly over his one opponent, a Reverend Mr Horne. However, there was some controversy as numerous people complained of guerrilla tactics at the polling booth. There were allegations of assaults and threats to voters, suggesting that if they didn't vote for Patrick O'Brien, they might like to leave town – quickly. Patrick even had to write to the newspaper, denying any such activity occurred:

> 'I would challenge your correspondent to bring forward a single voter who was offered the slightest intimidation if he voted against me.'[1]

Apparently no one did, but maybe that's because they were floating upside-down in the creek. As Patrick started his new life in politics and John and Mary raised a new life in Fitzroy, elsewhere in Melbourne a ragged old piece of real estate was given a new life. A disused paddock belonging to the police was presented to the Melbourne Cricket Club by Lieutenant Governor Charles LaTrobe. These days, that old paddock is where the MCG can be found.

Time moved on to 1854 and two members of the Kingdom family decided to move on as well. George's sisters, Frances and Elizabeth, together with Frances's husband, James Galliford and their daughter, Mary, set sail from Plymouth in May and arrived in Adelaide in August. I wondered if they had any intention of catching up with their brother after arrival in Australia – then they wouldn't have even known if he was still alive, let alone where he was. At any rate, their journey on the good ship *Thetis* appears to have been somewhat interesting as some excerpts from the ship's log indicate:

1. Adaption [sic] of ship for the conveyance of immigrants –
   In its present state very dilapidated, the rigging being old and bad, and leakage throughout the ship
2. Quantity and quality of provisions and water –
   The provisions and water were abundant and good with the exception of the pickles which were inferior

---
1. Patrick O'Brien, Letter to the Editor, *The Argus*, 28th June 1853

3. Conduct of Masters and Officers etc –
Kind and attentive, with the exception of the cook
4. Conduct of emigrants
The Cornish miners disorderly and troublesome with a few exceptions. No trouble with the farmers. The single females were in obedience with their reputations with the following exceptions, Mary Leuwin, Mary Bailie and Elizabeth Kingdom. Their conduct of the most depraved tendency – could not be kept from the sailors, viz, James McIntosh, the ship's cook and the 3rd mate. They could not be said to manifest any contrition for their behaviour [2]

Naughty girls, naughty cook, dodgy pickles. The mind boggles. Away from Adelaide, Great Britain found itself at war again, this time siding with Turkey as they fought the Russians in the Crimean War. The war would inspire many composers and poets, fascinated by the deployment of the Light Brigade against Russian artillery at Balaclava, which ended poorly for the Brigade. In the same war, a nurse named Florence Nightingale created a page in history for herself. Elsewhere, another page was created as an American politician named Abraham Lincoln made his first political speech. Also during the year, a man, who became famous for writing speeches, albeit in a more theatrical setting, was born. His name was Oscar Wilde and in later years he would test the patience of the judicial system, much as people were doing in Sydney. As you look through the colony's old cases, however, you have to wonder if the scales of justice were evenly balanced. In August, Mary Smith was indicted for stealing two pairs of trousers and received three month's hard labour for her sins. Elizabeth Bolton and Louisa Lloyd were sentenced to seven day's imprisonment for being idle and disorderly. Mary Ann Collins and Eliza Douglass were convicted of using obscene language in public and as they couldn't pay their fines, they were jailed for one month and two weeks respectively. Yet Hugh McMahon, who had been found guilty of striking and kicking his wife, declaring that he 'would gladly hang should he kill her', and then threw

---

2. Transcripts of ship's records of *Thetis*, Plymouth to Port Adelaide 1854, Emigration Department

her and their six-year old child out into the street – well, he was fined four pounds and went home.

Around the same time, the Colonial Secretary of New South Wales suffered a loss. A white wiry-haired terrier that he owned had either strayed or been stolen from his house at 16 Macleay-street, Woolloomooloo and he was offering a £2 reward for its return. The dog's name was Crab, and I would suggest that it had merely slinked away in embarrassment. While the Colonial Secretary fretted over his beloved pooch, the Commissioners for the City of Sydney had accepted the tender of John Aldred for emptying and cleaning all the privies and cesspools of the city. They also advised that any person who obstructed Mr Aldred while he was fulfilling his duties of filling his buckets, or if they removed 'night soil' by themselves, would be prosecuted.

Sydney was moving and shaking. It now boasted 3 sugar refineries, 14 soap manufactories, 2 distilleries, 12 breweries, 11 tobacco manufactories, 7 woollen cloth manufactories, 1 hat factory, 66 tanneries, 3 potteries, 10 iron and brass foundries and a gas works. The colony population was around 231,000 people, 139,000 horses, 1,500,000 cattle, 71,000 pigs and 7,929,000 sheep. 20,000 tons of potatoes and 34,000 tons of hay had been grown while 57,000 gallons of booze had been brewed. The Monarch Fire and Life Assurance Company of London were insuring third class inferior buildings with shingled rooves for 10-25 shillings per £100 per annum and £2800 was pledged in aid of the 'famishing Jews' of Palestine. And fifty people in Sydney were charged by police for allowing their goats to stray about public places. But in one goat-less part of the city, the Australian Museum was continuing to build its impressive collection: it advised the donations of twenty insects, three shells, a fungus from Wollongong, a fish from Port Jackson, two grass baskets, a specimen of a stick and a chicken with four wings and four legs.

Elsewhere in the world, life continued ... for some. Queen Victoria's court was rocked by the news that the wet nurse to the Prince of Wales had murdered her own six children by nearly decapitating them and then failed with a suicide attempt. With all due respect to the children, no doubt the Queen was grateful that the nurse had taken her troubles home instead of having a bad day at work. In America, Captain Van Buren and a party of twelve men took on a party of Comanche Indians and 'whipped them handsomely'. In country NSW, Richard Grainger, a man who was fond of becoming drunk and assaulting the Chinese men he had employed as shepherds, pushed his luck too far. After a quarrel one night, he fired a pistol at one of the men. It was then that the shepherds, Tsing Tsoon, Tah Sick, Hin Tick, Ly Tick and Sing Sing had decided they'd had enough. They held Grainger down, cut his throat and buried him in the sheep yard. Eventually one of the men, Sing Sing, sung to the police and they were charged with manslaughter. Back in Sydney, Neil MacInnes, a man who also appeared to be fond of a wee dram, went home one night and 'smote' his wife with a frying pan. He was released without conviction as she did not appear in court to substantiate the charge. Another chap, Richard Wenham, who was nearing seventy years of age, had been refused service at a pub due to his wild appearance. He went home in a huff and his wife found him the next morning – he had hanged himself in the privy. And lastly, and perhaps the saddest, is the story of two-year-old Emma Precious. Her mother had been in the habit of giving the child a small drop of rum occasionally, believing it to be good for her. One day, just before Christmas, Emma picked up the bottle of rum and drank the lot. The inquest decided that her death was caused by a shock to the nervous system.

Happily, there was new life as well. As mentioned earlier, compulsory birth registration hadn't commenced yet, so birth details prior to 1856 are hazy at the best of times and non-existent at the worst. In a town called Beveridge in Victoria, which is only thirty kilometres north of where John and Mary O'Brien were seemingly living, a child was born to a different set of Irish parents. The child's birth may have been 1854 or possibly 1855: history is not certain. What is certain is the child would become one of the most iconic figures in the Australian story. His name was Edward Kelly but in later years, he would simply be known as 'Ned'.

Also slipping under the radar of officialdom in 1854 was a girl born in Gostwyck. Her name was Frances (Fanny) Kingdom and George was her father. It appears that while George was tending the flocks of sheep, he was also sowing the wild oats. And who was the mother? Ah, yes. That question has caused Kingdom family historians some headaches. Some would have you believe it was a woman called Susan Smith and some would tell you it was a woman called Sarah, as this name was listed on Fanny's death certificate. But Fanny has no apparent birth registration, the baptismal records for the area are lost and even Fanny's marriage certificate has a blank space where the mother's name is to be written. To make things even more interesting, during my research I found there was a fatal flaw in both the Susan Smith and the Sarah theories; there is no record of them and neither of the ladies seem to have actually existed. So who was Mum and who was keeping mum on Mum?

A report appeared in the *Sydney Morning Herald* in December, under the banner of 'Armidale news':

> 'Most of the working hands who are not gold diggers, are employed at the shearing; consequently, our little town is, on the whole, rather dull.'[3]

I'm not so sure about that.

---

3. *Sydney Morning Herald,* December 4, 1854

Michael O'Brien

6. Family Ties

As 1854 drew to a close, there was trouble brewing on the goldfields of Victoria. There were some 25,000 miners digging in Ballarat; ships were left deserted in Port Philip and families were left deserted everywhere else as men scratched under the earth's crust in an attempt to find their fortune. The government found the activity very interesting and decided that they could make some money out of this too, so they decided to charge the prospectors a digger's licence. This was levied on a prospector whether they found gold or not and many men could not afford it. The goldfields were heavily patrolled by the police and anyone found without a licence was fined and in some cases, beaten up. Naturally, the miners found this scheme unfair and rebelled. Under the leadership of an Irishman named Peter Lalor, they built a barricade and fought the police and government troops. They were outnumbered and nearly thirty men died in the short battle. Lalor escaped the clutches of the law however he didn't escape a bullet wound in the arm and the limb was later amputated. The government launched a commission into the rebellion at the Eureka Stockade and while some men were charged, no-one was convicted. Reforms were introduced at the goldfields and Lalor soon became the MLC for Ballarat, thereby assuring his place in history and a seat near Patrick O'Brien in the Legislative Council.

Back in Sydney, as the number of licensed public houses in the city and surrounding districts approached 400, people were finding new ways to get into trouble. A man named David Jones was charged with embezzlement by his employers who just happened to be David Jones and Company – the forerunner of the department store that we love and can't afford to shop in today. Over a period of time, David Jones had been pilfering from David Jones and he had taken shirts, mackintoshes, hats, handkerchiefs and 66 yards of silk. Perhaps he had been planning to set up his own store – though I am not sure what he would have called it. And while we are talking about retail stores, in 1855 David Angus was born in Scotland. He would later move to Australia and join Mr Robertson in the book-selling business; it's probably just as well that neither of them is alive today to see the dusty pages of their crumbled empire.

In England, Lord Palmerston was Prime Minister; in Russia, Alexander II was Tsar while Tewodros II was Emperor of Ethiopia. Sir Charles Fitzroy was still Governor of New South Wales and Charles LaTrobe was Lieutenant Governor of Victoria. LaTrobe must have been grateful to see the end of the gold miner's rebellion but before he could put his feet up, it was the stonemason's turn to cause trouble. Melbourne was growing rapidly and needed more buildings but labour was scarce – most of the men were still trying to find gold. The remaining stonemasons were working their fingers to the bone and they felt they were entitled to better working conditions. They sought the radical new concept of an eight-hour working day, complementing eight hours of recreation and eight hours of rest. They called for action and reform and although they didn't build a stockade (and being masons you would think it would have been a more impressive stockade than the one at Ballarat), they downed tools and went on strike. Amongst them was my great-great-grandfather, John O'Brien, throwing his hammer and chisels to the ground, marching through the streets, protesting for a better deal. After some hemming and hawing from the employers, the stonemasons finally won the right to an eight hour working day. Many decades later we commemorate those early united workers and their brave stand, in the form of a public holiday called Labour Day. Back in Melbourne, John O'Brien, presumably in his eight hours of recreation, spent some quality time with wife Mary and as a result, after a day of labour, a son called Mathew was born. The O'Brien family was growing and the colony of Victoria was being good to them.

In Sydney, the concept of being good had flown out the window. The courts were busier than a one-legged man at an arse-kicking party and in one particular day's sitting in January, the judge would have been far from bored. Before him, he had four cases of embezzlement, two cases of uttering forged instruments and individual cases of murder, manslaughter, bigamy, bestiality, indecent assault on a female child, pick-pocketing, sheep stealing, cattle stealing, horse stealing, robbery with violence, wounding, assault on the high seas, obtaining money under false pretences, larceny, burglary, perjury and conspiracy. A lad named James Blackland was up on the bestiality charge. He was fourteen years old and had been indicted for having committed an 'offence against nature' with a dog. The jury found him guilty of rogering Rover but recommended him to mercy on account of his youth. The judge ignored their recommendation, donned his black wig and sentenced James to hang.

The drunkenness continued. A Charles Gerrard was charged with biting his own daughter while drunk, William Cooper was charged with using obscene language in public and Hugh McGuire was apprehended in the act of robbing a drunken man lying asleep in York-street. For the apparent minority of people avoiding the grog, the stores still had dazzling arrays of stock. At Alfred Fairfax and Co of 287 George-street, you could purchase Champion's Vinegar, Hill and Ledger's bottled gooseberries and barrels of prunes, while if you popped across the road to Crawley and Smith at 286 George-street, you could buy Peruvian guano in bulk at £17 a ton – that's if you were interested in a big pile of old shit.

On the 1st of January 1856, the island at the bottom of the continent, Van Diemen's Land, had an official name change and would now be called Tasmania. Way over on the western side of the continent the town of Perth became a city, while way out eastwards in the Pacific Ocean, Norfolk Island found itself with some new inhabitants. Previously the island had acted as a penal colony with only the worst of the worst sent there, but now the descendants of the *Bounty* mutineers, who had been living on a tiny lump of rock called Pitcairn Island, some 5000 kilometres east of New Zealand, had been granted permission to move there. It seemed that Pitcairn had become a hotbed of alcoholism, disease and murder and as Sydney already had enough of that, the British government made Norfolk available. Over 190 people made the journey west for a new beginning; within five years, a quarter of them had returned to Pitcairn. Perhaps the paradise they sought was the paradise they had left behind.

In New South Wales, the first colonial parliament opened and if you are ever asked in a trivia night at your local pub, the first Premier of NSW was Stuart Alexander Donaldson. However, he lasted less than three months in the position before resigning due to lack of support. He was replaced by Charles Cowper who managed to spend even less time in the job before Henry Parker took over. Victoria also formed a parliament; Dr William Haines was the first Premier and Patrick O'Brien joined the proceedings as the member for South Bourke.

As the colonies sorted themselves out politically, some countries around the world were beating the crap out of each other. Even though the Crimean War had ended with the Treaty of Paris in 1856, conflicts raged elsewhere. In America, no one was playing nicely. The Tintic War was fought between white settlers and native Indians in Utah and in Kansas, anti-slavery supporters took on pro-slavery supporters at the Battle of Black Jack. The British and French were in action again, this time fighting the Second Opium War against the Qing dynasty of China. And the British soldiers who weren't fighting the Chinese, were involved in the Anglo-Persian War. They were fighting the country we now call Iran, over a city named Herat, in a country we now call Afghanistan. 170 years they are back there again – some things never change.

Then, some things do. In Kilmore, Victoria, Owen/Eugene and Catherine had a baby girl. The child's name is not listed on the birth schedule but it does record that the girl is their fourth child so they hadn't been mucking around. Back in NSW, in August 1856, a Sydney publican named William Cole died. He had lived at 34 Lower Fort Street, constructed a row of Georgian buildings in Millers Point and he had run the Bee Hive Hotel on the corner of Prince and Argyle Streets for many years. In November 1848 his wife had passed away and in the following years of sadness he had found solace in the arms of another woman. He had found that much solace that they had three children together. The woman was Ellen Kennedy nee O'Brien. There is a lot more to this part of the story – a fascinating tale of wicked men, devious ladies and pots of money. I have included the tale at the back of this book in the Appendix.

In the New England area, one thing was changing dramatically – the population. At a place called Rocky River, not far from Gostwyck and Uralla, gold had been found. While it didn't quite attract the maniacal rush that Ballarat did, people still flocked there in droves. At one stage in 1856 the population of Armidale, just up the road, was around 800 while there were 5,000 people at Rocky River. The price of an ounce of gold had soared to £3 11s – around $300 in today's money, so you can see why the area became so attractive. One correspondent told the *Sydney Morning Herald* that 'there was no prospect of the gold fields being worked out for many a year to come'. Like most famous predictions, he was wrong and the rush started dying out during the following year.

Everything comes at a price. In November of 1856, in what the *Armidale Express* somewhat understatedly described as 'an accident of a very painful nature', five Scotsmen were killed when a mine shaft collapsed. Then there was the sad tale of George and Phoebe Brinsley, which I shall allow the relevant newspaper to tell because there is no way I could describe it the way they did:

> 'George Brinsley was charged with having feloniously slain, on the 29th June 1856, his wife, Phoebe. They had only recently arrived at the diggings and had not been successful. On the evening of the day named, the deceased was heard to accuse her husband of bringing her up to the bush to starve and said that she would take in needlework or washing, and keep herself but not him, and she called him a liar and a lazy vagabond. Towards morning the neighbours in the adjacent tents were aroused by a scream and upon rushing out found it proceeded from the unfortunate woman, who was standing near her tent with her throat cut. She was asked who had committed the crime but was unable to reply except by pointing to her husband's tent. She soon after expired. Upon going into the prisoner's tent, he was found lying on his bed, with his throat also cut; medical assistance was sent for and he revived. For the defence it was urged that when the violence of the deceased the previous night was contrasted with the prisoner's previous kind behaviour, it was more probable that she had first cut the prisoner's throat, and afterwards her own. The jury returned a verdict of not guilty.'[1]

---

1. *Maitland Mercury And Hunter River General Advertiser,* September 25 1856

Late in the year, the weather was warm and the crops were growing well under 'the influence of a moist bottom and a congenial sun'. One shepherd found more than a moist bottom after a big night of drinking. It seems the poor chap was staggering home and fell into Poison Swamp (an area that probably didn't attract too many tourists) and drowned in nine inches of water. It was thought that 'having fallen into the pool, he had not had the strength to get out'.

Across the land in Gostwyck, away from the excitement and/or the despair of the gold diggings, it seems George Kingdom had been out fossicking for other things. In late 1856, he was arrested with a man named John Doyle and they appeared in court on a charge of drunkenness. Doyle was cautioned and discharged while George was fined five shillings. Neither of these pisspots knew it at the time but George's son, Henry, would later marry John Doyle's daughter, Mary Ann, and would become one set of my great-grandparents.

Maybe my great-great-grandfathers had been celebrating. A girl named Jane Kingdom had just been born and George was the father. Like Fanny before her, the mother's identity was a mystery. The birth was seemingly not registered and a search through the various online trees created by descendants found that the descendants couldn't agree. This time the mother was listed on online trees as Sarah Kingdom or Mary Kingdom and even dear old Susan Smith was wheeled out again. Putting my detective's hat on, it was clear that the name 'Sarah' had appeared on later certificates so a family member from those relevant registration times had advised the names (believing the name to be correct or deliberately hiding the truth) to the person completing the certificate. 'Mary' didn't seem to appear anywhere apart from online trees and I could not find a single certificate with the name 'Susan Smith' on it; this made me think that she was not a fictional creation of the 1850's, she was a fictional creation of more modern times. There was even a listing on the Genserv genealogical site with a date of birth and death for Susan Smith. Could either of these dates be proved? In a word, no. Even though the concept of unwed mothers giving birth to bastard children was hardly new in Australia – a quick look at the First Fleet and you will find that most of the officers, aside from Governor Phillip, had children to convict women here as their wives sat at home warming their slippers in England. But in certain circles, there would still be shame attached and the mother would be judged. So if 'Susan Smith' hadn't been created by the family back then, she must have been created later and passed down through family folklore. I would say she had been created in a time when certificates weren't so easy to order and the Internet didn't exist. They thought the deception would just pass on down the family line.

Then I found a clue which led me to another and without trying to sound like a commercial for Ancestry.com, I believe I discovered the true identity of Jane Kingdom's mother, and possibly Fanny's, as well. The answer indicated to me just why these other names had been invented. In 1877, Jane Kingdom married Robert Frost in the Wesleyan Church in Armidale. On the marriage certificate, with details from the church register (and these details were supported by a later certificate), Jane's mother was identified as Susan Edmonds. Susan Edmonds, if you cast your mind back, was the maiden name of Susan Elliott. Whoops. Susan was married to John Elliott in 1856 – wasn't she?

That's when the clouds circled and the darkness set in. Where was John Elliott? Had he died? Once again, I turned to the online family trees and they all seemed to agree (for a change) that John Elliott died in 1855. It was time for me to track that event down but it would be challenging as the year fell into the pre-registration era. However, owing to the fact you couldn't go and plant your deceased loved ones under the petunias in the backyard because it wasn't consecrated ground, most deaths received a burial certificate from the relevant parish – unless, of course, if it was a suicide. Death by suicide generally meant you were expunged from the records after you had expunged yourself from life. I did find a record for a John Elliot dying in 1855(yes, one 't' but remember, spelling wasn't a priority back then) and another record for a John Elliott dying in 1853. The latter gentleman's burial certificate revealed him to be too young so was ruled out but Mr Elliot's certificate was an interesting, but terrible, document. It read:

Name:	John Elliot
Abode:	Factory Lunatic Dept
Age:	Unknown
Profession:	Lunatic
When died:	15 April 1855

Oh dear. Now I can think of a few people who should be called professional lunatics (they can mainly be found working in politics) but I've never seen the job title in writing before. The Factory Lunatic Dept was the old Female Factory prison which had been converted to form part of Parramatta Lunatic Asylum. As mentioned earlier, a display of habitual drunkenness would see you sent to the Asylum for a bit of a dry-out, but John had been in the country for less than two years – had he hit the sauce that bad or was there another reason? I did find the following:

> 'The greater number of the lunatics seem to come through the criminal gaols – for it appears that the friends of a madman prefer to transmit him through the Police Court and Darlinghurst [gaol], as it is the cheapest way. Any person apprehended showing mental derangement may be committed by two justices under the certification of two medical practitioners.'[2]

Of course, there was another issue – was this actually our John Elliott? I enlisted the help of respected researcher, Beryl Chesterton, to track down any records of Mr Elliot's admission to the Asylum. After a trip to the State Archives at Kingswood and a thorough investigation of the necessary books and registers, she came back with the result – nothing. There was no record of him and as Beryl mentioned, it appears that many patients were not recorded in those days – probably the 1850's version of the 'too-hard tray'. I further investigated Mr Elliot's burial in the hope of finding some information. The certificate had stated that he was buried in the Parish of Marsfield (that was a big help … not) and after sending what seemed to be three million emails and letters, he was found to be buried in All Saints Cemetery, Parramatta, where:

> 'Around 2000 people are known to be buried here, 1500 in unmarked graves. Poor, insane, abandoned, destitute and soon forgotten.'[3]

---

2. *Sydney Morning Herald*, 25th May 1855
3. Judith Dunn, *The Parramatta Cemeteries: All Saints and Wesleyan*, Parramatta Historical Society, 2007

Sounds lovely, doesn't it? Unfortunately, the book gave no further clues into the life and death of John Elliot.

So we had a problem. We have most of the family historians believing this John Elliot to be our John Elliott – and he may well be. On the other hand, there is not a scrap of evidence to support that it is him. Whatever the case, it was obvious that John Elliott wasn't on the scene in Gostwyck in 1856. Was there another clue as to what happened?

Sort of.

In the Police Gazette, published by the Office of Inspector General of Police, of 17th January, 1854, there is a report of a crime committed in Gostwyck. Mr H. Dangar, Esq, complained that two of his sponsored employees had absconded and their whereabouts were unknown. A £10 reward had been posted for their capture. One of the absconders was John Elliott. He was described as being '5'6" tall, aged about 27, bridge of nose rather flat and having a vacant stupid look'.

So if I went back and put two and two together, family folklore said that Fanny Kingdom was born in September of 1854. This means that she would have been conceived around January of 1854 – around about the time that John Elliott took off from Gostwyck. Did he walk in and find George and Susan in flagrante delicto? Or did Susan find comfort with George after John walked out? Or was there something else to throw into the mix?

While compiling information, I noticed that John and Susan Elliott's children, George, Mary Ann and Ann, all married and lived in the New England area. But there was no indication of the life-path of the youngest daughter, Emily. The last apparent record of her existence is the shipping log of her arrival in Sydney, aged two. After that, she has simply disappeared into the mist of history. Did she die not long after arrival, sending John into some kind of grief-based lunacy? Does this explain the 'vacant stupid look'? Maybe her death and the new environment he was living in were all too much for the poor fellow. However, I could come up with a complete page of theories and scenarios, knowing that all of them would be extremely difficult to prove.

But I remain convinced that Susan Elliott was the mother of Jane Kingdom, and by reading later certification, it appears she was probably the mother of Fanny, too. It seems that less than a year after their arrival in Australia, the lives of the Elliott family changed dramatically. I am also convinced that the name 'Susan Smith' is a more recent pseudonym, which leads me to hypothesize that someone, possibly still living today, knows the real story.

And they're not telling.

Michael O'Brien

7. Nice Day For a White Wedding

The year 1857 started with a bang:

> 'The gentleman who travelled along George-street in an omnibus, on Tuesday afternoon, about 5pm and who, in exchanging money with a fellow passenger, picked up a shilling that was dropped, is respectfully requested to communicate to the Herald office, as he (the gentleman) is accused of leaving the bus without paying his fare.'[1]

Believe it or not, that was printed on the front page of the newspaper. The layout of the *Sydney Morning Herald* in the 1850's was quite different to what we are used to today. The front page, and sometimes the second page, was for classifieds and advertisements. Prospective employers advertised their positions vacant in the space we now see filled with the latest bad news from here and around the globe. For instance, in January of 1857, Riley and Hopkins Sarsaparilla manufactory at 20 Pitt-street was looking for a soda water bottler; Mrs Hunt of Philip-street wanted 'a person competent to undertake a family's washing' while a 'sober man accustomed to the care of a horse and gig, and to garden a little' was needed at Mr Myles's place in Chippendale. The rest of the page was filled with shipping details, tradesman's ads and the odd (with emphasis on the "odd") classifieds such as:

---

1. *Sydney Morning Herald,* January 1, 1857

'Augustus, why did you not answer my last letter?'

or:

'If any man has any just claim on Mary Smith they must declare it before the 30th of August 1857 as Mary Smith intends to be married.'

Having finished reading the newspaper and knowing you were not Augustus and you didn't want to claim Mary Smith, you might have been feeling a bit peckish. Perhaps a trip to Osmond's Hotel on Pitt-street might be on the cards. The luncheon menu was an adventure in cuisine: oxtail soup, salmon au gratin, boiled fowls and ham, mutton cutlets with sauce piquante, stewed tripe a l'Anglaise, fried beans a l'Italiene and sauté of calf's liver.

After you somehow digested your luncheon, you may have wanted some entertainment. An exhibition at 30 Hunter-street would have shown you 'the Orang Otang, or Wild Man of the Woods, and a boa constrictor'. In April you could have watched the cricket match played between the Royal Surrey and the Emu Cricket Clubs, although that wouldn't have taken much of your time. The Emus batted first and were all out for 25 while the Surreys replied with an innings of 40. Emus batted again and did better in the second innings, scoring a total of 29 and set an impressive target of 15. The lads from Surrey managed to get the runs without losing a wicket.

If cricket wasn't your cup of tea, a stroll through the Botanical Gardens would have you arriving at the Sydney Poultry Club's First Exhibition of Poultry or if you fancied another type of bird, John North's place was the venue for you – well, it would have been if he hadn't been sentenced to two years hard labour in Parramatta Gaol for keeping a brothel.

Maybe you fancied a bit of extra cash so you could have kept your eyes peeled for lost property and claim the reward. Mr W. Brown of No. 8 Brougham-street had found a pig 'which would be returned if the owner paid expenses'. John Jones of Paddington had lost a brown pony; Henry Moody of Parramatta had lost a black horse; Ann Lane of Greendale hadn't heard from her husband in twenty years while Joseph

Zeutzins of No. 6 George-street was offering a reward of £1 for the return of his 'mottled cock'. No doubt he wanted that back in a hurry.

Perhaps all this activity was making you unwell and you were after a tonic. Holloway's Medicine was now Holloway's Pills and Holloway's Ointment but they still seemed to cure every ailment known to mankind. However, they had competition now. Watson's Worm Powders and Dayrell's Worm Lozenges could be purchased for the expulsion of worms while Pectoral Oxymel of Caragheen and Larmer's Pulmonic Mixture was available for coughs and colds. A concoction of Jamaica ginger and chamomile flowers could be bought at Heath's Family Chemist in George-street and it was guaranteed to remedy any 'distressing flatulence' that you had. Shaw's Invigorating Balm would give you a 'luxuriant head of hair'; Mr DeLissa's Valuable Tinted Spectacles would preserve your sight and his newly discovered Organic Vibrator would cure deafness. So once you could see and hear properly and you had stopped sneezing, coughing and farting, you could wander down to Mr Insley's Photographic Skylight Gallery. There you could have a collodion picture or a daguerreotype portrait taken of yourself – hopefully you had combed your luxuriant hair first.

All the excitement wasn't just in Sydney, you know. In England, the world's first soccer club was formed and called Sheffield FC. Also, Hugh Lowther was born in 1857 and I imagine you are probably thinking – who? He was an English sportsman and also the 5th Earl of Lonsdale and he is the man who they named the clothing company after … Lonsdale, that is, not Lowther. And speaking of the aristocracy, you might have noticed I haven't mentioned the residents of Buckingham Palace for a while. Good news! Queen Victoria gave birth to her ninth child, Princess Beatrice, who probably didn't wear ridiculous hats to weddings but did end up becoming the great-grandmother of King Juan Carlos of Spain.

The royal family probably escaped the Great Stink of 1858 in London but the House of Commons didn't. This phenomenon, which truly lived up to its name, was caused by the combination of a hot summer and the excessive flow of raw sewage into the River Thames. While a large number of people were suffering from the pong, a few lonely men were working on the bong – that is, the 14 tonne bell they called Big Ben. After some testing, they realised they had managed to crack the bell and they had to replace it with a lighter version. The replacement bell is still in use in the Tower of London today. As the bell makers worked on their donger, other chaps were working on their own projects: Albert Potts patented the street mailbox; Hyman Lipman patented the pencil with an attached rubber and Hamilton Smith patented the washing machine.

The Kingdom family had been a bit quiet up in Gostwyck but there's nothing like a wedding for kicking up your heels and having a good time. However, I have the feeling that the wedding held at a private house in Armidale on the 17th July 1858 was a fairly subdued affair. On that day, George Kingdom married Susan Elliott. The certificate for the marriage has many blank spaces and they are more conspicuous than the written information. There is nothing recorded for their birthplaces, their ages or their parent's names. However there is one interesting column – the conjugal status. George claimed he was a widower and Susan stated she was a widow. George hadn't seen his wife Charlotte for eleven years; and the seven-year rule applied. If a man or a woman hadn't seen their spouse for seven years, they could legally claim their marriage was over and remarry. It was a typical convict story; once transported, the life they had in the United Kingdom was over. Of course, George wouldn't have known that Charlotte wasn't burning a candle for him. As for Susan, she presumably last saw her husband John in 1854 and if he died in 1855, she was safe. One wonders how she knew though. I look at that certificate today and I have the idea that a lot of dust was swept under the carpet.

One point I must stress is that I am not sitting here in judgement. I can't as I don't know all the facts. Maybe Charlotte Kingdom was an unloving wife and she was having an affair with the Knowstone blacksmith. Maybe John Elliott is not the man who died in the asylum and he ran off with a large-chested seamstress he met on the ship. Maybe Emily Elliott did die young and Susan was the strongest of the pair emotionally and John reached for the booze for comfort. There are many possibilities and many decades have passed. I can only record what I know. And one thing I do know is that the new Mr and Mrs Kingdom had a son named Henry and he was born on 5th March 1859, less than eight months after the wedding. Henry, as previously mentioned, was my great-grandfather.

Down south in Melbourne, they felt that nothing of interest was happening in the north and the west. *The Argus* in January 1859 reported on the telegraphic despatches they had received from Sydney:

'Nothing has occurred today or yesterday worth mentioning.'

and Adelaide:

'The markets remain unchanged. There is no news.'

But there was news in the O'Brien family as Patrick, John's brother-in-law, had been appointed as a magistrate by the Commission of Peace. He and his fellow magistrates were kept busy. In one day in January, 21 people were arrested for drunkenness; John Brooks and Thomas Bezewing were charged with stealing a bell and some clothing; Richard Murphy, a private of the 40th Regiment was jailed for stealing a hairbrush; John Goodman was brought up for breaking a window of a Spanish restaurant in Elizabeth-street while drunk and Charles Jones was charged with stealing a quantity of spoons from the residence of the French consul. There was one additional drunkenness case, that of John McDonald. He had been brought into court three days after his arrest as he had not been deemed sufficiently sober to appear beforehand. When asked what he had to say for himself, he replied that 'he supposed his horse had carried him to the wrong shop but in all, he had been well treated'. McDonald was freed. The horse was not charged.

The court also had to deal with a strange case of three men in a boat. The three, Messrs Ferrie, Gowan and Ritchie had intended on spending a few days on the River Murray for a spot of shooting and fishing. They had procured a boat and went out onto Lake Moira. At some stage, Mr Ferrie was in the bow of the boat and took aim at a pelican. Mr Gowan said, 'Here take my gun, you might miss him with yours'. He was in the act of handing the gun over when it went off and Mr Ferrie was shot through the heart. The pelican survived; Mr Ferrie didn't.

In May of 1859 it was all go. The Port Phillip Farmer's Society held the Melbourne District Annual Ploughing Match at Mr Blair's farm at Moonee Ponds. In the city, Madame Sohier's Waxwork Exhibition could be seen at the Royal Charter Hotel while the future could be seen at Madame Carole's, Clairvoyant, at 114 Collins-street. Someone who didn't have much future to be seen was Catherine Sorahan, who died on the 9th of May from inflammation of the lungs. In keeping up with tradition, her surname on the death register is spelled 'Sorraghan'. Her daughter, Rosanna, would be known in future years as Soraghan, Sorraghan and Sorrighan. For an added treat to me as a future researcher, Rosanna's second husband was named John O'Brien.

In his grief, Mr Soraghan might have wanted to get away and see the world in 1859 and there were many options. The Peninsular And Oriental Steam Navigation Company would sail you to Kangaroo Island for a fiver while Mauritius would cost you £50, Alexandria £100, Malta £110, Marseilles £115 and Southampton was £120. That fare to Southampton equates to around $10,600 in today's money and included steward's fees, wine, bedding but not the hotel expenses in Egypt. You could have also sailed to England on the *Oneida*, which had an advertisement that boasted 'an unusually favourable opportunity for passengers proceeding to England as there was every prospect of a rapid and agreeable voyage'. Prospect? That's like boarding a plane today and hearing the captain announce – 'Hi! Thanks for flying with us! We really hope to get to our destination in comfort!'

Maybe you preferred a jaunt in your new homeland. Gilles, Nicholson and Co would steam you to Hobart for £7 and W. P. White and Co would take you to Sydney for £8 or only £3 if you travelled in the steerage section. Even closer to home, the Geelong and Melbourne train service ran three times a day; Hansom's Patent Safety Cabs would transport you within Melbourne for a couple of shillings or you could just do it yourself – Mr Carter of 71 Queen-street had a 'plucky mare' for sale at only £28.

Two months after Henry Kingdom's birth in Gostwyck, John and Mary O'Brien brought another soul into the world. His name was John Joseph O'Brien and he was born in Kilmore. His uncle Patrick, the former MLC for Kilmore and current MLA for Bourke, was becoming more involved in the community. When he wasn't politicking or judging, he was a member of the St Patrick's Society. This benevolent group had been established to promote education, help the destitute and promote prosperity in the new land. In July, he addressed the society's monthly meeting and suggested they contribute £100 towards the publishing and purchase of a new Irish dictionary, being compiled by the Archaeological and Celtic Society of Ireland. Patrick had never forgotten his Irish heritage. A note written on the letter that started me on this quest, mentioned that Patrick was related to William Smith O'Brien, an Irish patriot and activist who had been convicted of treason in 1849. Originally sentenced to be hanged, drawn and quartered, his punishment was commuted to a period of exile in Tasmania. I haven't found any evidence that they were related and seemingly, as every second man and his dog are named O'Brien in Ireland, it's a needle in a haystack job.

In August of 1859, Patrick addressed a meeting at Conran's Hotel in Hawthorn and declared that he was not in favour of government aid to religion and he disapproved of pensions – except to judges. Hmm. Later that month, the Victorian people went to the polls. Patrick appealed to his constituents and 'stated his willingness to support their interests in the ensuing Parliament'. His constituents didn't listen. He may have had the Irish voters on his side but no other bugger wanted him. In the election, he was soundly beaten and finished fourth in a field of five and that was the end of Patrick O'Brien's parliamentary career. He could now concentrate on his day job: selling booze to people and jailing them when they got drunk.

Some family trees have beautiful leaves and some just have a bunch of nuts. Remember it is the nuts that make the tree worth shaking.

                                                                         Author unknown

Michael O'Brien

8. THE ROOT OF ALL EVIL

In the preceding decade, the British had shown they were always up for a spot of biffo with Johnny Foreigner, so it comes as no surprise that a group of colonists fought a war in 1860. The surprise was that the war was in New Zealand and the British were fighting native Maoris in what was known as the First Taranaki War. Elsewhere, the second Opium War was being fought in China and Lord Elgin and his forces found themselves at the Gardens of Perfect Brightness in Beijing. Lord Elgin obviously didn't find them bright enough so he ordered his men to set fire to them and they were burned to the ground. And not content with fighting them on the beaches and the flower beds, the British launched the first ocean-going, iron-hulled armoured battleship, the HMS Warrior.

In America, they weren't fighting but they were warming up. Abraham Lincoln had been elected President and he was keen to abolish slavery. However, in the southern parts of America they were just as keen to keep slavery so the storm clouds started to threaten. In another part of America, a man named Joseph Smith created the Reorganised Church of Jesus Christ of Latter Day Saints by reorganising the previous Church of Jesus Christ of Latter Day Saints that had been reorganised by his father, also named Joseph Smith. Confused? So were they. The reorganisation also led to storm clouds as Smith's followers, who were practising polygamy, or multiple marriages, fought with the traditional Mormons and non-Mormons who were quite happy with just the one wife. America was a kettle that was approaching boiling.

Life in the Past Lane

Back in Australia, two chaps decided that they would set off on an expedition. They would start at Melbourne, walk to the Gulf of Carpentaria and then come back again. This would be the first attempt to cross the continent in a south-to-north direction. It seems that early explorers had lost interest in the east-west route; Ludwig Leichhardt hadn't returned from his attempt in that direction and as twelve years had passed since he departed, he was somewhat overdue. Anyway, these two chaps, Robert O'Hara Burke and William Wills, left Melbourne with a party of 19 men, 23 horses, 6 wagons, 26 camels, a cedar-topped oak table and a Chinese gong. 15,000 people gathered to see them leave and those 15,000 people would never see them again. Out of that enormous party, one man made it back to Melbourne alive, over a year later.

September of 1860 brought sadness to the O'Brien family. They were living in Nicholson Street, Fitzroy when John and Mary's daughter, Mary, died at the age of seven. The little girl died of scarlatina or scarlet fever. The disease causes a bright red rash which can cover the whole body, then the skin dies and flakes off. It was a common illness of the time and it would have been horrific to watch your child slowly succumb. John O'Brien had worked hard in his twenty-one years in the colony; he had chiselled away at the stone that would build a city, he had fought for what was right for the working man and he had kept his family safe and secure in the new world. Then his daughter dies and everything collapses. I can't help feeling that little Mary's death had a profound and severe effect on John; an effect that may have pushed him close to the edge, as the next decade would show.

On the 14th March 1861, John O'Brien became the treasurer of the Eight Hours Association, the society that was still working on improving employment conditions. In April, the Association ran a fete to raise money and they managed to collect £151 – some $13,000 in today's coin – so it must have been one hell of a chocolate wheel. John's duty was to take the money to the Colonial Bank and deposit it, which he did partly. Later, he was asked to attend a meeting of the Association and produce the receipts. John met with the secretary of the Association and told him that he had received a letter that required him to go into the country and he would be back on the following Saturday … which he wasn't. In fact, several Saturdays went past and there was no sign of him. The Association placed an advertisement in *The Argus*, asking him to attend meetings. There was no sign of him. The Association decided to check the bank and found that John had not banked all the money and had kept £37 ($3200) for himself. But where was John?

The simple answer is that he took off to Sydney. What isn't so simple to answer is – why was he alone? He had left his wife (who incidentally was pregnant again) and his two boys behind. We cannot know if he had a plan to meet up with them at a later stage but it seems unlikely. He was a man on the run but that would change, and change quickly. John was arrested in Sydney in June.

> 'J. O'Brien, treasurer of the committee for the eight hours movement, who absconded from Melbourne, has been apprehended and remanded back. He will leave today by the **City Of Sydney**.'[1]

His arrest in Sydney gave me my first and only chance of picturing my great-great-grandfather. He was listed in the Gaol Description and Entrance Book of Darlinghurst Gaol. In the days before mug shots, this was the best they could do. John was 5'6", had black hair and blue eyes. The Victorian Police Gazette added – 'medium build, dark complexion, black whiskers all around the chin and no moustache, usually wears dark clothes'. Fantastic – most people have family photos of their ancestors; I have police reports. And apparently, my great-great-grandfather was a Goth.

John was dragged back to Melbourne and charged with embezzlement. In the United Kingdom, they had recently reviewed their criminal law acts and had decided to go easy on the death penalty. It would only be handed out for cases of murder, piracy, high treason … and embezzlement. Whether this information had reached these shores is unknown but whatever way you look at it, John was in serious trouble. The court case dragged out for over a month as witnesses were found and points of law were argued. John's defence team (he had two lawyers

---

1. *The Argus*, 17th June 1861

representing him – was that some help from brother-in-law, Patrick?) – did the best they could, throwing the blame back at the Association by accusing them of shonky accounting procedures. The case came to a climax in mid-July and John was found 'guilty of larceny'.

> 'On being asked what he had to say why sentence should not be passed upon him, the prisoner said he had been twenty-three [sic] years in the colony, and he had never been before a judge or jury in that time. Mr Wintle, the governor of the gaol, knew him to have been a hard-working man. In answer to questions by the Chief Justice, he said that he recollected the man's face as having been employed in the buildings about the gaol, but knew nothing more of him. He had never been an inmate of the gaol. The Chief Justice said he believed it was the prisoner's first offence and he would give him the benefit of the doubt.
>
> Sentence: Twelve month's imprisonment, the first week of each alternate month in solitary confinement.'[2]

Four months into John's sentence, Mary O'Brien gave birth to a son named Thomas.

Back to a man who knew all about spending time in gaol for larceny while their wife gave birth to children - George Kingdom. In the period that John was on the run from the wallopers, George and Susan had another daughter and they named her Elizabeth. It looked like life was settling down in Gostwyck, but it was unsettling in London. Queen Victoria's mother, Princess Victoria of Saxe-Coburg-Saalfeld, had passed away and not long after, the Queen's beloved husband, Albert, died. He was only 42. Albert was also a member of the Saxe-Coburg family – actually, he was his wife's first cousin. They had nine children. It is not known if any of them had six fingers or could play the banjo.

While Victoria grieved, America seethed. The divide over the slavery issue had become geographical. Eleven southern states seceded

---

2. *The Argus,* 17th July 1861

from the United States and formed the Confederate States of America. When Confederate forces attacked a Union fort in South Carolina, it was on for young and old. The Civil War began and would be fought over the next four years. The Americans were outdoing the British; they wouldn't bother with travelling to kill people – it was easier to kill their own neighbours. It is estimated that over 600,000 soldiers died in the war and it is unknown how many civilians lost their lives. Mate against mate, state against state.

But we will finish 1861 on a happy note as the people of Melbourne watched the running of the first ever Melbourne Cup. The winning horse was Archer. The colonists were becoming fond of races. On the 26th January 1862, they celebrated Anniversary Day – which is what we now know as Australia Day. Seventy-four years had passed since the arrival of the First Fleet. Sydneysiders had to wait until the 27th to enjoy the festivities as the 26th had fallen on the Sabbath. Hundreds of people gathered at Sydney Cove to watch the Anniversary Day Regatta. There were numerous races involving skiffs, dinghies and yachts while the courses consisted of routes around Fort Denison and Goat Island. Some spectators were aboard the steamship *Kembla* as they had seen the advertisements for 'lunch provided with fowls and pastry at 2 shillings a head with lemonade, ginger beer and soda water'. However, it appears that they might have been better off staying on land:

> 'A large number of the passengers were completely drenched by the seas that broke over at midships and a still larger number of people succumbed to the motion of the vessel and the smell of tobacco with portions of the ship presenting somewhat the appearance of a very uncomfortable hospital.'[3]

The following day, the port was back to normal as the cargo kept arriving. Imports received included 49 packages of boots, 1 case of books, 390 barrels of cement, 171 packages of gunpowder, 2 pianos, 9 tons of salt, 220 cases of wine and 14 casks of grease.

---

3. *Sydney Morning Herald,* 28th January 1862

And the city's entertainment was back to normal as Mr Joseph Jefferson, the celebrated 'eccentric comedian', played at the Victoria Theatre along with a 'screaming farce' entitled 'Rooney's Blunders'. If eccentric comedians and screaming farces weren't your style, you could have popped down to the Prince of Wales Auction Room at 126 King-street East. There you would have seen the 'PETRIFIED BLACK FELLOW' that had been found in a cavern in South Australia. As the 'great sensation and excitement caused by his removal had not yet subsided', they tried to calm you down by also displaying a 'gigantic 200-year old CROCODILE' which was at a 'monstrous' length of nineteen feet and a 'SKELETON' from the Fitzroy River, though they didn't mention what the skeleton was of. Maybe you liked your exhibitions to be a bit more alive so you could have gone to see Mary Jane Young at 603 George-street. Mary was advertised as a 'native female Dwarf Prodigy' and was apparently thirteen years old, 35 inches high and weighed twelve stone. For those metrically inclined, that's 88cms and 76kgs. Admission to see Mary was a shilling.

There was also entertainment of an outdoor nature. At Watson's Bay Menagerie, 'Mr Billings will perform with the lions and put his head into the monster's mouth'. Show times were 3pm and 4.30pm with feeding time at 4 o'clock – which was probably only necessary if the lions hadn't eaten Mr Billings's head. Cricket was also popular as a visiting English XI played various colonial teams. The matches did seem a bit unfair on paper as the colonial teams used twenty-two players – not that it helped them much as they were soundly beaten. Perhaps the colonial side was more interested in the drink breaks than the game. But support for the sport was slowly increasing and an editorial in the *Sydney Morning Herald* opined:

> 'If each of these noble exercises – cricket and swordsmanship – were properly patronised, so as to become permanent institutions amongst us, and generally available, the natives of this colony would, as far as physical development is concerned, rank among the most athletic and active people of the world.'[4]

---

4. *Sydney Morning Herald*, 28th January 1862

Well, he got his wish with cricket – not so sure about the swordsmanship, though.

As the year progressed and if you were after a spot of culture, Sydney was your town. In June, Dr Berncastle addressed the Philosophical Society and read an 'elaborately compiled and interesting paper' on the cave temples of India. John King, the sole survivor of the Burke and Wills expedition, gave a talk at the Museum of Illustration in Pitt-street on the 'fate and sufferings' of the pair and maybe an insight into what happened to the cedar-topped oak table and the Chinese gong. His namesake, Mr W. King, with the assistance of his daughters, was 'prepared to give private lessons in dancing at any hour' at his residence in Liverpool-street, in case you fancied a waltz at three o'clock in the morning. And if you didn't, the Victoria Theatre was now featuring the nautical drama, 'The Dumb Girl of Palermo' and the admired burlesque, 'Nymph of the Lurleyburgh'.

Of course, you could not go to any of these events wearing a bunch of old rags, so it was fortunate that David Jones, the department store, had just received twenty-four cases of clothing. You could take your pick from the dazzling assortment of Elysian Derby coats, Inverness capes, Piccadilly Paletots, Orkney hand-knitted hosiery, Leicester cashmere pantaloons and fleecy-lined dog-skin gloves. And if you were a Freemason, you could also purchase your Master Mason's Apron there.

While all this sounds lovely, New South Wales was still a dangerous place to live. All sorts of things could happen to you and none of them were nice. Early in the year, a young man named Dobbs, of the Newcastle Volunteer Rifles, lost the middle finger of his left hand while he was on parade, as the charge in his rifle exploded while he was fixing the bayonet. Elsewhere, a girl named Jane Pritchard was burnt to death at Burwood when her clothes caught fire while she was engaged in washing. A forty-six year old man, named Thomas Williams, died from violent bleeding of the nose; Mr Lynch of Cowra was killed by a kick from a horse; another Mr Lynch, this one from Wagga, was killed by being gored by a cow; John Drew of Bathurst drowned when he fell into a well and Mary Selwood of Windsor died from injuries sustained when she fell onto a fire while intoxicated.

The sad story of Margaretta Ryan Maroney also happened in 1862. Margaretta was fifteen years old and was in the employ of Mrs

Foot of Bathurst. Mrs Foot had ventured into the water-closet of her premises where she found a newly born infant. The baby died and it was discovered that Margaretta was the mother. The teenager was charged with murder. She was indeed fortunate that the jury showed sympathy towards her youth; she was convicted of manslaughter and sentenced to two years hard labour in Bathurst gaol. Not so lucky in the court that day were two Chinese men who had been charged with breaking into Sofala Post Office and stealing money. The two men, Ah Chong and Cum Fat, were found guilty and went away for a long time.

There was a bloke living in New South Wales at the same time who probably wished he could rob a Post Office and that was George Kingdom. George was broke. In October of 1862 he filed for insolvency as he had run up some serious debts with the local businesses. At the time of the application, his personal balance sheet was very unbalanced. He owed £52 ($4500) to various storekeepers, fruiterers and publicans and his personal asset listing consisted of £2 of furniture and wearing apparel and six shillings worth of fowls. His declaration to the court was a sad story:

> 'On this third day of November one thousand eight hundred and sixty two – George Kingdom of Gostwyck in the Colony of New South Wales, sheep watchman, being duly sworn maketh oath and saith as follows. I am the person who petitioned his Honor [sic] the Chief Commissioner of Insolvent Estates that my estate should be surrendered for the benefit of creditors. I account for the insolvency for the following reasons. About two years ago the floods swept away all my crop of wheat worth eight pounds and also about two tons of potatoes worth sixteen pounds together with everything I possessed. I had also bought a horse a short time previously for which I paid twelve pounds, which died at the same time; I was thus left almost destitute. When endeavouring to obtain some goods in Armidale for the support of my family I warned those who supplied me that from my destitute condition and large family some considerable time must necessarily elapse before I should be able to pay for the

goods … my unfortunate position they would not press me for payment but would be satisfied to accept it whenever I could obtain means to pay. My salary is only eighteen pounds per annum and I have a family of four children and a wife to maintain out of that sum; yet since the time of my incurring the debts alluded to I have always gone to my creditors on receiving my half years pay and divided it among them as far as it would go; my creditors have become impatient and have all pressed me at once, so that I am compelled to seek the protection of the court.'[5]

The weather (and other issues) had destroyed George's fiscal state and at the end of 1862, it was still wreaking havoc. A heavy hailstorm at Gostwyck in December caused damage to wheat and fruit crops and severely weakened trees in the area. An old man named Davy was out looking for bullocks just before Christmas when a large branch fell off a tree, smashing him on the head. He was killed instantly.

The colonists liked a garden … as long as it didn't kill them. A visit to J.G. McKeon, wholesale and retail seedsman at 242 Pitt-street, would provide you with a choice selection of garden seeds. Purchases at John Purchase's at Parramatta would deal with all your fruit tree requirements. There were 11 varieties of orange tree as well as 4 types of lemons, 18 pears, 15 peaches, 45 apples and a selection of pomegranates, custard apples and mulberry bushes. When you'd had your go around the mulberry bush, ornamental trees and flowering shrubs could be bought at Guilfoyle and Sons Exotic Nursery at Double Bay. And to keep everything nicely nurtured and fertilised, Campbell's Patent Animal Manure was only £4 a ton.

In Victoria, Patrick O'Brien was too busy for horticultural pursuits. Great-Grand-Uncle Pat was elected chairman of the Hawthorn Bench of Magistrates in early 1863 and he was flat out coping with the crime wave. In one session of his court, the crims were lining up. Samuel Coles was charged with permitting a horse to wander; James Nolan, Michael O'Callaghan, John Baxter and James Davis were all charged

---

5. Affidavit to Commissioner of Insolvent Estates by George Kingdom, 3/11/1862, signed with his mark.

with allowing their cows to wander while Mary Garde sought £5 damages from Alexander Mayne as his goats had wandered onto her property and destroyed half an acre of potatoes. In the non-wandering crime category, Patrick O'Mara was charged with having no name on his dray and William Burchfield, alias 'Happy Tom', was indicted for indecently exposing his person in a public place.

So while Patrick O'Brien spent his days telling Happy Tom to put it away, he spent his leisure time putting real estate away. He already owned Kincora Hall and seventeen acres of land at Hawthorn which cost him £220 (or $19,500) a year in rates and he also bought five land lots at Echuca in an auction. He was a true descendant of Brian Boru. And not content with his attempt to buy most of Victoria, he ran for parliament again. Patrick appeared at an elector's meeting in Brighton in 1863 and *The Argus* had this to say:

> 'He was anxious that as few obstacles as possible should be thrown in the way of the transfer of property. He then called attention to the fact of the Imperial Government contemplating the establishment of a transport settlement in Australia. He should strongly oppose any such settlement. The colonists had come hither as free men ('some of us', shouted a voice) and as free men they ought to live. Let the people of Great Britain and Ireland keep their criminals at home. Why should Australia be deluged with the worst characters of the mother country?'[6]

Patrick's one and only opponent for the parliamentary seat was a Mr J.P. Bear. He seemed to think that he had the support of the voters in the district and he was 'perfectly satisfied that Mr O'Brien had entered a futile contest. He had known Mr O'Brien for many years and he was sorry that he was not better advised'.

Smug fellow, wasn't he? And as it turns out, completely correct, as well. Two weeks after the meeting the voters went to the polls and by and large, voted for Mr Bear. In Brighton, where Patrick had spoken so eloquently, he received only five votes. In Hawthorn, the town Patrick

---

6. *The Argus,* 22nd May 1863

loved and just about owned, he received 53 votes while Bear scored 120. And in the village of Snapper Point, forty-eight kilometres to the south of Melbourne, Patrick did not receive a solitary vote. Mr Bear comfortably claimed his seat in parliament.

Why did I bring up Snapper Point? Well, that is where John O'Brien was living after his stint in prison. He had probably moved his family down there, away from the people of Kilmore he had betrayed and the stern disapproving countenance of his brother-in-law. After all, Patrick was making speeches about free men and criminals – having a crook in the family was embarrassing. So, it appears that John didn't vote for Patrick, but it wasn't just bad blood in the family. To be a registered voter in Victoria in 1863, the law required that you should own property to the value of £1000 or more. John would not have made that qualification.

Patrick's unbearable loss to Mr Bear was not his only problem. Along with his land holdings, he also owned the Duke of York Hotel in Collins-street, Melbourne. He had leased the hotel to an Edward Butler and in August, Butler was applying for insolvency. It seems Patrick was charging an annual rent of £700 ($62,000 today) and Butler had discovered that the business potential was somewhat overstated. His average daily taking was £2 and that would have only just covered the rent, let alone any other expenses. Butler's lawyer criticised Patrick for his conduct and said that 'he was the very cause of his client's ruin'. The judge responsible for the decision on the insolvency case probably ruined a few of his other clients over the years. He was Sir Redmond Barry and he is best known as the magistrate who sent Ned Kelly to the gallows.

It was a trying time for Patrick and there was more bad news to come. Catherine O'Brien, his mother-in-law, my great-great-great-grandmother, died at the age of seventy-two. She had been living in Fitzroy, possibly in the house that John and Mary and family had also lived in. Catherine's death certificate is extremely difficult to read but the main cause of death appears to be 'exhaustion'.

Catherine O'Brien was buried in Melbourne General Cemetery in August but life went on in Melbourne. However, they didn't seem to get quite as excited about their entertainment the way Sydney people did. The theatre listings in *The Argus* for the 20th of August 1863 were:

| Apollo Music Hall | A concert |
| Royal Princess Theatre | Mr and Mrs White |

Wow. Then, perhaps the people were all at the Bourke-street Menagerie. That day, Thomas Jones, who was employed to feed the animals, had been rushed to Melbourne Hospital. Apparently he had taken his job a smidge too literally as he approached the lion's cage. A lioness had seized his arm and 'tore it severely'. Thomas should have taken some lessons from Mr Billings at Watson's Bay.

Christmas came and brought some happy news to my immediate O'Brien family. On Boxing Day, John and Mary had another daughter and she was named Mary. Shopping for presents and yuletide catering seemed to be quite easy in Melbourne – you only had to go to one shop. A spree in Alex McFarlan and Co at 18 Flinders-lane East would see you sorted: there you could buy Glenury whiskey, Fulton's Ale, Cramp Suter's sherry, Moffat's hams, oatmeal, cheese, ling, herrings, soda ash, tobacco, brown paper, table linen, cambric handkerchiefs, Crimean shirts, stationery, paper bags, Robey's thrashing machines, hydraulic presses, bookbinder's presses, miner's safes, nuts and bolts, iron tram rails, barrowman's ploughs, pig iron, saw benches and washing machines. If nothing there tickled your fancy, you could go to James Service and Co, 139 Bourke-street West and fill your Christmas stockings with Sinclair's hams, cheddar cheese, arrowroot, Polson's corn flour, Tainsh's jams, Batty's red cabbage, fresh herrings, Findon haddocks, homeopathic cocoa, Jordan almonds, Wotherspoon's Superior Confectionery, Nelson's gelatine lozenges, sulphuric acid, Belmont sperm candles, rifle powder, galvanised iron, griddles, Dunphy's Stout, Campbelltown whiskey, paper hangings, sugar bags and McDougall's Patent Sheep Dipping Composition.

It was all you needed for a cosy Christmas … and apparently it was the last cosy Christmas that John and Mary O'Brien had together.

Michael O'Brien

9. Through A Glass Darkly

It is 1864 and we are about to enter a hazy time in this branch of the O'Brien family. The dark period starts in this year and the lights come back on again about five years later – dimly. Only snippets of information are known from this span; the one thing that I think it is safe for me to say is that my great-great-grandfather, John O'Brien, ran amok.

I can only guess at his state of mind. He was about thirty-seven; he has a wife and four children but he has lost both his parents, two sisters and his first-born child. He has also spent time in jail which included the dreaded solitary confinement – a week spent in a cold and dark cell with only his cold and dark thoughts for company. Many a man went mad during solitary confinement, being reduced to a mumbling and dribbling shadow of the man he used to be. I don't know if this happened to John – but I believe something might have snapped. We will see shortly.

Up north, the Kingdom's had been very quiet in Gostwyck although they had celebrated the birth of another son during the previous year, when William Edmund was born. William's birth was close to the tenth anniversary of his mother's arrival in Australia. Susan Kingdom nee Elliott had been busy in that decade: one husband lost, one new marriage, one child lost, five new children born. George Kingdom had 'lost' his wife before all that; now he had lost his money as well but gained a new wife and five children. Swings and roundabouts, really.

In February 1864, a boy named Andrew Barton Paterson was born but he would later be better known as 'Banjo'. A month later, some engineers in Sheffield, England, probably wished they hadn't been born. After they had finished building the Dale Dyke Dam, they filled it with water for the first time. It broke. Hundreds of millions of gallons of water cascaded through towns and villages. Over 800 houses were destroyed and nearly three hundred people were drowned, with some bodies floating through the countryside for days. Water, water, everywhere and not a drop to drink.

In Australia, bushrangers were becoming all the rage. In May, Ben Hall and John Gilbert were involved in a fierce gunfight at a hotel in Koorawatha, in western New South Wales. At least they picked the right venue – the hotel was called the Bang Bang Hotel. They survived the shootout but their days were numbered. If you chose to be a highway robber in that period, you also chose to walk around with a target on your chest and a price on your head. Under the laws of the day, the police were actively encouraged to shoot bushrangers rather than bring them to trial. The following year, Hall, Gilbert and Dan Morgan were all dead – gunned down by the police. While these Australian outlaws met their maker, an American comrade-in-crime was making his name as a ruthless and violent bandit. He was Jesse James.

The US Civil War ended in 1865 as did the life of US President Abraham Lincoln, when he was shot dead at a theatre in Washington. The man who sent Lincoln to his salvation was John Wilkes Booth and around the same time, his namesake in England, William Booth, formed an organisation called the Salvation Army. It was also the year of a serious train crash in Kent where ten people were killed and forty-nine were injured. One of the survivors was Charles Dickens.

1865 also marked the birth of a boy christened George Frederick Ernest Albert. His family tree is more like a family forest. He and his cousins, Nicky and Willie, were destiny's children. Within fifty years, three little boys had three little toys. Cousin Nicky would be known as Tsar Nicholas II, Emperor of Russia, Grand Prince of Finland and King of Poland; cousin Willie would become Kaiser Wilhelm II, German Emperor and King of Prussia while Georgie would be greeted as – His Majesty George V, by the Grace of God, of the United Kingdom of Great Britain and Ireland and of the British Dominions beyond the Seas, King, Defender of the Faith, Emperor of India. George and Willie would end up at war with each other while Nicky would die in a hail of Bolshevik bullets. I hope they enjoyed their childhood.

The year also saw a bakery open in Newcastle, NSW, selling biscuits and pies to residents and visiting ship's crews. The bakery was very successful, the baker even more so. His name was William Arnott and his name still holds pride of place in stores today even if the financial reward now goes to an American soup manufacturer.

1866 saw another addition to the Kingdom family in New South Wales when a son, James, was born. In the United Kingdom, in old south Wales, the people had adopted an anthem. It has the delightful title of 'Mae Hen Wlad fy Nhadau', which is easy for them to say, and if we want to make it easy for us to say, we call it 'The Land of My Fathers'.

George Kingdom was in his fifties now and obviously still had a spring in his step. John O'Brien, approaching forty, definitely still had a spring in his step – or should I say, side-step. He appeared in court again in March of 1867, having been summoned to answer a complaint. This time the complainant was his wife, Mary. She stated that he had refused to provide her with a means of support and had deserted her. She also stated that he was quite able to maintain and support her. The court agreed and ordered John to pay £1 towards her maintenance. Now a few questions arise. Firstly, even allowing for the different monetary values, what the hell was £1 going to buy? Secondly, why had John deserted Mary? Finally, as the case was heard in the Sydney Water Police court, what were the O'Brien's doing in Sydney?

Just over a year later, the questions remain unanswered and John remained unrepentant. He was brought up on a warrant to the same court. This time he was charged with 'being about to leave the colony with intent to defeat an order of Court for the support of his wife, Mary O'Brien'. It looks like John was about to do another runner but the wallopers caught him again. (I have to say, that as a criminal mastermind, John was rubbish.) This time, John was ordered to find security of £11 or be sent to jail for twelve months.

What was he up to? It appears that after the birth of his daughter, Mary, in late 1863, John spent some time in Sydney. Whether he was commuting back and forth or he merely took off and moved north is unknown. What is known is that at some point between 1864 and 1868, John met the woman mentioned before - Ellen Cunningham. Where and how he met her is a mystery, but it brought about the end of John and Mary as a married couple.

Divorce in Australia in the 1860's was not common. To go through the legal motions in the courts was an expensive exercise. Also, John and Mary were Roman Catholics and divorce doesn't feature highly on the 'Ticket to Heaven' list. If they had lived in America, they could have gone to the state of Nevada, where the city of Reno had been founded. Reno would find fame as the home of the quick and easy divorce. Although it's clear that one man, Brigham Young, never visited Reno. He had assumed the mantle of leader of the breakaway Mormon Church after the murder of founder, Joseph Smith, Junior. In 1868, Young married his twenty-seventh wife. He believed polygamy was his ticket to heaven. I would tend to agree – after all, he was going through Hell on Earth.

It seemed that everyone was coming to New South Wales now – even royalty. In 1868, Prince Alfred, Duke of Edinburgh and fourth child of Queen Victoria, was in Sydney and had been invited to a picnic at Clontarf by the NSW Governor, the enchantingly named Somerset Richard Lowry-Corry, the 4th Earl Belmore. The royal prince found a place for himself in Australian history as he became the first person in Australia to be the victim of an attempted political assassination. Henry O'Farrell, an Irish alcoholic, had been recently released from the lunatic asylum – obviously prematurely. He went to Clontarf, pulled out a gun and shot the prince in the back. The shooting led to a wave of anti-Irish feelings as O'Farrell initially blamed his actions as being an order from the Melbourne Irish nationalists – this excuse was later dropped as his lawyer decided he was a nutter and went for the insanity plea. As the prince recovered, the parliament decided to build a structure to display their gratitude at the prince's recovery. The structure became a hospital and is still visited today – it is the Royal Prince Alfred Hospital in Sydney. The Governor (who didn't even see the shooting) was honoured with the suburb of Belmore being named after him. O'Farrell was honoured with a one-way ticket to eternity, courtesy of the hangman's noose.

Later that year, there was a Chinese man in a western NSW jail who avoided the hangman's noose – but not his own. The man, named Ah Hung (but according to the newspaper was also known as Teapot) had received a two-year sentence for stabbing one of his fellow countrymen. He must have found the idea too depressing as he wrapped his ponytail around his neck and attached it to the door hinge of his cell. Hung was found hanged the next morning.

It was another exciting year for inventions as the typewriter, the stapler and the measuring tape were patented. It also brought the installation of the world's first traffic lights. Set up outside the British Houses of Parliament, they were operated by a policeman manipulating hand-turned gas lanterns. Within a month of their introduction, they exploded.

In 1869, two gold prospectors from Cornwall were quite lucky. Working in Victoria, they found a gold nugget just under the ground's surface. Dusting it off, they realised they had found the end of the rainbow. The nugget was that heavy that no scale existed that could weigh it so they had to break it into three pieces. Its tallied weight was recorded at over two thousand troy ounces or around 70kgs. The prospectors were paid just over £9,000 ($801,000) for the find. The same find today would fetch them over $3,500,000. The nugget was christened the 'Welcome Nugget' and if you wish to go and see it, you can't – it was melted down and shipped to England.

There was no luck for John and Mary as they battled in court. The *Sydney Morning Herald* published an article that year which described the growing problem of deserted women. Amongst other comments, it read: 'The theory of the common law in England is that a married woman has no legal existence. Of course, it follows that she has no property, for a being who [sic] does not exist cannot possess anything.'[1] On the day that was published, Mary Elliott, eldest daughter of Susan and John, who had been waiting quietly in the wings while her mother and stepfather took centre stage, joined the ranks of the non-existent. She married a man named Henry Frost who, twelve years earlier, had undergone an unpleasant experience. His father, Charles, had left the family home in 1857 in a state of drunkenness, which was quite common, but he had not returned for a fortnight, which was less common. The Armidale area was searched thoroughly and eventually twelve-year old Henry found his father's coat by Armidale Creek. Shortly after he found his father's body floating in the water. Charles Frost's inquest decided that he had 'supposedly drowned himself whilst suffering from the effects of intemperance'. Twelve years later, Henry and Mary's marriage began a curious link between the two families,

---

1. *Sydney Morning Herald,* 11th March 1869

which we will see more of shortly. But there was probably another familial link that Susan Kingdom possibly could have lived without and that is the adventures of her brother-in-law's son, William Monckton.

A few years after the combined South Petherton forces of the Elliott, Edmonds and Monckton families arrived in New England, William Monckton snr passed away. His widow, Hannah, married again in 1860 but there were problems between the stepfather and William Monckton jnr. William left the family home to find fame and fortune; while he didn't rake up much of the latter, he achieved quite a lot of the former. He met up with a man who would change his life forever. The man was the bushranger, Captain Thunderbolt.

Will joined the bushranger in his robberies and his vendetta against the colonial government. He spent nearly a year with the man who was either feared or admired, depending on which way your sympathies lay. The police were frothing at the mouth and wanted Thunderbolt's head on a platter; being covered by the Felon Apprehension Act, they could just about do that. However, the bushranger had received the people's compassion for his cause and some of his victims were actually excited and grateful that he had robbed them. Thunderbolt had apparently been driven to a life of crime after a vindictive legal system ruined his chances of a normal, peaceful existence.

His marauding subsistence in the north of the state had largely been a solitary one. While he may have been glad of the company, he actively discouraged Will from accompanying him. Thunderbolt knew that if they were caught, the police would dispense justice under the 'protection' of the Act. The rozzers were tooled up and the 'shoot first, ask questions later' policy was in full swing. But Thunderbolt and Will Monckton roamed the countryside between Barrington Tops and New England, holding up merchants and mail coaches. They would converse with their victims while removing their valuables from them. Will did eventually leave Thunderbolt and gave himself up to the police. In April, he was brought up on three charges – attempt to rob under arms, horse-stealing and larceny. The judge told him he was a 'perfect young vagabond' and sentenced him to hard labour in Darlinghurst Gaol for twelve months. You might be thinking that in this time of bushranger eradication that Will Monckton was fortunate to receive only a year in jail. He had one thing in his favour – Will was only fourteen years old.

While Will languished in prison, being a fresh-faced boy amongst the colony's most deprived and depraved, the career of the shepherd was being discussed, when one was reported missing in Gostwyck:

> 'It shows the necessity of establishing a Bushman's Home, or some similar refuge, for this class of worn-out station servant-men who have toiled beneath the scorching noon-day sun in summer and slept on the frosty ground during the long winter nights and become feeble-limbed and decrepit and either die in their hut or linger out a painful existence in the wards of some Sydney infirmary.'[2]

No doubt Henry Dangar didn't use this article on his recruitment drives but it does indicate that George Kingdom and his colleagues didn't have a cushy day job.

Sydneysiders had their problems, too. The classifieds of the Herald in March display the anguishes:

> 'Lost: A £10 note between the Bank of New South Wales and the Savings Bank. Reward to finder.'

Surely the finder already had a reward. Hah, I thought, you can kiss that tenner goodbye ... until I read three lines down in the same column:

> 'Found: A sum of money. Apply Mr Wise, Savings Bank.'

I don't believe it. But it wasn't just moolah that was missing:

> 'Archie. I want to see you before you go. M.C.'

> 'Would the woman who was at the Home yesterday call again at once.'

---

2. *Maitland Mercury and Hunter River General Advertiser,* 5th August 1869

Well, obviously she had run off with Archie … and maybe they had taken someone else with them:

> 'To Edward Wilson Beach – write to your mother, stating where you are.'

I must stress that none of these are products of my imagination and if I was going to stress back then, a visit to Elliott Brothers (no relation) would be beneficial. They were supplying the 'celebrated' French medicines of Grimault & Co. There, soluble phosphate of iron could be purchased along with iodized syrup of horseradish (containing horseradish, iodine, watercress and scurvy-grass) and if you suffered from asthma, they recommended Indian cigarettes made of cannabis. It wouldn't fix your asthma but then you probably wouldn't care.

Michael O'Brien

10. THE WRONG SIDE OF THE BLANKET

January of 1870 was unremarkable. A Mr Gale flew a balloon in a gale from the Domain to Marrickville. A paper was published on the merits of using lime in the manufacture of sugar. The secretary of the Agricultural Society of NSW warned colonial vine-growers about the insect *Phylloxera Vastatrix* and the Society of Bellringers had an anniversary dinner at Randwick. Oh, but there was one piece of excitement - my great-grandfather was born. Frank O'Brien was born on the twenty-fourth in Derwent Street, Glebe. His father was John O'Brien and his mother was Ellen Cunningham. The birth certificate highlights in bold letters the fact the Frank was illegitimate.

Three months later, there were two weddings to celebrate in New England. Mary Elliott's brother, George, married Annie Frost, who was Henry Frost's sister and Mary's sister-in-law. So, George was now his sister's brother-in-law as well as being her brother and trust me, this part of the story is only going to get more complicated later. Mary and George's sister, Ann, bucked the trend and married a man named Lockyer.

In May, New England was again in the news with the announcement that Captain Thunderbolt had been shot dead by a young constable named Alex Walker, at Kentucky Creek. No doubt the Governor, the members of parliament and the Police Commissioner had a sherry or two that night. Over the last two years, they had to endure the public outcry of the attempted assassination of the Duke of Edinburgh and the anti-Irish backlash that crime produced as various nefarious outlaws rampaged around the state. Thunderbolt was probably one of the last 'Mr Big's' (allowing that a certain Ned Kelly hadn't begun his career yet) and the powers-that-be needed him out of the picture. And shooting him dead saved the cost of the trial.

But there was just one teeny problem: was the dead man actually Frederick Ward, the man police believed to be Captain Thunderbolt? The wallopers weren't sure what Fred Ward looked like. There was only one person who could clearly identify the corpse and that was young Will Monckton. Will had just completed his twelve-month sentence and was on his way back to New England. He was quickly marshalled over to Thunderbolt's body at Uralla and was asked if it was Fred Ward. He replied it was and the officials rejoiced. Thunderbolt was buried in the old Uralla cemetery and that was that. However, nearly 150 years after the burial, debate continues as to who the dead man actually is. Or was.

Several months after the burial of Thunderbolt, the colony received the news, via a ship called the *Wonga Wonga,* that France and Prussia were at war. This obviously made some people nervous and the residents of Waverley and Woollahra expressed an interest in forming a volunteer rifle company. A few gentlemen at Parramatta decided to do the same thing. But there was one gentleman who was oblivious to the news of the war; he knew nothing about it because he had been at sea for a quarter of the year. That gentleman was the Duke of Edinburgh, Prince Alfred.

He returned to Australian shores in September and was delighted that no-one shot him. He was given the news of the Franco-Prussian war and put his serious hat on as he toured proposed sites of additional fortification in Sydney Harbour. Then having got the formalities out of the way, he boarded a coach pulled by four horses, proceeded to Sans Souci and spent a pleasant afternoon shooting pigeons.

To mark the centenary anniversary of Lieutenant Cook's landing in Australia, the Agricultural Society of NSW had planned an exhibition. They wanted this to rival the Great Exhibition of London in 1851 and it was held in October at Prince Alfred Park. Thousands of people flocked to the exhibition under sunny skies. What to see first? There was a whole acre dedicated to a display of agricultural implements and machinery. There were 130 separate exhibits featuring horses and 186 for cattle. Further along were arrays of St Bernard's, Spanish fowls, Brahma pootras, Burdekin ducks, turkeys, pigeons, canaries and rosellas. There were presentations of locomotives, fire engines, phaetons, landaus, velocipedes, aerated water machines and drain pipes. The arts were covered as well with an assortment of paintings, statues, bronze figurines, photographs and musical instruments – this included a set of bagpipes made from tulipwood, whale's teeth and the skin of a goat. Prince Alfred was thrilled with proceedings and even lent the exhibition an animal off his own ship. It was an elephant, which must have been a fascinating beast to have on board a sailing vessel.

Eventually the Duke (and his elephant) sailed off and the Exhibition finished. The excitement died down and everyday life continued. The NSW Governor undertook a tour of the colony – no doubt to tell the people how well they were doing (even if they weren't) and wasn't it nice that the government had gotten rid of all those nasty bushrangers. But in those limousine-less days, the Governor had to do it tough. When he left the Shoalhaven area, he had to cross the river on a log, with a guide rope, up to his knees in water after sending his horse across first.

At the end of April 1871, the Catholic Bishop of Melbourne held a consecration ceremony for the Church of the Immaculate Conception. Remarkably on the same day, a baby was born who was the result of a less than immaculate conception. His name – William O'Brien and his parents were John O'Brien and Ellen Cunningham. William was born in Cardigan-street, Carlton – Carlton, Victoria, that is, which is a long way from Glebe, NSW. Why were they in Victoria? Was John trying to escape the clutches of his wife, Mary or her demands for financial support or the law or all of the above? I can't believe that brother-in-law Patrick, still meting out justice to the ne'er-do-wells, was overly chuffed to see John back in Victoria.

Coincidentally, an Irish labourer named Patrick O'Brien was arrested on charges of wife desertion. His wife claimed that he had left her 'in the shaugharon' – which is not another way of spelling Sorahan, but it did have court officials wishing they had an Irish dictionary. It simply meant that she had been left to wander – but she didn't wander alone as there were four deserted children as well. [Remarkable parallels to John O'Brien's current life situation here.] The husband claimed that he had been driven out of home by his wife's bad behaviour and she had broken his heart. When he was told that if he didn't return to his wife, he would have to contribute a weekly sum for her support, his heart quickly mended and back home he went.

John and Ellen had left the streets of Sydney and so had good behaviour. A July report in the *Herald* refers to the misconduct of idle and rowdy 'hobble-de-hoys' (a quaint old way of saying gawky, awkward youths) roaming the town and being rude and offensive to the elderly, women and children. And if that wasn't bad enough:

> 'The orange peel nuisance is becoming and insufferable grievance and has occasioned several painful accidents, one of which has proved fatal. The filthy and careless custom of throwing the rind of the banana upon the pavement is equally complained of by city people and disregarded by the city police.'[1]

Come on. Poor old PC Plod can't deal with all the drunks, the boisterous hobble-de-hoys as well as the lethal orange peels and have time to worry about banana skins. Sheesh. They also had all the dead bodies, which included a man named Hunt, who had been killed when he was hit by a train in Penrith. The police found no fault with the train driver or even Mr Hunt but as for Mrs Callaghan, the gatekeeper on the train line, well, she was charged with manslaughter. Still, could have been worse – the cops could have been on the island of Tanna, in Vanuatu. In late 1871, a Mr Grut was murdered by the natives – who then disposed of any evidence by eating him.

As a brig named *Velocity* sailed into the south coast town of Eden with 220 barrels of sperm, apparently elsewhere in the colony political correctness didn't exist. In Newcastle, the buildings previously used as a reformatory school for girls had been given over to the medical profession. The buildings were now called the Public Lunatic Asylum for Imbeciles and the Institution for Idiots. I imagine they dispensed with the idea of colour brochures for these places. Elsewhere in mental health issues, an 'entertainment' was given by some amateur minstrels to the inmates of the Gladesville Home for the Insane. The crowd went mad.

---

1. *Sydney Morning Herald*, 4th December 1871

In 1872, the English parliament knew that booze was a problem and they needed an Alcohol Licensing Act to control the Great Unwashed. They decreed that pubs would have to close at midnight and publicans would be fined for adding salt to the beer – a common practice as it increased thirst. The Act also banned people from holding a loaded firearm or to be 'propelling' a cow or a horse while drunk. There are no statistics for that time of how many people took their cow to the pub but there could be no doubt that DUI [droving under influence] was a serious social problem.

The government probably sent out the new legislation with the new NSW Governor; Sir Hercules Robinson would take over from Somerset Lowry-Corry. This appointment meant that the four mainland colonies of the time were being governed by titled gentlemen: the 1st Baron Rosmead, the 2nd Marquess of Normanby, the 6th Baronet Fergusson and the 3rd Viscount Canterbury. Poor old Tasmania had a bloke called Charles. Slightly further down the chain of command, Henry Parkes became the Premier of NSW, Charles Watt was appointed as the colony's Inspector of Kerosene and Mr Riley took over from Mr Peevor as the Scab Inspector of Geelong. Hand-picked, presumably.

While we are in Victoria for a moment, it's worth mentioning that a Mrs Bloor of 31 Napier-street, Fitzroy, had advertised her services in *The Argus*. She was a self-proclaimed 'lady physicienne and accoucheuse' which made her useful in pregnancy matters. It is unknown if Ellen Cunningham ever visited her but she certainly would have cause to. John and Ellen were parents again as Kate O'Brien was born on May 29. They were leaving no stone unturned – and possibly no mattress either.

May 29, 1872 was a big news day in the southern colony. The public were livid that smoking had been banned within the Botanical Gardens, yet every second vendor within the Gardens was selling cigars. It was also the day of the very first meeting of the Melbourne Hounds. Quite unlike the dog racing meetings of today, where greyhounds chase an electrified fake bunny around a track, these early gamblers used a live dingo as a lure. They would release it and allow their hounds to chase the startled creature. The course was a little longer than what we are used to; the first meeting saw the dingo run for nine miles over railway tracks and stone walls. The punters would follow on horseback in an exuberant manner – one horseman was so exuberant, he fell off his steed and broke both his arms. Mercifully, after running out of puff, the dingo was captured alive. But dingoes weren't the only four-legged beasts that were hiding from mankind. The Warrnambool Meat Preserving Factory were busy that month with their latest offering – tinned rabbit. The demand was so great, some 2600 rabbits were shot in one day to supply the factory.

Some humans were nervous too. A Mrs Hooke of Richmond walked into her local police station and informed the wallopers that her husband had threatened to kill her. The lads had heard this sort of tale before but accompanied her back to her house for a bit of a look-see. There they found Mr Hooke drunk as a skunk, and he seemed to have several suspicious bulges about his person. They searched him and found he was carrying a tomahawk, two razors, a knife and three bottles of poison. The police decided that Mrs Hooke might have a case and they arrested her husband.

On the same day Kate O'Brien greeted the world, her Uncle Patrick greeted the judicial system again. He wasn't back there as a magistrate but as a complainant. It seems he had another unhappy tenant in another one of his hotels. George Gallogly, financially struggling under crippling rents, had met his landlord, Patrick O'Brien, outside the hotel. He told Patrick that he could only pay half the money he owed him and he was in the process of auctioning off his effects. He was then heard to say: "I'm as good a man as you, blind Paddy O'Brien, and I will do for you yet.' An employee of the hotel testified that Gallogly had said previously, "that if O'Brien was in the country he came from and had used the tyranny he had towards him, he would have been shot long ago". Gallogly was found guilty of threatening Patrick and placed on a bond – his final words to the court were that he "would not dirty his hands on O'Brien". Patrick O'Brien had been in Australia for thirty-three years; from his humble beginnings and a potential early death in Ireland, he had built himself up to be a very wealthy landowner and businessman. With his success, he was good at making friends ... and equally as good at making enemies.

Several weeks later, in Sydney, a crowd was gathering. They had begun to assemble around 7.30am but they weren't being allowed to enter the gates till 9.00am. This led to fighting and a scrambling for positions which disgusted many. So what was this event? This year's Exhibition? A cricket match with the touring English? Mr Billings and his lions? No, it was a hanging at Darlinghurst Gaol – well, two actually. The men responsible for the case known as the Parramatta River Murders were about to feel the full extent of the law. George Robert Nichols (real name Robert Fitzgerald but also known as Mitchell) and Alfred Lester (aka James Froude) had confessed to the murders of William Walker and John Bridger. Both of the victims had been robbed, stripped, killed then thrown into Parramatta River. The crowds, after their long wait and struggle for the best viewing position, were finally treated to the sight of Nichols and Lester falling through the trapdoors. Lester's noose killed him instantly but Nichols took longer to die, his body twitching violently. Still, it was a good day out for the people and it beat sitting at home, drinking rotgut and kicking the goat. If the crowd had been at Bathurst Gaol a fortnight earlier, they would have had a real treat. A man named John Conn had just been hanged for murder and the gaol-keepers were taking down the body. Through some 'mismanagement', the prisoner's head was wrenched from the body and remained in the rope.

1873 arrived and the British army, who had previously thought that the African continent might be a jolly nice spot for a bit of a war, were fighting the Ashanti Empire, in the land which is now called Ghana. General Garnet Wolseley led his forces against the tribesmen under the Ashanti ruler, the Asantehene, or if we give him his full moniker, Otumfuo Nana Kofi Karikari. The Ghanaians lost the brief war and were forced to pay 50,000 ounces of gold in compensation to the British. In today's values, that would equate to about 85 million dollars. Needless to say, Kofi Karikari was deposed shortly afterwards.

Meanwhile in Canada, the North West Mounted Police were formed, bringing justice to the region and allowing the future creation of Dudley Dooright. South of there, a circus created by Phineas Taylor Barnum opened in New York and was christened the 'Greatest Show on Earth'. One of the other greatest shows on Earth at the time was the New York Stock Exchange and it went into meltdown when banks closed and investors panicked. Who said history never repeats?

Back in Australia, a member of George Kingdom's flock was leaving the nest. Fanny, George and Susan's eldest daughter, married a gentleman by the name of Dugald Cameron. As Fanny was only nineteen she had to obtain the permission of her father to marry as she was under the age of twenty-one. Her husband, who was born in Ardnamurchan, Scotland, didn't need any such formality – he was 37. However, even though he was nearly double his wife's age, he was of good breeding stock; he ended up fathering twelve children and the last was born when he was sixty-two years old. But it's not as if the Armidale region needed his help with population growth – that received a boost when gold was found on the Gostwyck property. In the blink of any eye, sixty miners were digging two and a half miles from the head station and some of the shafts were fifty feet deep. A mining boom is good for the economy; the baker's and the butcher's carts were returned empty to the town as they would sell out of produce as soon as they reached the diggings.

Mining companies were quickly being set up as the hopeful entrepreneurs of the time sought fortunes. In 1873, a person could buy shares in any of the following: Queensland Tin Company, Sydney Tin, City of Sydney Quartz, Great Southern Gold, Biraganbil Gold, Murchison Gold, Marshall's Rich Vein Gold, West Sydney Gold, Buckinbah Copper, Queen Tin, Stanthorpe Tin, Marcolini Gold, Dayspring Amalgamated Gold, Barton's Reef Gold, Darby's Creek Tin, Long Drive Gold, South Star No 3 Gold, Brown's Creek Gold, Glen Innes Tin, Ironbarks Golden Gully, Benedick Gold, Waratah Gold of Sally's Flat, Comet Gold, Lion Reef Gold, Phoenix Gold, Gulgong Gold, Ajax Amalgamated Gold, Fortuna Gold, Cornucopia Gold, Lord of the Isles Gold and even Wombat Gold. Or you could just buy a bottle of rum and piss all your money up against the wall – which was probably the same result for a lot of early investors.

While all those people were digging big holes in Australia looking for little rocks, one white explorer managed to find a bloody big rock without even using a shovel. William Grosse was on an expedition and came across an enormous lump on the landscape of Central Australia. The local natives referred to it as Uluru but Grosse, in a gross display of brown-nosing, named it after his boss, Sir Henry Ayers. For some reason, when Europeans and the British find a large piece of geography, they feel they have to climb it. The traditional owners of the rock and its surrounds do not climb Uluru due to its spiritual significance.

Tourists couldn't give a toss about spiritual significance and have only recently been prohibited from clambering over it.

The aboriginals were busy in other areas at this time and they were helping the white settlers with another issue – one that caused much debate. In March of 1873, a Mr Thompson of the Wagga Wagga area, reported seeing 'a great hairy animal that was about the size of a goat, that jumped into the water on his property and disappeared below the surface'. Rather than suggest he may have had too many drinkies the night before, the experts moved in. It was hypothesised early in the piece that goats were not amphibious, which was a brilliant observation and one hopes they didn't have to do many tests of the theory. It was suggested that there was a large type of otter residing in Australia so perhaps the beast was that. Others suggested it was a seal that had swum upstream. One man decided that as it was too big to be a platypus, it must be a bunyip.

It should have ended with that, but up in Queensland, an animal was spotted climbing a tree. It was said to look like a kangaroo, be more agile than a bear and chattered like a monkey. Once again the experts put their heads together and decreed that it was a 'ridiculous notion' to suggest that the animal was a kangaroo as they couldn't climb trees. Therefore, they decided, this animal was a bunyip.

Now, a bunyip is a mythical creature from Aboriginal lore and please take note of the word 'mythical'. Depending on what account you read and who told what to whom, a bunyip has been described as an amphibious animal that is the size of a calf. Or a hippopotamus. (This description must have lost something in the translation – I don't know how many Aboriginals of the 1870s would have seen a hippo.) It was also described as an aquatic animal that had grey feathers and swam like a frog or a creature that was a cross between a bird and an alligator that could stand upright on its back legs. So there you have it – a bunyip in the nineteenth century was a kangaroo that resembles a goat or an otter and it had feathers and could climb trees and swim underwater and make monkey noises. Brilliant.

The members of the NSW Parliament weren't overly concerned with bunyips. They were more worried about the correct use of punctuation. One politician mentioned a sign that he had recently seen outside a barber shop that read: "WHAT DO YOU THINK, I WILL SHAVE

YOU FOR NOTHING AND GIVE YOU A DRINK" People had been entering the shop, receiving their shave and being surprised when asked for payment. The barber finally realised his sign should read: "WHAT, DO YOU THINK I WILL SHAVE YOU FOR NOTHING AND GIVE YOU A DRINK?" The politicians all laughed heartily at the anecdote and then voted 'No' to an Act of Punctuation. However, they did approve the opening of the Divorce Court which opened in August at the Criminal Court House in Darlinghurst. On opening day, there weren't any cases for trial and the Under Sheriff presented the magistrate with a pair of white gloves. Then presumably, they just sat there and waited.

Down in Victoria, John O'Brien and Ellen Cunningham were keeping up with the annual production rate as a son, James, was born. Unfortunately, little James contracted bronchitis and died twelve days later.

Michael O'Brien

11. But Wait … There's More

In 1874, Patrick O'Brien stood for parliament again – I know, I know, some people just can't be told. There were two seats available for five men to contest; needless to say Patrick came fourth and missed out. Edward Cohen, the Commissioner of Customs, received three times the votes Patrick did. The second-place getter was George Seth Coppin, who doubled Patrick's tally. Mr Coppin's occupation on the ballot form was – 'comedian'.

It seemed that poor old Pat was going to have one of those years. Some joker had outpolled him at the elections and a woman named Margaret Cummins was playing him for a fool. Margaret was trespassing on one of his blocks of land in Melbourne. She had taken possession of a small hovel and was living there happily with her dogs, cats and goats. Patrick took her to court where she acted as her own defence counsel, launching into a lengthy tirade on the evils of society and Patrick O'Brien himself. She claimed that someone had tried to burn her 'house' down and also poisoned her dog. She had performed a rudimentary autopsy on the dog and discovered a lump of poison as big as her fist. The magistrate took a good look at the eccentric lady and her dishevelled appearance, deduced she would not have two pennies to rub together and fined her forty shillings. Failure to pay would mean a month's imprisonment. She pulled out a purse, paid the considerable fine in full and walked out of the court.

1874 was a year for the births of some influential people: the writers W. Somerset Maugham and G.K. Chesterton; the explorer Ernest Shackleton; Pharaoh Tutankhamen's discoverer, Howard Carter and future political powerhouse Winston Churchill were all born. John and Ellen also managed to produce another child when a son named Cornelius John was born. As his birth records have been difficult to trace, I am unsure of the locality of his birth but it appears to be somewhere in Victoria. To complete the baby shower, the year also saw the birth of Georgina Kingdom – no, it wasn't to George and Susan, but to their unmarried second daughter, Jane. It appears from later evidence that George and Susan may have tried to pass the child off as their own, to save any embarrassment.

While the Kingdom family was growing and the gold rush was still enticing people to New England, a young German man found a way to get himself into the Armidale history books. Seventeen year old Gottlieb Eichhorn followed an old woman home in early 1874 then brutally bashed her and left her to die, which she subsequently did. Even though Eichhorn was considered to be a 'half-simpleton', he was charged with murder and sentenced to hang. His parents visited him in prison, verbally abused him, shook his hand and told him goodbye. Several days later, Eichhorn became the first person to be executed in Armidale.

In the rest of NSW, people were finding other ways to die. A young man named Joseph Leahy was killed at Mort's Dry Dock by an accidental blow from a sledgehammer; the charred bones of an itinerant broom-seller were found near Haslam Creek and a man named John Shepherd, who was better known as Bandy-legged Jack, was found drowned near Campbelltown. Perhaps one of the strangest coroner's findings was handed down at Appin, where a man was found to have died from the effects of 'Icelandic Worms' that had been introduced into his system by drinking water frequented by dogs. Other people tried hard to die but failed: Thomas Foster of Phillip-street was badly burned when a torpedo exploded in his shop (an odd choice of retail product) and Fred Cohen was seriously injured when his gun exploded while he was shooting birds on the harbour shore. Karma, perhaps.

For the people who weren't being blown up or succumbing to Nordic nasties, there was a news story that was capturing attention. Andrew Hume had returned home from a two-year expedition in a search for the remains of Ludwig Leichhardt and his missing troop. This was some Herculean task; Leichhardt hadn't been seen for twenty-six years and of course, no-one knew how far he had crossed the continent. Hume, however, had some news. He had found Leichhardt's body, his watch, a quadrant, a piece of his journal and … his brother-in-law. While this was stunning news, there were some problems. Leichhardt's brother-in-law spoke little English and was now living with an Aboriginal tribe, yet somehow, he had managed to dictate an account of the ill-fated expedition – but Hume had lost it. He remembered the good bits though and it seems the Leichhardt expedition had reached a place called Sturt's Creek. There had been rumblings within the ranks and the majority of the party mutinied, clobbered Leichhardt and took off. The mutineers were all killed by natives and Leichhardt finally died of his injuries. His body, as per the custom of the local tribe, was placed in a tree.

There was some debate as to the accuracy of Hume's discovery. He declined to allow any examination of the documentation in his possession. The watch he had brought back was shown to Leichhardt's friends and they claimed it wasn't his. The government were asked if they proposed to take any action to verify the story and their only reply was that they were thinking about it. Several months went by and Hume wanted to clear his name so he organised another expedition to bring back the brother-in-law and any more evidence. Sadly, not long after he set off, he died of thirst. Now we will probably never know.

The year ended with more people getting into strife as fifteen people were dragged before the magistrate at the Water Police Court and charged with the shocking offence of playing cricket on a Sunday.

1875 arrived, ran its normal course and apart from the Brits taking a break from war, European royalty marrying each other and the Americans shooting Indians, lynching blacks and chasing Jesse James, not much happened. There was a concern in Sydney, though, and it was an observation that the people, particularly children, were getting sick. Steadman's Teething Powder was using a shock tactic in its advertisements as they led with a headline that screamed: 'MASSACRE OF THE INNOCENTS'. Underneath it suggested more calmly that their product was superior, and less fatal, than the others as it didn't contain opium. Another medication to be sampled was Udolpho Wolfe's Schiedam Aromatic Schnapps and a good slurp of that would fix your fevers and debilitating sickness.

But prevention is better than cure and a letter to the SMH editor in April pointed a finger at the problem:

> 'In the olden times there were no sweeter spots for a bath than Woolloomooloo Bay, Sydney Cove or even Darling Harbour. Forty years ago, the water in those places was as clear as it is in Coogee or Bondi. Now thanks to the ignorance of civilisation, all that is changed. The inhaling for an hour of the odours of the Tank Stream outlet at the Queen's Wharf, Blackwattle Swamp, Fort Macquarie or Darling Harbour is enough to give any one typhus fever … Undoubtedly much of the illness prevailing in Sydney is caused by the suicidal system of drainage … Our people suffer to live in hovels, in foul lanes, in cellars, surrounded by filth. We stand by while our children grow up weak, sickly and diseased.'[1]

This anonymous letter from many years ago serves to remind us that the Sydneysiders of that time didn't have chaps coming round at 4 o'clock in the morning to empty the wheelie bins nor did they have Royal Doulton flush toilets, Harpic Ducks or lavender scented air fresheners. What they had was a pile of waste in the yard, a pot to piss and shit in and a water source to throw the whole stinking lot into. Typhoid and scarlet fever were prevalent.

In the last quarter of 1875, it was reported that 228 children under the age of five had died. Scarlet fever claimed 32 and typhoid 19 but they weren't alone in providing family heartbreak. Heart disease claimed 28, pneumonia 29 while 49 fell to phthisis or tuberculosis. Another worrying figure was the seven children who died from the effects of alcohol and/or delirium tremens. It was a lottery if your child survived. Sadly, it appears that John O'Brien and Ellen Cunningham had moved back to Sydney and their son, William, became one of the 228. He died of scarlet fever in Cumberland-street, Sydney, in October. He was four years old.

---

1. *Sydney Morning Herald,* 29th April 1875

In 1876, a man living in Ultimo who had the unfortunate name of William Bastard, advised the population of the death of his daughter-in-law and invited them to her funeral. Two months after the burial, there was another bastard named William in Ultimo as John and Ellen produced another child. He was born William Smith Cunningham; the name was partly in honour of his deceased sibling and partly in honour of the Irish activist, William Smith O'Brien. Statistics on the birth rate of the colony had been published and revealed that some 7,532 children had been born between 1865 and 1874 (John and Ellen were regular contributors to this statistic). 4%, or 301, of those children were illegitimate. This was a lower percentage than the mother country – England's illegitimate births accounted for 6.1% of the total.

It is unknown if Mary was still receiving financial support from John. Their children would have now been aged 21, 17, 15 and 13 – at those ages, the four of them were probably part of the workforce. But there were numerous other men being ordered by the courts to pay maintenance for deserted families. A quick search found an Alfred Cullett being ordered to pay seven shillings a week, John Briley five shillings, Samuel Williams eight shillings and for a dash of irony, a William O'Brien (no relation) was paying six shillings a week to support his illegitimate child. For the children born out of wedlock, or living in a broken home, a begrudged payment from a father was better than the alternative 'solution' some parents carried out.

In July, a woman near Cardiff was charged with the manslaughter of her four-year old illegitimate child. The youngster was found to have suffered malnutrition, severe bruising and four broken ribs. A servant girl in Melbourne was also charged with manslaughter after she suffocated her own child and a woman named Williams was charged with murder when she held her illegitimate child in her arms – and cut his throat.

1876 is an important year in American history. It marked the centenary anniversary of George Washington and his army fighting the British in the War of Independence, which the American colonists won. It was also the year of the infamous Battle of Bighorn, which the American colonists lost … really, really, badly. In true white colonial style, the United States government announced that all Native Americans should not be allowed to wander around freely and they should be despatched to closely watched reservation areas. Naturally, this idea didn't overly enthuse the Indians and many skirmishes resulted. In a previously peaceful part of Montana, General George Custer led over two hundred men into a battle against a force of Cheyenne and Sioux warriors. It didn't go well. The natives, led by chiefs including Sitting Bull, Crazy Horse, Black Moon and Rain-in-the-face, annihilated Custer's men and then mutilated the bodies. The ambitious general is believed to have been felled by a female named Buffalo Calf Road Woman. Custer's two brothers, brother-in-law and nephew were also killed. The Native Americans briefly celebrated the victory, not knowing they would spend the next 150 years paying for it.

While the wild frontier was a dangerous and unforgiving place, those living in the American metropolis had their hazards as well. In December, a fire broke out in New York's Brooklyn Theatre and 295 people were killed. The following day, by uneasy coincidence, the first American crematorium opened in Washington. And for those people who hadn't been incinerated, or were about to be, a chap named Albert Spalding started a small sporting goods company with an ambition to one day keep the masses entertained. He appears to have succeeded.

1877 arrived and Jane Kingdom, daughter of George and Susan, obviously thought she better marry the father of her child, Georgina, so in March, off to church she went. Georgina's father was Robert Frost, who was the brother of Henry and Annie Frost. Those two had previously married Jane's half-brother and half-sister so that meant that Jane's half-siblings were also now her in-laws. One could be forgiven for thinking that there were only two families in Gostwyck; the Kingdom/Elliott's and the Frost's. But believe it or not, this part of the story still hasn't ended.

March also saw the first ever cricket test match played between Australia and England. Australia managed to win the match by 45 runs and managed to do so without the use of Snicko, Hawkeye, KFC Classic Catches and Tony Greig sticking his car-keys into the pitch. Several months later, another great sporting tradition began: Wimbledon. The All England Lawn Tennis and Croquet Club held their first tournament as a field of 22 players battled each other for supremacy. The final was watched by 200 spectators who paid a shilling to get in. As the crowd ate their strawberries and cream,

Spencer Gore beat William Marshall in straight sets and became the first Wimbledon champion.

While Gore and Marshall stood in the sun and swatted their balls across the net, elsewhere in Great Britain, life was not so splendid. In Blantyre, Scotland, the local coal miners had been fearful of their safety inside the mine they were working. They approached the mining company to express their concerns and to seek a compensatory pay rise. Once the company management had stopped laughing, they refused the pay rise and told the miners to get back to work. Some miners took action and went on strike – they were sacked immediately. However they may have been the fortunate ones. The rest of the miners went back to work and several weeks later there was an enormous explosion within the mine. Over two hundred miners lost their lives (the youngest was 11) and ninety-two women were widowed. Some months later, the mining company took legal action against thirty of the widows – their husbands were dead, they had no income and could not pay the rent on the cottages they had leased from the mining company. The widows and their children were evicted. Two years later, the mining company erected a monument at the site of the tragedy.

The year also provided a remarkable insight into the lives of people living on the island of Houat, off the coast of Brittany. 219 people resided there but one of them had supreme power – the parish priest. Apart from his spiritual duties, he was the mayor and the municipal council. He was also in charge of the military fortifications and settled disputes over fishing hauls. When he wasn't doing all that, he was the island's policeman and he dealt with the troublesome revellers at the pub – at which he had the monopoly of supplying wines and spirits to. And bizarrely, he was the key-holder to the one and only oven on the island – the islanders would have to bring flour to him if they wanted to bake bread.

It sounds like a job that Patrick O'Brien would have enjoyed but in late 1877, he wasn't enjoying much. His devoted wife of thirty-eight years, Sarah, passed away in Hawthorn. The official cause of death was jaundice, probably indicating liver disease. Patrick and Sarah had nine children but four of them had predeceased Sarah. Friends of the family were invited to meet at Kinkora Hall, the family home, and then follow the remains to the Church of the Immaculate Conception in Hawthorn while the burial was at Melbourne Cemetery. With Patrick's standing in the community, there was probably an impressive procession.

It is unlikely that Sarah's brother, John, was there. Living in NSW, he was still dealing with his constantly growing family … sorry, families. It must have been a challenge to find the money to keep a wife, mistress and eight children. He probably wished that he had the luck of a man who attended an auction at Young. At the forced sale of a distressed family's effects, he bought an old chair for a shilling. He decided to reupholster it and upon removing the original fabric, he found a will, deeds to a property and over £900 in notes, gold and valuable trinkets.

But not everyone was lucky in the country. A teacher wrote to a Yass newspaper and told them of his hardships. He had to attend two different schools on alternate days. The two schools were eight miles (nearly 13 kilometres) apart and to go from one to the other, he had to ride a horse for four miles, row a boat across a sea inlet for a mile and then walk the remaining distance through wild bush. At least he could count himself fortunate that he wasn't on the Wiseman's Ferry punt in April when it flipped over on the Hawkesbury River. Two men and twenty-four horses drowned. And he wasn't at Goulburn races when a cow walked onto the track and collided with a racing horse. The horse was killed and the jockey was severely injured. There was no report on the cow.

I have been disappointed in all my expectations of Australia, except as to its wickedness; for me it is far more wicked than I have conceived it possible for any place to be.

Henry Parkes, 1896

12. Thursday's Child Has Far To Go

In 1878, Gilbert and Sullivan's operetta *HMS Pinafore* premiered in London and brought happiness to many - but two other ships in the capital didn't. A pleasure boat called the *Princess Alice* collided with a coal freighter on the River Thames. Unfortunately, an hour before the collision, the river authorities had opened the sluice gates and 75,000,000 gallons of raw sewage was released into the river, quite close to the crash scene. 650 people lost their lives in the heavily polluted waters.

Back in Australia, a certain Ned Kelly and his merry men were running rampant. In April, a policeman had been wounded (so he said) as he tried to arrest Dan Kelly but it was the shooting of three policemen at Stringybark Creek that lathered up the government. They offered a £500 reward (around $40,000 today) for each member of the gang – captured dead or alive. A subsequent bank robbery in Euroa saw the figure raised to £1000. To put that in comparison, a wharf labourer in Sydney was being paid one shilling an hour in 1879 … or about four bucks today.

While some probably dreamed of the riches to be had by capturing the Kelly's, others just dreamed. A Scottish-born composer, Peter Dodds McCormick, had been working on a little ditty and decided it was time to release it. He named the song 'Advance Australia Fair' and most people thought it was a pretty hip tune. Even the government liked it although they took a while to show their appreciation; twenty-nine years after McCormick wrote the song, they gave him £100 for it. So while he would have made more money by shooting Ned Kelly, his words have not been forgotten. Actually, that's not quite right; the original song was four verses long and when it was introduced as our anthem, it had been cut to two verses. And the anthem we know is not the same as the one he wrote. The first verse remains largely untouched but the second copped a right old rewrite. Here's the original:

> 'When gallant Cook from Albion sailed,
> To trace wide oceans o'er,
> True British courage bore him on
> Till he landed on our shore.
> There he raised old England's flag
> The standard of the brave.
> With all her faults we love her still
> Britannia rules the wave.
> In joyful strains then let us sing
> Advance Australia Fair.'

Stirring, isn't it? Yet, the second verse we now sing … well, someone must be able to sing … is quite different:

> 'Beneath our radiant Southern Cross
> We'll toil with hearts and hands
> To make this Commonwealth of ours
> Renowned of all the lands.
> For those who've come across the seas
> We've boundless plains to share
> With courage let us all combine
> In Advance Australia Fair
> In joyful strains etc'

You can see all the British references have been removed and you can also enjoy the sheer poetry of – 'For those who've come across the seas, we've boundless plains to share' – that is, unless you are an asylum seeker. Maybe that's why no-one sings the second verse today. However, there is one other interesting point: you can sing the whole of our National Anthem to the tune of 'House of the Rising Sun'… and vice versa.

Back in 1878, if you liked Mr McCormick's tune, there were several ways for you to perform it. You could purchase a Zeitler and Winkelman's Powerful-toned Walnut piano and that would set you back £55. W. H. Paling's Music Warehouse in George-street was offering lessons in pianoforte, violin and cello. You could also go to Hereford College in Glebe-road, where private lessons were given in music, singing, dancing and … wax flowers. Or perhaps a visit to 213 Macquarie-street would be preferable, as there you would receive lessons in singing and piano from Signora DeBaraty Ferrari.

I would suggest that John O'Brien and Ellen Cunningham were probably not worried about music lessons as they had a young family to look after and as a matter of fact, on the first of August another joyful bundle arrived into their lives. Leopold Bede Cunningham was born at 424 Harris-street, Pyrmont and his birth certificate has provided another mystery. Under the heading of previous issue, it states that there are 3 males and 1 female living. That would be Frank, Cornelius, William Smith and Kate – no problems there. But the certificate also notes something that is echoed on future certificates – three deceased males. I have found and mentioned the first William and James, but who was the third one? After many months of fruitless searches, a possibility arose. An illegitimate child named Alfred Ernest Cunninghame died in June 1869. He was 14 months old. On the certificate, his father wasn't stated, and his mother was noted as Ellen Cunninghame. Strangely, the informant was listed as – "Ellen Brian, late Cunninghame". Even more of interest is that she gave her address as Derwent Street, Glebe – the same address as given for the birth of Frank, my great-grandfather - less than six months later.

John O'Brien would have been about 51 in 1878 and he had fathered five children with Mary and apparently eight with Ellen. If they had all lived, he would have had more than a soccer team. Therefore, it's only fitting to mention the formation of two soccer teams in England in 1878 – Fulham St Andrew's Church Sunday School Football Club and the Newton Heath Lancashire and Yorkshire Railway Football Club. These club names are obviously a bit of a mouthful so in future years, changes would be made. The former mentioned team was just shortened to Fulham; the latter would go on to dizzy heights in world football – they are now called Manchester United.

In 1879 the reward for each member of the Kelly Gang was raised to £2000, or twenty national anthems, as they had robbed another bank, this time at Jerilderie. John and Ellen took a year off baby production and the Kingdom's of New England were behaving themselves. Down in Melbourne, perhaps Patrick O'Brien was feeling a bit lonely after Sarah's death so eighteen months after his loss, he married Mary Agnes Hayes. Paddy would have been in his early sixties, probably worth a small fortune and he didn't do things by halves. The service was performed by the Archbishop of Melbourne in his private chambers.

In the Sutherland Shire, south of Sydney, a large area of natural bushland was proclaimed as – The National Park. It is the world's second oldest national park, after Yellowstone in the USA. Seventy-five years later a visiting monarch, Queen Elizabeth II, passed by the area in a train on her way to Wollongong. Apparently, this was enough to get the park relabelled – The Royal National Park.

British military forces must have been feeling a bit bored, so they picked a fight with some Russians in Afghanistan and took on some Zulus in South Africa. In the latter conflict, the British invaded the area known as Zululand and found themselves involved in the Battle of Isandlwana. There, with their rifles and 7-pounder cannons, they met the army of King Cetshwayo kaMpande, who were equipped with shields, clubs, spears and some old rusted guns. While the British force had an advantage with their apparatus, they had a shortfall elsewhere – men. The British numbered around 1,800; the Zulus had over 20,000. Blind Freddy would have seen that was a bit of a problem, but not the British. Tally-ho, old boy, once more into the breach.

They were massacred. It's all very nice having a rifle but they are very hard to reload when you are being disembowelled by an assegai and your skull is being jellified by a hundred blows with a club. However, the British being British, picked up whatever of themselves was left, dusted themselves off and went on to fight further battles in Zululand. There they were more successful and with the aid of Gatling guns, they stormed the capital of Zululand. In celebration, they burned the capital to the ground and slaughtered all the Zulu wounded.

However, there was another conflict to come for the British and it would happen at Moore Park, in an area now known as the Sydney Cricket Ground. The touring English cricket team were playing a match against a New South Wales selection. Everything was spiffing until a NSW batsman was given out by one of the umpires. In that time, both teams would select an umpire each and the English had chosen a Victorian. He was the man who gave the batsman out but the decision was questioned by the batsman. As there were no third umpires or review procedures, the batsman was out and that was his bloomin' lot. However some of the crowd didn't like the decision and they vented their frustration by running onto the field – about 2,000 of them. The spectators (including a young Banjo Paterson) invaded the field and assaulted the Victorian umpire and several English players. The other umpire tried to restore order but was fighting a losing battle – he was destined for bigger things anyway; his name was Edmund Barton and he would become Australia's first Prime Minister.

The English captain was escorted from the field by two of his players using the stumps as protective weapons. Most of the cricketers suffered cuts, bruises and torn clothing. Unsurprisingly, play was abandoned for the day. The two captains met the following morning and agreed to play on. NSW were quickly dismissed and England won the match. Then they promptly cancelled all their remaining games in Sydney. The incident became known as the Sydney Riot of 1879 and received vitriolic media coverage in London, with one of the main concerns being the claim that the NSW police just stood and watched the riot. It also became front page news in Australia, knocking the Kelly Gang's activities further back into the paper. The game of cricket would not see such outcry again until Bodyline or the day Trevor Chappell rolled one down the pitch to a New Zealander.

As the sun set at Moore Park, a ship named the *Peterborough* sailed into Sydney. It was packed with Irish immigrants seeking a new home. One man, Daniel McAuliffe, arrived with his wife and eight children. He and his wife were born in County Cork, as were his two eldest. However they must have tried their luck elsewhere before Australia; the remaining children were born in North America. The second-eldest daughter was named Ellen; she was 13 years old and already working as a servant. Say hello to my great-grandmother.

So in with the people and out with everything else. Not content with just supplying the needs of its population, the colony of New South Wales was also exporting home-grown goodies. In May of 1880, a ship named *Sydenham* set sail for London with a dazzling array of cargo. The freight included 548 bales of wool, 3,167 bags of copra, 50 tons of shale, 6,780 ingots of copper, 193 bales of leather, 1,615 bags of bark, 3,623 hides, 12 tons of bones, 13 tons of hooves and 40 packages of hair. Waste not, want not. The ship sailed off with its curious assortment as Ellen Cunningham added to her own curious assortment – Sydney Augustus, her ninth child with John O'Brien. Ellen was thirty-two years old.

In Victoria, time and luck had run out for the Kelly gang. The four of them had holed out in an inn at Glenrowan and they were keeping hostages. The gang had been advised that a small army of coppers were on a train and heading their way so they sabotaged the tracks. However, a quick-thinking local had alerted the police and a train wreck was avoided. The coppers surrounded the inn and a volley of shots rang out through the countryside. Ned Kelly, wearing his iconic suit of armour, advanced towards the police, apparently oblivious to the fact that his limbs were unprotected. His defiant march came to an end with several wounds to his arms and legs. Inside the inn, things weren't much better – in fact, they were a whole lot worse. Joe Byrne had been killed by the gunfire and according to a witness, Dan Kelly and Steve Hart had committed suicide. The inn was set on fire and the remains of the Kelly gang were toasted.

Two hostages were killed that day, one of them an eleven year old boy. Only one policeman was injured, receiving a minor flesh wound which caused him to run from the scene like a startled rabbit. He was later suspended from the police force for his cowardice, yet curiously he collected a portion of the reward money – some £800 or around $45,000 in today's coin. Even more curious was the fact that the brave fellow who had alerted the wallopers to the danger awaiting their train, probably saving some or all of their lives – he only received £550. And even more inflammatory was the awarding of £50 each to several native trackers. The money was taken back from them as 'it was undesirable to place money in the hands of people who can't use it'.

Ned Kelly recovered from his wounds and was able to stand trial in front of Judge Redmond Barry. Even though there was considerable public support for Kelly, he stood a snowball in hell's chance of earning a reprieve from execution. Barry donned the black cap, sentenced Kelly to hang and ended his judgement with – 'May God have mercy on your soul'. It is reported that Kelly replied – 'I will see you there when I go'.

Kelly was hanged on the eleventh of November; Redmond Barry died twelve days later.

1880 also heralded the opening of the first stage of the Sydney Town Hall. The site, as previously mentioned, had previously been the location of the colony's first cemetery. During the construction of the Town Hall, builders were required to remove the buried remains to Rookwood Necropolis. The headstones were not moved as it was considered to be too difficult to match them with the remains. So at Rookwood, they decided to build one big monument to honour the dead. Not one person's name is written on the monument. It also turns out that the builders may have been a little neglectful in their duties – during renovation work at the Town Hall in both 1991 and 2003, it was discovered that some remains had been left behind.[1]

But there was also life in the town in 1880 – Sydney's society loved forming societies. In August, the monthly meeting of the Eastern Suburbs Horticultural Society was held and a certificate was presented to Mr J. B. Durham for his cabbage. And in the following week, the annual dinner of the New South Wales Poultry, Pigeon and Canary Society took place in a hotel in York-street – I wonder what was on the menu.

In 1881, a census was taken in Australia. The population was recorded as 2,250,194 – well, there were actually more people than that but Western Australia refused to count aboriginals. New South Wales had 751,468 souls with 224, 939 living in Sydney but Victoria led the way with 862,346 people of which 282,947 lived in Melbourne. Sydney's population might have been greater if a smallpox epidemic didn't rage through The Rocks but at least the government were assisting to stop carnage in another way: legislation was passed to close pubs on a Sunday and to cease trading at 11pm on weekdays.

All was quiet on the O'Brien and Kingdom front but it was far from quiet on the western front. The American Wild West was living up to its name. In April of 1881, fear was caused when an armed gang of Mexicans rode into the town of El Paso, Texas. They were looking

---

1. History thanks to the Sydney Town Hall website

for two missing men who were eventually found dead on the property of a suspected cattle rancher, named John Hale. Two men associated with Hale were accused of murdering the Mexicans and an inquest was held. After a day's proceedings, Hale and a man named George Campbell argued with a deputy and shots were fired. Across the street in a restaurant, quietly eating his lunch, sat the town Marshall, Dallas Stoudenmire. He heard the shots and like John Wayne, he sprang into action. He ran out into the dusty street and pulled out his six-shooters. He shot dead an unfortunately-situated innocent Mexican bystander who had been running for cover. Probably murmuring – 'Whoops' – to himself, the Marshall swivelled and shot Hale between the eyes. He then spun around in the other direction and shot Campbell in the stomach, causing a fatal wound. Meanwhile, three Texas Rangers allegedly stood around watching the carnage, believing Stoudenmire had everything under control.

Three days later, a friend of Campbell and Hale sought revenge against Stoudenmire. Like all good cowboys, the friend got himself plastered at the saloon and then crept up behind the Marshall with a shotgun. Sadly for him, he slipped, fell backwards and his shotgun discharged into the air. Stoudenmire turned and fired eight shots. One of the shots blew off the would-be assassin's testicles and the freshly-created soprano bled to death.[2]

Four months after Stoudenmire's Rambo-like heroics, a gunfight broke out into the less-than-optimistically-named town of Tombstone, Arizona. History and Hollywood has billed the gunfight as the "Gunfight at the OK Corral". To be historically and geographically correct, it should be billed as the "Gunfight near the OK Corral, Around the Corner and Down the Street", but that doesn't sound as dramatic and would look funny on the movie poster. Anyway, several outlaws and assorted cowboys took on the law, represented by Wyatt Earp, his brothers and a gambling-mad dentist by the name of John Henry Holliday, better known as 'Doc'. In the gun battle, over thirty shots were fired, three outlaws were killed, two Earps and Holliday were injured and Wyatt walked away unharmed.

---

2. *Dallas Stoudenmire, El Paso Marshal,* Leon Claire Metz, University of Oklahoma Press, 1979

Later in the year, murder charges were laid upon the Earps and Holliday, but they were acquitted. They were only acquitted in the eyes of the law, however and not in the eyes of the people. The next six years were littered with retribution killings from both sides as Tombstone ran short of tombstones. Today, you can visit the town and watch a daily re-enactment of the battle, performed by actors who can't get into the movies … or you can watch re-enactments performed by actors who did get into the movies, as they appear in one of the eighteen different films about the event.

No rest for the wicked as a sheriff named Pat Garrett shot dead a twenty-one year old man named William Henry McCarty, Jnr. McCarty was also known as Henry Antrim, William H. Bonney or just simply Billy the Kid. One Australian newspaper described him as 'New Mexico's Answer to Ned Kelly' but this is a little unfair on Ned. In Billy's short but brutal life, he is estimated to have killed between fifteen and twenty-six men. Interestingly, Billy's exact burial place within the cemetery is unknown due to floods destroying the cemetery and his gravestone has often been the target of thieves. Then some say that doesn't matter anyway, as he isn't in that cemetery. In 1949 a man named Brushy Bill Roberts claimed to be Billy the Kid … um … which is eleven years after a man named John Miller claimed he was Billy the Kid. While at least one of them had to be wrong, being a descendant might have been profitable. In 2011, a 2" x 3" photograph, believed to be an authentic picture of Billy the Kid, sold at an auction for 2.3 million dollars.

Last but not least, as time moved onto 1882, the train-robbing, bank-robbing and murdering outlaw named Jesse James was finding the heat from the authorities a bit much. He was hidden away in a house in Missouri, sharing it with his wife and the only two men left he could trust, Charley and Robert Ford. Jesse's judgement was misplaced, however as Robert Ford had been running back and forwards to the sheriff, organising the outlaw's capture and his receipt of the reward. On the morning of April 3, Jesse dressed, ate breakfast and noticed some dust on a picture on the wall. He reached for a chair, stood on it and dusted the picture. As he did the cleaning, Robert Ford drew his gun and shot James through the back of the head, killing him instantly. Ford then rode into town, eager to claim the reward only to find disappointment as he was charged with murder. Ford was found guilty and sentenced to hang. Two hours later he received a full pardon, was given a portion of the reward money and he vamoosed out of town. He spent the next ten years bragging about his exploits, even concocting a stage show, until he was shot dead inside a Colorado saloon.

To carry on with the posthumous tradition, in 1948 a 101-year old man named J. Frank Dalton came forward (probably slowly) and claimed he was Jesse James. He was put through a thorough questioning by surviving James relatives and got most of the answers wrong. He shuffled off in disgrace. In 1995, the remains of Jesse were exhumed and subjected to a DNA test, which indicated that the body in the grave was in fact, Jesse James.

So while our own Captain Thunderbolt's remains and final resting place has been the subject of debate and controversy, there aren't too many other similarities between American outlaws and Australian bushrangers. The streets of Sydney, Melbourne and even Armidale were somewhat quieter than the blood-soaked streets of Arizona and Missouri.

Back home the Colonial Secretary, Sir John Robertson, had angered a few people in the south. He had stood up in parliament and stated that New South Wales should have all the trade with the rest of the world while Victoria should take a back seat and become a cabbage garden. But he wasn't the only person who hated Victoria. In March of 1882, a man named Roderick McLean had sent some of his poetry to Queen Victoria. Apparently she returned it with a less-than-positive response to his creative work – so he decided he was going to shoot her. His assassination attempt was thwarted and he was charged with high treason which if he was found guilty of, would mean a fairly unpleasant execution. However the jury decided he was not guilty due to insanity and he spent the remaining thirty-nine years of his life in Broadmoor Asylum.

In Sydney, larrikins were running amok. Around 600 of them had an all-in-brawl in Cumberland-street in the early part of the year. Two policemen were injured by stones that had been thrown at them. Several months later, young men ran up and down Crown-street in Surry Hills, chucking stones at houses. Several plate glass windows were smashed, furniture was ruined and one man was hit in the head while he ate his supper. At least he wasn't in the USA at the time when a storm hit Iowa and hailstones were measured at 17" (43cms) and weighed in at 1.75 pounds (800gms). Having one of those scone you while you were eating your scones could ruin your appetite. But it might have been the least of your worries - the following day, the storm upgraded to a tornado, ripped through the state and killed 130 people.

Heading towards Christmas, the police authorities had become bored with all the unclaimed goods that had accumulated in the storeroom of the Central Police Court, so they held an auction. There was tinned fish, baby's clothing, tricycles, trinkets, old saws, modern philosophy books, Chinese wearing apparel and a ball gown amongst the assortment. According to the *Herald*, -

> 'The purchasers were as motley in appearance as the collection of articles was varied. At the sale's conclusion, a long line of men and women, carrying pots and pans, bundles of ragged clothing, cross cut saws, door mats, concertinas and gingham umbrellas, filed out of court, rejoicing in the possession of their bargains'.3

This sort of retail activity still happens today but it is known as a 'Boxing Day Sale'.

So while the townspeople shopped, the new arrivals kept arriving. One particular ship that arrived late in the year was packed with immigrants seeking work – and most of them didn't have to seek hard. At the time, applications and requests from employers far outweighed the available employees. The general rate of annual wage was between £30 and £40 (around $2400-$3200 today) with board and lodging for unmarried men, while married couples could expect to pick up about £70 ($5600) per annum. Work was that easy to find that tradesmen would leave the ship, walk into the city, get a job, walk back to the ship and grab their bags.

> 'Energy and hope were written upon every face . and when leaving the vessel that had borne them from England,

---

3. *Sydney Morning Herald,* 22nd November 1882

with its crowded cities and hard struggle for existence …
cheer after cheer was heartily given.'[4]

Was everyone joining in the cheers that year as they revelled in prosperity and happiness? Could I picture John O'Brien and Ellen Cunningham jumping for joy? Was Mary O'Brien thrilled with her lot? Were George and Susan Kingdom gambolling gaily around Gostwyck? Probably not, but did they have the worst of it?

In Goulburn, a labourer named William Morin had been charged with stabbing a woman, in whose house he had been a lodger and in whose care he had left his children. Mr Morin was described as a strong fellow, in the prime of his life, but alcohol had ruined him. His wife was also seemingly addicted and she was already in jail serving a three month sentence. Morin received six months for the assault, which meant the Morin's four children, aged between 3 and 9, were left with nothing. Arrangements were made to forward them to the Destitute Asylum. It is unknown if the Morin's ever claimed their children back.

A domestic servant named Peter McGregor, aged 58, was discovered lying under a tree in Moore Park with his throat cut. The four-inch long wound, caused by a razor, was self-inflicted. He had been out of employment for several months and a year earlier, his wife had been struck dead by lightning. He had decided to put an end to his misery but a policeman had found him. He was taken to the hospital where he recovered.

An old woman, shoeless and ragged, was brought before the Bench in the Central Police Court, charged with having been drunk and using bad language. "Let me have Christmas out, your Worship," she cried out. "It is twenty years since I spent Christmas outside of the lockup or the gaol, your Worship."[5] The old lady had quite a bit of form as a drunkard and had spent the greater portion of her life doing short stints of incarceration. On this occasion the judge ordered her to be imprisoned for fourteen days and she would be freed just before Christmas. So, providing she didn't get locked up

---

4. *Sydney Morning Herald,* 5th July 1882
5. *Sydney Morning Herald,* 11th December 1882

in the interim, she would spend Christmas Day at liberty for the first time in twenty-one years.

Joy to the world.

1883 heralded the introduction of two famous Australian brands. Alfred Thomas Bushell founded his tea business in Brisbane and in Tasmania, Boag's Brewery was formed. A Scot named James Boag had bored of the Victorian goldfields, moved to Tassie and started to make beer instead. James went into partnership with his son named James who had a son named … James. The third James took over the operation when the first two passed away and unsurprisingly, his son took over from him. Surprisingly, his son was named George. However, today there are no Boag's family members left in the business and it is now owned by a Japanese brewing company.

During the year, it seemed that a couple of chaps named O'Brien had been imbibing a few too many Boag's products or perhaps, they had a few other issues. In February, a 'lunatic named O'Brien' created a disturbance in the Police Court at Murrurundi. Appearing on a charge of 'being a dangerous lunatic', he stood up in court, knocked the books stacked on the lawyer's table flying and approached the judge. "What are you doing?" asked O'Brien. "Am I a murderer? I'll soon see about all this." He then picked up an inkstand and threw it at the judge. The inkstand missed but the ink didn't. As the judge wiped the ink off his robes and face, the police led Mr O'Brien away.[6]

Later that year, a man by the name of John O'Brien (oh dear) walked on the board the warship *Cerberus* that was docked at Melbourne's port. He demanded to see the officer in charge. When the officer arrived, O'Brien informed him that he was the King of Spain and he had come to take possession of the vessel and all of the Irish informers he believed to be aboard. The ship's officer cottoned on rapidly that O'Brien wasn't the King of Spain and was just a nutter. He had O'Brien arrested by passing police. The alleged Spanish Royal then told the cops that his name was O'Brien and he was the Earl of Inchiquin. The boys in blue cottoned on rapidly that he wasn't and they took him away. In a thought-provoking twist, this John

---

6. *Sydney Morning Herald*, 21st February 1883

O'Brien's description bore some similarities with my John O'Brien. A coincidence, surely?

1883 was not a good year for children's variety concerts or for taking holidays on tranquil islands. In June, a concert was held in the Victoria Hall in Sunderland, England. All was going well until the end of the show when it was announced that children with certain numbered tickets would receive a prize upon leaving. Not wanting to miss out, the majority of the thousand-or-so children present raced to the exit door – to find a gap only wide enough to allow one child through at a time. The children at the front were crushed by the weight of the crowd behind them. The event that started as a pleasant afternoon's entertainment resulted in the death by suffocation of 183 children.

In August, some people may have found themselves basking in the sun on the golden sands of a beach on a small island called Krakatoa, near Indonesia. Their holiday would have been ruined however, when the volcano on the island erupted. The force of the explosion has been compared to 10,000 times the force of the atomic bomb dropped on Hiroshima in WWII. After the explosion, there wasn't much left of the island nor was there much left of the 20,000 people who lived nearby. The resulting tsunami wasn't particularly nice either and it is believed the final death toll was around 100,000 people. Up to a year after the eruption, skeletons were washing up on the coast of Africa.

Back in non-volcanic Sydney, the population was increasing and expanding outwards from the city. The colonial government had to find ways of transporting these people around and the rapidly growing rail network seemed to be popular. The government called for tenders for a stretch of railroad between the Hawkesbury River and Gosford plus a twenty-six-mile long line through Coalcliff in the Illawarra district. A gentleman named Mr Blunt won the Hawkesbury tender with a quote of £293,021 16s 8d or around $24,000,000 in modern money. The lowest tender for the Illawarra line was £318,526, 2 shillings and 8 pence – around $25,500,000. These figures seem remarkably cheap by modern standards: nowadays, the costs of feasibility studies, environmental impact reports, steering committees, planning applications and Occupational Health and Safety evaluations would have eaten up that kind of money before they even drove a spike into the ground.

While the railways extended, the inner city tramways were causing some problems. In May, the mayors of Sydney and Glebe paid a visit to the Commissioner of Railways. They wanted to make a complaint about the dust in Glebe-road that had been caused by the trams. They considered it a nuisance and they wanted his staff to water the road. As the Commissioner of Railways was named Mr Goodchap, they probably sniggered and said – "Look, Goodchap, be a good chap and …"

For some, the dust was the least of their concerns. A Mr Bolger was run over by a tram in Petersham and had both of his legs amputated. Then a seven-year old girl named Annie Harris was hit by a tram on Botany-road. At the hospital it was discovered that she had a compound fracture in her right arm – so they amputated it. They also found a contusion on her face but luckily they chose not to cut off her head.

If the O'Brien-Cunningham family ever rode on the public transport network, not only would they probably fill a carriage by themselves but they would also have to decipher the timetables. In April, the *Herald* published some amendments to the Southern and Western lines:

> 'The train leaving Sydney at 5.15am will leave at 5.30am. The 1.30pm Saturday train will run daily. The 5.30pm train will leave at 5.27pm and will not stop at Petersham or Stanmore. An additional train will leave Sydney at 5.31pm for Newtown and Petersham only. The 5.50pm train will start two minutes later and will not stop at Petersham and the train leaving Petersham at 5.35am will leave at 6.12am, starting from Ashfield at 6.04am. An additional train will leave Homebush at 5.54pm and an additional train will leave Petersham at 5.27pm and the 5.42pm train from Petersham will leave at 5.50pm.'[7]

Got all that? Good. Stand aside, doors closing!

---

7. *Sydney Morning Herald,* 30th April 1883

Michael O'Brien

13. Last, But Not Least

We haven't been north for a while so it was time to check in on the Kingdom's. George and Susan were in their sixties and their daughters, Fanny and Jane, were going forth and multiplying – Fanny had given birth to seven children by now. Then of course, there was the ever confusing Kingdom/Elliott connection with the Frost family. In 1884 it was about to become a little more convoluted. It seems that George Elliott (Susan's son) had suffered a tragedy in 1880 when his wife Annie (Frost) passed away. She had managed to provide him with six children in ten years but without her, what was George to do? Well, in 1884, he married Jane Frost (not to be confused with the Jane mentioned above, whom by marriage was also Jane Frost). No, this new Jane Frost was the sister-in-law of that Jane Frost and the sister of the deceased Annie, which meant she was the sister-in-law of her new husband, George, who was the half-brother of Jane Frost – the old one, not the new one. George and Jane went on to have ten children which means those children were stepbrothers and stepsisters to their own cousins. It also means that as far as the first six children were concerned, their stepmother was their aunt and their father was also their uncle. I imagine that poor old George Kingdom found all this a bit too hard so he went out and tended the sheep.

George wasn't the only one to have weddings on his mind as John O'Brien's brood from his marriage with Mary were leaving the nest. In an eighteen month period during 1883-84, John Joseph, Mathew and Thomas O'Brien all tied the knot – thankfully to no-one named Frost. It seems that the three boys had different viewpoints: John Joseph married Clara Allen in the Catholic Church at Woollahra; Mathew married Elizabeth Knight at a Congregational service in Bethel House while Thomas married Susan O'Neill in the Registrar's Office in Elizabeth-street. It is unknown if John, the unholy father, turned up to any of these services or if he was even invited. Mary was presumably there so it may have spoiled the mood somewhat.

The average cost of a wedding in 2008 was $49,200. The figures aren't available for 1884 but I sense they were doing it a bit cheaper than that. Braun's of 376 George-street were offering engagement rings for 28 shillings (around $105 today), diamond rings were £2 8s and a lovely 18ct gold wedding ring would set you back one pound or about eight bucks today. Farmer and Co. sold white Duchesse satin, suitable for wedding dresses at £2 6d a yard (or $154 a metre). A hall was available for weddings at 239 Parramatta-street with 60ft of space, a 'splendid' floor, card rooms, kitchen and a piano – all for one quid a night. If you wanted something a bit more up-market, the Bondi Coffee Palace and Restaurant offered first-class wedding dinners – 'supplied at the shortest notice', which was probably useful for this family.

And what to buy the happy couple who have nothing? Harris and Ackman, auctioneers at 179 Pitt-street, offered many fine items you could purchase as wedding presents. They had dinner services, breakfast sets festooned with blue and gold forget-me-nots, Worcester vases, Tunisian ware, picnic baskets, Grotesque figurines, decanters, liqueur sets, Wedgwood Jasper Ware biscuit boxes and for that special touch – hand-painted and profusely-decorated chamber pots.

A wedding is a special occasion but for some people outside Australia, it was very special. In September, a Polish Jew left his home in Russia to attend his brother's wedding in Paris. Upon arriving at the train station of his destination, he was asked for his ticket. The Pole couldn't speak French, didn't understand and the station official became annoyed. Very annoyed. Without warning, he knocked the man to the ground, handcuffed him and had him taken to a dark and dirty cellar. He was detained there for four days without food. A rope was put around his neck, firecrackers were let off in his face and buckets of water emptied over his head. He was finally released when the mayor of the town heard of the incident, sensed the damage to the local tourism industry and went down to the station to free him.

Still in Paris, we briefly go back to 1867 where a gentleman by the name of Augiot had married his beloved and was enjoying the reception and his prospects. During the festivities, Augiot was informed that a man outside the hall wished to speak to him. He excused himself to his bride and ventured out to talk to the visitor. No-one at that wedding reception saw Mr Augiot alive again. Seventeen years later in 1884, a hunter clambering through a mountainous area of Spain found a skeleton. Papers in the remnants of the clothing indicated that the body was Augiot. It was rumoured that before he married, he had been in a liaison with a Spanish woman. After he decided to marry his French sweetheart, it seems the senorita wasn't best pleased.

In Bulgaria, shortly after the discovery of Augiot, a beautiful wedding took place in a winter wonderland. After a charming service, the wedding party climbed into decorated carriages and rode off to the reception. As the weather conditions were poor, the carriages kept close together, and the lead driver took a short cut across a frozen river. Alas, the weight of the carriages was too much for the ice and it gave away. The entire wedding party plunged into the icy water and thirty-four people drowned. Only one man, a musician, survived.

We lastly move over to America; more specifically, Platte City, Missouri. William Montgomery had been engaged to a young lady by the name of Alice Cooper. (No, not that one.) Several months into the engagement, Montgomery announced he was breaking it off. Miss Cooper was very sad. The following day, Miss Cooper, her relatives, the town judge and forty-odd townspeople rode out to Montgomery's farm. After hearing a knock at his door, Montgomery opened it to find Miss Cooper and fifty men armed with shotguns standing in his yard. He was then given a choice: marry Miss Cooper and be happy ever after … or the townspeople would be happy to send him to the hereafter. He chose the former and the couple were married on the spot.

John Joseph, Mathew and Thomas had a more peaceful start to their married lives but now they needed somewhere to live. Sydney's rental market was quite active in 1884. The couples could have chosen a cottage at Alexandria (with water laid on) for 8 shillings a week (around $30 today), a six-roomed house at Surry Hills for 15s, a six-roomed house at Pyrmont for 16s, a place at Moore Park (furnished, four rooms, kitchen, bath) for 25s or a house at Waverley with four rooms, kitchen, large yard and ocean views for 14 shillings a week or about $52 today. You could not rent a roofless kennel for that price in 2020.

I doubted John O'Brien was present at any of the weddings but he was most certainly present at the registration of his next child. John was listed as informant and he signed the register. He advised that Maud Ellen O'Brien was born on the 24th August 1884 and the family now lived in Burlington-street, Ultimo. He also advised that he was a contractor and he was 51 years old – considering he was 11 when he arrived in 1839, he's shaved a few years off there. But then it gets more mysterious. He advised the mother of Maud was Mary Sullivan, his wife – surely by now, it was a bit late for him to be worrying about reporting an illegitimate child. As for previous issue, he states 5 males and 1 female living (which tallies) and FOUR males deceased. What? We know of two (James and the first William), we know a third one popped up when Leo was born and now here was a fourth. Curiously, no other certificate I have seen mentions the fourth deceased boy and most agree that there were three. Had John miscounted? – To be fair, he was running out of fingers. Was he drunk? Was he in a poor mental state? We don't know. It was just another conundrum he left for his descendants.

It is possible that John was a bit doolally but he had plenty of company. In Great Britain, a very odd Welsh gentleman by the name of William Price had also just fathered a child. Nothing remarkable about that … apart from the fact he was 83 years old, the child's mother was forty years younger and he christened the child Iesu Grist – for those of you unfamiliar with Welsh, that translates to 'Jesus Christ'. This baby Jesus died in 1884 and William, a firm believer in Druidism, considered the burial of a corpse to be wrong as it polluted Mother Earth. So he took his dead son up a hill, built a funeral pyre and prepared for a cremation. As cremation was frowned upon in Victorian Britain, Price was stopped by several villagers. They then informed the rozzers who arrested Price and charged him with illegally disposing of a corpse. But in court, the prosecution had some trouble finding the relevant law that decreed cremation was illegal – mainly because there wasn't one. Price was freed, walked home and completed the fiery farewell of Jesus. This set a precedent for future cremations in Great Britain.

Mr Price may have been a smidge eccentric but he wasn't as bad as the Reverend Mirehouse, a rector in Lincolnshire. He had found himself in a dispute with England's Home Secretary over the planned closure of a graveyard in his area. In November, he took his protest to a new level – he mailed a package, marked 'Perishable', to the Home Office. When they opened the package, they found the corpse of a stillborn child.

In Victoria, Australia, the people had problems of a different nature. Several publicans had chosen to honour a resolution that had been adopted and they closed their doors on a Sunday. Well, didn't that stir up the people? Newspapers were full of stories of the grumbling among the poorer classes who were 'deprived of their dinner beer'. As not much else was happening, the papers were probably grateful of something to print. Let's look at the Country News from the Herald on the 25th of August:

> 'Walgett: Business is dull. The weather is fine.
> Newcastle: 10,000 cigars were seized by Custom's officials from the house of Sam Hoy.
> Braidwood: Caterpillars are appearing in great numbers in the district.'

But at least they could report on the Hampstead Aerated Water Manufactory in Queensland being destroyed by fire or the 'immense attendance' at the Poultry and Dog Show in the Exhibition Building of Melbourne, where they remarked there was an exhibit of a fine collection of … cats.

John O'Brien and Ellen Cunningham may not have had time to read the newspapers; they were probably still trying to count how many children they had. And as children get sick, they need treatment and medication so it was exciting that there was a new development in Pitt-street. Washington H. Soul had opened a dispensing department and Mr Thomas Ellis, a member of the Society of Druggists in London, would be dishing out drugs and preparations to the public. John and Ellen could have purchased Dr Thompson's American Coltsfoot Cough Linctus, Dr Jones's Magic Corn Paint, Clayton and Co.'s Millefleur Toilet Powder, Chlorate of Potash Lozenges, Langton's Concentrated Compound Extract of Red Jamaica Sarsaparilla, William's Patent Clothes Renovator (I imagine the family had a few hand-me-downs), Carbolic Jujubes (for sore throats), Mason's Perfumed Carbolic Acid (for disinfecting cesspits) and if John wanted to grow a moustache or cover his bald patch – he could buy a bottle of Dr Barbarossa's Cantharides and Russian Bear's Grease Oil, lovingly made from the oil produced from melted-down bear's fat.

The children may have had a sour taste in their mouth after sucking on Carbolic Jujubes, so they could have been taken to Kellett and Alford's at 14 Barrack-street. Those gentlemen were busy auctioning off 245 tons of confectionery which included mixed lollies, peppermints, liquorices and barley sugar. But don't get in the wrong bidding war – they were also selling off 30 cases of damaged wire nails.

Retail was all the rage in the growing metropolis of Sydney and in 1885, the *Herald* waxed eloquently on the subject:

> 'Merchant's vans are staggering under the loads they bear and the muscle and sinew of the land are strained in transporting goods from the vans to the warehouses, where busy hands unpack them and place them glitteringly before the public gaze. The shops are fascinatingly bedecked. A great and grand transformation has taken place. Small shops have disappeared and with the mighty progress the colony has made, large emporiums have taken their place. In connection with one of these, no less than 650 hands are engaged and it is said to be the largest retail establishment in the world.'[1]

The writer was referring to the Hordern's emporium which was exciting the Sydney shopper and loosening the purse strings. In this same environment, two brothers had opened a drapery store in George-street and dreamed of one day being as successful as Hordern's. Well, their dream came true and they not only rivalled Hordern's for size, they outlasted them. Albert Edward and Joseph Neal Grace saw their business grow rapidly and they also saw that expansion into the suburbs was the way to go. While Hordern's disappeared, Grace Bros lasted for another century until they were swallowed by a competitor and their stores re-branded as Myer.

---

1. *Sydney Morning Herald*, 19th December 1885

Another retail giant of the time was Mark Foy but he was in a spot of bother. In October of 1885, the Draper's Association held a meeting and formally requested Mr Foy to reconsider his trading hours. They were concerned for his employees and the 'evil effects which long hours of toil had upon them'. Mr Foy remained unfussed and refused to make any adjustments. His shop stayed open till 10pm for five days of the week. Then trading hours were debated in parliament with mixed opinion; one politician obviously liked his late-night shopping and he condemned the idea that shops should close by 7pm as it was a 'gross infringement of liberty'.

Foy wasn't the only shopkeeper in trouble, though. An Alfred Michaels was fined £5 for attaching pieces of lead to the bottom of the plates on his scales while Patrick Kirby was fined on another matter. He was an undertaker in Hunter-street and it appears he was keeping decomposed corpses and body parts in his shop. The resulting foul odour was wafting throughout the neighbourhood and the locals were not pleased.

But maybe Mr Kirby's customers weren't the only thing on the nose. A gentleman named Hirst wrote to the paper with his concerns:

> 'That we are generally speaking a dirty and unwashed people is a disgrace…Look around and where can our masses, and especially those who need it most – the labouring classes – obtain a really good, refreshing and cheap bath? Nowhere, sir!…Can you imagine anything more grateful to the brainweary [sic] business man, the fagged-out shop assistant and factory hand or the dusty toilworn workman, then to be able, for a small fee, to step in at the end of a day's labour … a good bath?'[2]

Meanwhile, the Great Unwashed of America were about to unwrap a present. The French had chosen to celebrate American independence by the sending them a really large gift – but neglected to mention it would have to be assembled. By the time all the containers arrived in New York Harbour, the Yanks were looking at 200 tons of metal and

---

2. *Sydney Morning Herald,* 1st September 1885

a complicated assembly diagram. Like a massive IKEA project, it was put together over a year and placed on a pedestal. The French had christened it 'Liberty Enlightening the World' but that was quickly shortened to the Statue of Liberty.

Initially she was the colour of copper but over time, the elements have oxidised her to a greenish tinge. But she has survived the weather and a bomb attack by German saboteurs; however the resultant explosion caused the stairway up her right armpit to be closed off. Then, when they were checking the damage, they noticed the arm had been put on incorrectly and her head was off centre. This meant that on windy days, a ray protruding from her crown would pierce her arm – which is probably something you don't want to see or hear if you are a tourist up there. In 1929, there was another shock for tourists when a man jumped out of the crown's viewing area. His fall was marginally disturbed when he bounced off her left boob but the plummet continued till he hit the ground in a poor, tired, huddled mass.

While the New Yorkers were putting Miss Liberty together, their Canadian neighbours were battling with the local Indians. In April, an incident known as the Frog Lake Massacre occurred when Cree Indians killed nine settlers. The Canadian government weren't overjoyed with the act and they had the natives rounded up and charged with treason. They were found guilty and sentenced to hang so Wandering Spirit, Round The Sky, Bad Arrow, Iron Body, Little Bear, Crooked Leg, Man Without Blood and the delightfully-named Miserable Man were despatched to the Happy Hunting Ground.

Natives weren't the only beings the Canadians were killing, though. The legendary Jumbo the Elephant, star of Barnum and Bailey's Circus was on tour in the north when she was hit by a train and died of the injuries received. She was stuffed – figuratively and literally – and donated to a university in Massachusetts where she stood proudly until a fire in 1975. Today, her ashes reside in a peanut butter jar at the university but her legacy lives on; her name has become part of our lexicon.

In the year after the elephant's demise, the President of the United States raised a few eyebrows. Grover Cleveland became the first, and only, President to marry while in the White House. The eyebrows were raised because President Cleveland was 49 and his bride, Frances Clara

Folsom, was 21. She became the youngest First Lady and still holds that record today.

Another American destined for notoriety was John Pemberton, a morphine-addicted US Civil War veteran. He had just invented a drink to try and cure his drug addiction and he named it Pemberton's French Wine Coca. The government had installed legislation concerning temperance and abstinence from the demon alcohol, so Pemberton was forced to create a non-alcoholic version. After experimenting with various formulas, he finally released it for public consumption and declared it would cure drug addiction, headaches and impotence. One hundred and forty years later, you can still buy the drink he invented – it is called 'Coca-Cola'.

Over in Europe, they were busy inventing other goodies. A man named Karl Benz had just developed the Benz Patent-Motorwagen, thought to be the first vehicle propelled by a motor. It had three wheels, solid rubber tyres, a rear-mounted engine and a top speed of 16kmph. There was no air-conditioning, GPS or cruise control and the only airbag was Mrs Benz sitting in the passenger seat.

While the Germans celebrated that genius, they got rid of a man they considered less than a genius. King Ludwig II of Bavaria was deposed by his parliament as he was considered to be quite loopy. The forty-year old king was taken to a castle south of Munich to live out his days. In June of 1886, his ex-Royal Highness went out for a walk and so began a mystery that remains unsolved today. He had taken his doctor with him on the stroll and their plans were to walk around the local lake. Three hours later, they were both found dead in the lake. The subsequent autopsy proclaimed the deposed king had committed suicide by drowning – yet no water was found in his lungs. A local villager testified that he had heard a gunshot yet no bullet wounds were found. To add to the mystery, the doctor's body showed signs of strangulation and wounds to the head.

Away from all the excitement overseas, NSW found itself under the leadership of a new Governor. The Governor was born in 1843 and at birth, his name was Robert Wynn. Upon his father's death in 1868, he became the 3rd Baron Carrington and on his mother's death, he was instated as joint Lord Great Chamberlain of England. Before his move to Australia, he had served as Captain of the Honourable Corps of

Gentlemen-at-Arms and was made a Knight Grand Cross of the Most Distinguished Order of Saint Michael and Saint George. Not bad, so far. When he finished his time in Australia, he scored a few more jobs such as Lord Privy Seal, Lord Great Chamberlain and Lord Lieutenant of Buckinghamshire. Wow. By the time of his death in 1928, Robert Wynn had become Charles Robert Wynn-Carrington, 1st Marquess of Lincolnshire, Earl Carrington, Viscount Wendover, KG, GCMG, PC, DL, JP. And wouldn't you know it – his only male heir, Albert Edward Charles Robert Wynn Carrington, was killed in WWI so all those titles were declared 'extinct'.

And while John O'Brien's governor was picking up honours, so was his brother-in-law. In 1886, Patrick O'Brien was approaching seventy and was a very wealthy man. On St Patrick's Day, Patrick donated £1000 ($75,000) to the building fund of St Patrick's Cathedral in Victoria. The local archbishop was grateful and as a reward for his service to the Catholic Church, Patrick was made a Knight of St Gregory the Great. This honour had been conferred by the Pope himself.

Patrick was chuffed by this. He hadn't been in the best of health and the honour picked him up. In 1887, he decided to go on a tour of Europe and Great Britain and revisit the country of his birth. He left his Kinkora House estate at Hawthorn and sailed off. But while in London, Patrick O'Brien passed away. The obituary in *The Argus* highlighted his career, mentioning his involvement with the colonisation of Victoria, his career as a judge, his service to parliament, the St Patrick's Society and the Catholic Church. He was also described as one of 'the richest men in the colony'. This is an understatement. His estate in modern money was worth in excess of thirteen million dollars. Patrick's remains were brought back to Victoria and he was buried at Melbourne General Cemetery. The family grave was quite crowded; Patrick had already buried his first wife, his mother-in-law and seven of his nine children.

In the same year of Patrick's death, Queen Victoria celebrated the fiftieth anniversary of her perch on the throne. She was 68 years old and had survived her husband, two children and seventeen prime ministers. There was a procession for her anniversary, a thanksgiving service at Westminster Abbey and a banquet in which 50 kings and princes were invited to.

The day was also celebrated in Australia with the biggest knees-up happening in Sydney. The Mayor of Sydney, Mr Alban Riley, held a jubilee ball at the Sydney Exhibition Building. This former fine structure no longer exists but if you were to go to the pool in Chalmers Street, near Central Station, you would be in the area where it stood.

The ball was no small affair; there were 4,000 invited guests. No gate-crashers were permitted – a "Card of Entrée" had to be produced at the Devonshire-street entrance and people were encouraged to obey these instructions, 'if they wished to avoid unpleasantness at the door'. If you managed to get past the heavies, you would have been greeted with a sumptuous sight. Chinese lanterns were draped from the domed ceiling, pillars covered with evergreens, bangalow palms on the balconies and flags of every nation festooning the walls. But there were a couple of little problems: the capacity of the hall was so pushed that only half of the people could dance at any one time and there were no chairs.

Out the back, however, in a special room, sixty people were seated and having a lovely supper. This little group consisted of the power brokers of Sydney and included the Governor, the Mayor, Henry Parkes and some fellow named Sir William Ogg, who was a director of English, Scottish and Australian banks. They scoffed away happily, proposing endless toasts and making more speeches than what's heard on an Oscar night.

For those not invited to the Mayor's Exhibition Hall shindig (like my ancestors), Jubilee Day was honoured by a fireworks display. Twelve square miles of an area surrounded by Fort Macquarie (Bennelong Point), Kirribilli, Cremorne, Bradley's Head, Shark Island, Goat Island and Fort Denison was used for the display while 300 men were employed to set up and discharge the bangers. It all started with a 50 gun salute from Fort Denison and the people watched on in awe. They had gathered around the harbour shore; the Man O' War Stairs, Dawes Point, the north shore, Mrs Macquarie's Chair and the rocks at the frontage of the Botanical Gardens were covered with people. No-one has been able to supply an attendance figure as the tram officials had given up counting (or had run out of fingers) but the crowd could probably be numbered in the tens of thousands.

Elsewhere in Sydney, the children of the Randwick Asylum were given a special luncheon. The kids sang the national anthem, gave three cheers for the Queen, three cheers for the Governor, then tucked into roast beef, vegetables and a plum pudding. Then, as some nice man named Mr Stedman had donated 182lb (83kgs) of lollies to the Asylum, the children probably went berserk. As they didn't have much else to celebrate, you wouldn't blame them.

There were other events in the city, designed to cash in on the Jubilee and suck up some tourist shillings. At the Gaiety Theatre, the Cogill Bros Minstrel and Burlesque Company were playing, after a matinee performed by the Children of the Jewish Education Board and Sabbath School. The YMCA Musical Society had a concert featuring Signora Lardelli and Herr Schmellitscheck and his organ recitals. Not to be outdone, the Australian Waxworks, situated opposite the cathedral, had daily shows by Arthur Francis, the Ventriloquist and Zingari, the Gypsy Queen, the 'popular' mind reader.

But for some, the party never got going as life beat on the same drum. In the Police Court, John Montgomery was fined £10 for stealing four chickens, Peter Shields copped a month's hard labour for assaulting his wife and John Kearney was fined a quid for using insulting words on the Balmain ferry.

What about the rest of New South Wales? What did they get up to for Victoria's anniversary? Well, not much. The towns of Albion Park, Bourke, Canowindra, Cowra, Crookwell, Hay and Wallerawang all advised that there was no bugger home, as they were all in Sydney, so there would be no festivities. But in Adelong, there were church services and fireworks; Camden just had church services while Kiama just had fireworks. Cobar had a procession of members of Friendly Societies; two hundred children marched around the market square in Berrima; a bullock was roasted in Maclean; a bowling tournament was played at Parramatta; a picnic was postponed at Walgett due to the rain; West Maitland's streets were gaily decorated with bunting while at Windsor, 'the Queen's health was drunk, followed by lusty cheers'.

The year also marked the ending of a remarkable journey – one which had taken nearly three years. In April of 1884, a thirty-one-year old Englishman named Thomas Stevens had thought that it might be fun to ride a bicycle across America. So he bought himself a penny-farthing bicycle; packed a bag with some socks, an extra shirt, a raincoat and a .38 Smith & Wesson, and pedalled off from San Francisco. Four months later, he arrived on the other side of the country ... and for some astonishing reason, decided to keep going. The man and his bike boarded a ship sailing to England and after he arrived in Liverpool, he rode to London and boarded a ferry to France. He then rode through Germany, Austria, Hungary, Serbia, Bulgaria and Turkey. He stayed there for a while as he replaced tyres and waited for the local bandits to return to their mountain hideaways.

He then crossed Armenia, Iraq and rode into Iran, where he met the Shah. He was refused permission to enter Siberia and was kicked out of Afghanistan. Undaunted, he managed to find his way to India, rode to Calcutta, caught a steamer to Hong Kong and then rode across China. Another boat carried him to Japan, which he duly pedalled across before finally catching a ship back to California. He was the first man to ride a bicycle around the world and he wrote a book about the experience, which bore the imaginative title of *Around the World on a Bicycle*. He also wrote several magazine articles, including *Wild Pea-Fowls in British India*.

The book was more popular.

Life in the Past Lane

14. WE'RE GONNA PARTY LIKE IT'S 1888

So there were the folks in Sydney, getting over the excitement of Queen Vic's anniversary, and what happens? Another party, that's what! January 26, 1888 – European settlement's one-hundredth birthday. Here we go, here we go, here we go. For this party, there were some different activities planned.

The NSW government took some old grazing land south-east of Sydney and turned it into a public park. They called it Centennial Park and it was officially opened by Henry Parkes. The former cattle pasture and swamp was once famous for being the location of a duel, fought between the colony's first Premier, Stuart Donaldson, and the Surveyor General, Thomas Mitchell. Both men survived the duel. I must say it is a fascinating way for politicians to settle their differences and it would be delightful to bring back the duel today. Who would you want shot first?

During Centenary Week, the foundation stone of the New South Wales Parliament House was laid and Henry Parkes was in attendance. There was an inter-colonial band contest (Parkes was there, too); a children's music festival (yep, there as well); horse racing at Randwick (you guessed it, there again) and feasts provided for inmates of charitable institutions – which remained strangely Parkes-less. Mayor Riley also gave a banquet for 130 of Sydney's oldest citizens.

The week also featured an agricultural show at Moore Park. As there was an inter-colonial cricket match being played and an Anniversary regatta being held on the harbour, the crowds were down a bit. However, they received a treat on the 27th: a man rode up in a carriage and yelled out to the people queued to get in. He told them the park was public property and therefore entry was free. Some 1,500 people thought that was a good deal and they pressed forward, breaking the gates down and entering the show. It took the police some time to restore order; they never discovered who the mystery man was.

Once inside, the people were treated to a myriad of activities: animal displays, horse jumping, trotting races and a working dairy. There were interesting exhibits as well: John Brush & Co was showing saddles, harnesses and boots; Messrs Willacy and Hornby of Paddington were demonstrating their Liquid Manure Spreader while there was an unveiling of Wolseley's Steam Sheep Shearing machine.

England also had some excitement in 1888 as the first professional Football League competition started. This is the great-grandfather of today's Premier League. In the first year, there were only twelve teams: Accrington, Aston Villa, Blackburn Rovers, Bolton Wanderers, Burnley, Derby County, Everton, Notts County, Preston North End, Stoke, West Bromwich Albion and Wolverhampton Wanderers. In the following five years, the competition expanded to include a second division. New teams were founded and some of them would be unfamiliar to supporters today but once upon a time, crowds would flock to see the likes of Middlesbrough Ironopolis, Loughborough, Leicester Fosse, Burton United, Gainsborough Trinity and Bootle.

The more astute football fan or even the geographical wiz would note that there wasn't a team from London mentioned above. It would take half a decade for a side from the capital to be admitted and that was only after some shady dealings by the owner. The team was Woolwich Arsenal; they still play today, without the 'Woolwich' in the name and without many Englishmen in their jerseys. In any case, the London of 1888 was preoccupied with something other than football – a series of murdered prostitutes and the enduring mystery of Jack the Ripper.

The police agree that there are five murders in the Whitechapel area of London that can be attributed to Jack the Ripper, however they also concede there may have been as many as eleven. At last count, there are over a hundred theories on the identity of the killer – including the Duke of Clarence and Lewis Carroll. I'm not going to tell you who I think Jack the Ripper was simply because I wouldn't have the foggiest idea, however that hasn't stopped a truckload of authors writing a truckload of books with different opinions on who the murderer was. What that means is that all of those books but one must be a load of codswallop – and there's no guarantee that anyone has got it right. The mystery of Jack has inspired many writers and publishers and even other murderers; since 1888, we've had the French Ripper (1894), Düsseldorf Ripper (1913), Blackout Ripper (1942), Jack the Stripper (1964), Yorkshire Ripper (1975-80), Rostov Ripper (1978-90) and the Camden Ripper of 2002. The difference is that all of those Rippers have been caught.

Were the Australians of the time reading accounts of these terrible crimes, discussing the case around the nineteenth century equivalent of the water cooler? In our times, when a juicy newsworthy event happens, we are bombarded with CNN 24/7 coverage with windswept reporters and action replays ad infinitum. But things were different in 1888; reporters used quills and newsflashes came by ship. Then, sometimes the newspaper editors couldn't be arsed. From page 7 of a 14 page edition of the *Sydney Morning Herald,* 10th September, 1888:

> 'Four women of the unfortunate class were murdered by a man believed to be a maniac. The bodies of the victims were horribly mutilated. The murders have caused quite a panic in Whitechapel.'

And that's it. Possibly there might have been more coverage if the women were from a more fortunate class. Fifteen days later, the papers decided to give the people an idea of what the English authorities were thinking:

> 'It is the belief of the coroner who inquired into the Whitechapel murders that the victims were killed at the instance of an anatomist who desired to obtain some of the organs for medical exhibition in America.'[1]

---

1. *Sydney Morning Herald,* 25th September 1888

But it wasn't all just gruesome murder in London – they had industrial action as well. In July, there was a strike in the Bryant and May match factory. The action started when a worker was dismissed but then the workforce, consisting of 1,400 women and children, protested. They objected to the poor pay, 14 hour working days and the fact that some of them were becoming sick and eventually dying from the phosphorus they were using.

It wasn't a good year for U.S. foreign policy and international relations, either. President Grover Cleveland declared that the Chinese 'were impossible of assimilation with our people and dangerous to our peace and welfare' – though he did stop short of invading China to search for Weapons of Mass Destruction.

1888 was a mixed year for picture makers. A man named George Eastman registered the trademark 'Kodak', thereby establishing the beginnings of an empire. But in Europe, Dutch artist Vincent Van Gogh had been suffering from a few mental issues. In December, he cut off the lower portion of his left ear, wrapped it in a newspaper and gave it to a prostitute named Rachel … as you do.

Men destined for fame and infamy were born in this year. Irving Berlin, Squizzy Taylor, Raymond Chandler, T. E. Lawrence (Lawrence of Arabia) and poet T. S. Eliot all entered the world. The man who invented television, John Logie Baird, was also born; if he had known that his invention would spawn *Big Brother* and *I'm A Celebrity, Get Me Out Of Here,* he might have given his tinkering away and become an accountant. 1888 also was the year that saw the birth of a man who would become the patriarch of one of the great American families – Joseph Kennedy. He went on to father nine children but there would be pain along the way: he had a son killed in WWII, a daughter killed in a plane crash, another daughter lobotomised, a son become a candidate for the U.S. Presidency and assassinated while another son became the U.S. President and was also assassinated. Joseph lived through it all.

A woman who had also once celebrated several births appeared again on our radar. Mary O'Brien, the wife that John had deserted more than twenty years ago, was doing it tough and apparently her family weren't interested. In April, she was admitted into St Magdalen's Women's Refuge at Tempe. The refuge was run by the Sisters of the

Good Samaritan of St Benedict and they provided accommodation for destitute women. Mary, who was in her fifties, was found a 'situation' at Rosebank Convent, Five Dock.

In Armidale, the town was abuzz. Two ministers of parliament, Messrs Abigail and Inglis, were in town for a tour. They visited schools, an orchard and a boot factory. They received deputations for such matters as an extension of land for the cemetery and the supply of a boring machine ... to be used outside of the cemetery. In the evening, they were treated to a 'champagne spread'. The ministers spent the night in a train carriage at the railway station – read into that what you will – and left for Glen Innes the next morning. There is no record of the gentlemen attending any weddings in the district which is a shame; they might have been guests at my great-grandparent's wedding. Henry Kingdom married Mary Ann Doyle and I wonder how many drinks old George Kingdom had that day.

Onto 1889 and those wacky European royal families were at it again. The Crown Prince of Austria, Rudolf, was thirty years old and married to Princess Stephanie of Belgium. He was also having an affair with a seventeen-year old Baroness, Marie Vetsera. His father ordered him to end the affair and Rudolf obliged – somewhat dramatically. He acquired a pistol, shot Marie in the head and then shot himself. His family appeared to be destined for tragedy; his mother was murdered nine years later by a crazed Italian with a sharpened nailfile and his nephew was murdered sixteen years after that. His nephew's killing would cause quite a reaction – the nephew was Archduke Franz Ferdinand and his death sparked World War I. Strangely enough, if we go back to three months after Rudolf's suicide, a boy named Adolf Schicklgruber was born in Rudolf's Austria. The boy's father would later change the family name to Hitler and the boy went on to create World War II.

In 1889, Sir Henry Parkes was Premier of New South Wales. It was the fifth time he had formed and led a ministry but it was also the twenty-sixth ministry to lead in thirty-three years. This is not exactly a formula for political consistency but when have politicians ever worried about that? Sir Henry had some things on his mind and he wanted to air them, so at a dinner in Tenterfield in October, he made a speech. The important part was:

'The great question which has to be considered is whether the time has not arisen for the creation on this Australian continent of an Australian government. Australia now has a population of three and a half million people and the American people numbered only between three and four million when they formed the great commonwealth of the United States. The numbers were about the same and surely what the Americans had done by war, the Australians could bring about by peace.'[2]

"Hear, hear", the people cried out … but not all of them. Two years after this speech, Parkes presented the NSW parliament with a bill dealing with the formation of the Commonwealth of Australia. Half the parliamentary members supported it while the other half blew raspberries and called for a vote of no-confidence. Parkes then resigned as Premier. As for the other 'great commonwealth of the United States' in 1889, there was a change of President as Benjamin Harrison replaced Grover Cleveland. It was later discovered that Harrison had secured the position with the use of fraudulent balloting. Sound familiar?

Elsewhere in NSW politics, the Minister of Works had given instructions for the construction and repair of various roads within the colony. He estimated the cost would be in the region of £60,000 ($4,500,000) a month. But Mr Garvan, who was the Colonial Treasurer, said there was a bit of a problem with that. It seems that New South Wales had a budget deficit and was 'overdrawn' by the sum of £1,300,000 or around 97 million dollars today. Mr Garvan said that he couldn't guarantee the payment of wages for government employees so fixing potholes was put on the back burner. Does any of this also sound familiar?

The government also had issues with a typhoid outbreak in Newtown and the drinking water of Parramatta was being criticised. As it was supplied to the townspeople for their domestic purposes, the fact that the water was 'milky-coloured, with a putrid smell and full of specks of floating matter' left a lot to be desired.

1889 was the year that a woman named Louisa Collins entered the record books. Her husband, Michael, had been to the doctor six

---

2. *Sydney Morning Herald,* 25th October 1889

months previously, complaining of stomach pains. The doctor couldn't find what was wrong and sent him home. Twenty-four hours later, after an explosive attack of diarrhoea and vomiting, Michael Collins died. The doctor carried out a post-mortem and found green fluid in the man's stomach, which was later identified as arsenic. His wife, Louisa, was questioned and several questions were raised. Louisa had married Michael in April of 1887 after her first husband died in February of 1887. Witnesses testified that the first husband had died of a stomach complaint. But the most damaging evidence of all was the glass found on Michael's bedside table. The residue in the glass was tested and found to be containing a product called 'Rough On Rats' – a popular pesticide which was 95% arsenic.

So, not looking good for Louisa, you would think – but the people of the day were divided. She was charged with murder and underwent a trial but after some deliberation, the jury couldn't agree on a verdict and was dismissed. A second trial was arranged but once again the jury was undecided. While the Attorney General considered a third trial, the coppers charged Louisa with the murder of her first husband. Amazingly, this jury was also unable to come up with a decision. So they legal boys went for a third trial on the murder of the second husband. This time, finally, the jury found her guilty. The judge donned the black cap, told her that he 'held no hope of mercy for her on earth' and sentenced her to hang.

However, a large percentage of people were not having this. They organised petitions to parliament, they arranged public meetings and rallies at Town Hall, and they formed deputations and met with the Governor. Their point was simple: women, barred from voting and sitting on juries, should not be held accountable to the same laws as men. They argued, they wrote letters to the paper, they jumped up and down and shouted.

It didn't do them, or Louisa, any good.

In 1889, she became the first woman to be hanged at Darlinghurst Gaol and the last woman to be hanged in New South Wales. If her death sentence caused controversy, her death caused even more. The trapdoor on the scaffold wouldn't open and had to be hit with a hammer; when she finally dropped, the noose nearly tore her head off.

A year later and the Australians weren't the only ones having difficulties disposing of their murderers. In New York, a man named William Kemmler had been sentenced to death after he murdered his de facto wife with a hatchet. Authorities were keen to try a new form of execution – the electric chair. The day before Kemmler's demise, they successfully tested the chair by electrocuting a horse – though how they got the horse to sit in the chair is not documented. The following day, Kemmler had his head shaved and was strapped in to the lethal furniture. He said a few final words then a switch was flicked and 1,000 volts flowed through him for seventeen seconds. The power was switched off and a doctor pronounced Kemmler dead. But he clearly wasn't a very good doctor as other spectators noticed that the murderer was still breathing. Officials then called for the power to be switched on again. 2,000 volts and eight minutes later, Kemmler finally left this world - while most of the spectators had left the room due to the smell of burning murderer.

As 1889 came to a close, there was a serious incident at the Christmas horse race meeting at Uralla. It appears that prior to the running of the last race, a dispute erupted between a young man named Andrew Fraser and George Kingdom's old drinking mate (and now also a great-great-grandfather of mine), John Doyle. The dispute developed into fisticuffs and at some stage, John fell to the ground and hit his head. The gathered crowd noticed that he wasn't getting back up; a closer inspection revealed that he was quite dead. John Doyle was 43, leaving a wife and numerous children. Fraser was charged with manslaughter; the last race at Uralla was called off.

1890 was the year that Banjo Paterson's celebrated poem, 'The Man from Snowy River', was published and was also the year that a famous best-selling novelist visited Australia. Robert Louis Stevenson, author of such page-turners as *Dr Jekyll and Mr Hyde*, *Treasure Island* and *Kidnapped,* arrived in Sydney in February. He was not in the best of health, suffering from tuberculosis, and had recently purchased land in Samoa to see if some sun might help his condition. He planned to spend five or six months touring Australia and having a bit of a looksee. Stevenson told the *Herald* that he wasn't planning on writing a novel based in Australia but he was keen to read some Australian literature as he was unfamiliar with it. He also intended to study some poetry and Marcus Clarke's *For the Term of His Natural Life*.

If you were inspired by Stevenson's visit and wanted to read one of his books, William Maddock's of George-street was the shop for you. There, you could purchase copies of *The Wrong Box* and *The Master of Ballantrae* for five shillings each. If the work of RLS wasn't your cup of tea, you could also buy Mrs Paton's *Nooks and Corners* for six shillings, *Mrs Bob* by J.S. Winter for 2 shillings, Edna Lyall's *A Hardy Norseman* for six bob and nine bob would get you a copy of *The Evolution of Sex*.

When Stevenson left Australia, he sailed back to Samoa. Halfway into the journey, his cabin on the ship caught fire. The crew declared that the best way to deal with the fire was to toss anything that was burning into the sea. Mrs Stevenson just caught them as they were about to throw a box overboard. This box contained an unpublished manuscript, which later became his work entitled *In the South Seas*. While she saved his book, she couldn't save him. His health deteriorated in Samoa and he lived for only four more years – his last words reportedly being, 'Does my face look strange?'

Because of the distance and the lengthy travel time, Australia wasn't high on celebrity's visiting lists, yet in 1891, another bright young novelist landed on our shores – albeit reluctantly. "I only came here because the steamers happened to touch here", Joseph Rudyard Kipling told a correspondent from *The Argus*. Kipling was some time away from writing his best-known books, *Kim* and *The Jungle Book*, but he was building a reputation as a writer and someone who was not afraid to speak his mind. He had just come from New Zealand where industrial strike action was slowing the country down and he was asked his opinion of the situation:

> 'I never was in a place where they talked more about work and did less of it. But then you don't know what work is in this part of the world... You don't suppose this eight hours work, eight hours rest and eight hours recreation is going to last, do you? Why, the Chinese must come in and swamp you. People who can live on nothing and sleep

with their heads hanging over the side of wheel barrows are dangerous.'[3]

Kipling was not only a social commentator; he was a man of adventure and excitement:

> 'When I was in San Francisco, I was lucky enough to see two shooting affrays and three fatal accidents. One day, I saw a Chinaman whose eye had been gouged out by a European. The blood was spurting in torrents but nobody seemed to take any notice but myself.'[4]

Gosh. Today's visiting celebrities just say that the weather's nice, koalas are cute and the girls are pretty.

---

3. *The Argus,* 13th November 1891
4. ibid.

*I was human, very human
and if in the days misspent,
I have injured man or woman,
it was done without intent.
If at times I blundered blindly
bitter heart and aching brow,
If I wrote a line unkindly,
I am sorry for it now.*

Henry Lawson
The Last Review 1904

Michael O'Brien

15. Red Sky In The Morning, Shepherd's Warning

While on a tour of Japan in 1891, a Russian named Nikolay Alexandrovich Romanov was attacked by a Japanese policeman. The copper swung a sabre at Romanov's head but only caught him a glancing blow off his face. The would-be assassin was then over-powered by two rickshaw drivers. The policeman, Tsuda Sanzo, was manacled and raced off to be imprisoned for the rest of his life – all four months of it. Soon after his close shave, Romanov became Emperor Nicholas II of Russia.

As Nick survived the attempt on his life (well, that one, anyway), other world rulers were dropping off like flies. Charles I, the third King of Wurttemberg, and Dom Pedro III, the last emperor of Brazil, breathed their last. It was also a time to grieve in Hawaii as the last reigning king, the delightfully named David La'amea Kamanakapu'u Mahinulani Nalaiaehuokalani Lumialani Kalakaua also passed away, well before Spell Check was invented.

Closer to home, there was sorrow within the Kingdom family as Georgina Kingdom died at the age of seventeen. According to the obituary in the *Uralla and Walcha Times*, she had spent her life living with her grandparents at Gostwyck, even though she was Jane Frost nee Kingdom's daughter. She may have grown up thinking that Jane was her sister, not her mother. This wasn't an uncommon practice.

At the time, Australia, and indeed the rest of the world, was in the grip of an influenza epidemic. The experts of the day believed that the epidemic started in Russia in 1889 but it had spread across the world and it was a killer. 'Death, the stern mower, has again been busy in our little community' wrote the *Maitland Mercury and Hunter River General Advertiser* in November of 1891.

A woman named Sarah Blick quilled a letter to the same paper that month and suggested the epidemic was a 'cleansing from God as moral pestilence had taken possession of the country'. She decreed that a quick read of the Bible would find a quotation from Jehovah – 'Unless ye repent, ye shall all perish'. While Ms Blick sounds like a right barrel of laughs, she also mentioned that a diet of broth, arrowroot and gruel would bring you back to health and presumably back from eternal damnation. However, H.J. Kolk's of Armidale were of the opinion that as soon as the influenza attack comes on, the patient should go to bed and drink a tumbler of 'MICROBE KILLER' every hour. George Buxton of Maitland had other ideas – he said the cure for influenza and most other diseases could be found by smoking cigars and cigarettes … bought from his establishment, of course. I can't see this theory being popular today.

The epidemic killed hundreds across the country and on October 30th, it claimed a victim within the Kingdom family. Old George Kingdom, patriarch of the family, died from influenza. George had survived starvation in England, survived two years on a filthy rat-infested prison hulk, survived the heat and financial hardship he had found in this country and managed to bring up a family as best as he could. I can visualise George on the Gostwyck pastures, sitting on a rock, watching the sheep feed on the green grass of New England. Did his thoughts ever drift back to old England? Did he remember the wife he left behind or the mates who joined him in dangerous poaching missions during the cold nights? Did he think of the life he might have led if the long arm of the law hadn't sent him across the world? George wasn't any richer in wealth than he would have been in Devon but he was probably richer in spirit. He wasn't perfect – but these weren't perfect times.

While George was laid to rest in the Old Uralla cemetery, not far from the remains of Captain Thunderbolt (or whoever), what was happening down south with the O'Brien family? Well, the simple answer is – we're not sure. In the Sands Directory (a kind of phone book without phone numbers) of 1888, John O'Brien is listed as living at Burlington Lane, Ultimo – an area of Sydney that, as John Birmingham mentions in his book, *Leviathan,* Henry Parkes had described as a 'region of human slaughterhouses'. However in 1889, only 'Mrs O'Brien' aka Ellen Cunningham is listed at that address. Family folklore has it that John abandoned both families about this time – although in reality, he had abandoned the first family more than twenty years ago. Some say he went back to Ireland, some say he died in a destitute asylum, some say he was still alive in 1900 and some (namely me) have no idea. We do know that at his daughter's wedding in 1901, he is listed as deceased. So, it appears sometime between 1888 and 1901, John O'Brien passed away – where and exactly when is unknown. His whole life seems to have been an enigma; it's probably only fitting that his death was, too.

In 1891, a man stood up and demonstrated why politicians should be seen and not heard. He loudly decreed that the outlook, in regard to the establishment of the federation of the Australian colonies, was not promising. His name was Alfred Deakin and twelve years after uttering this, he was the Prime Minister of that same federation.

As the year faded away, so did a group of people in Melbourne:

> 'The departure of the London Gaiety Company by the Melbourne express yesterday was witnessed by an immense crowd. There was much cheering and confusion.'[1]

At the same time, there may have been some confusion caused by an advertisement in the Maitland newspaper:

> 'For real satisfaction, ask Fry Brothers to
> furnish your home for £20.
> Fry Brothers, undertakers, West Maitland.'

They didn't say what they furnished your home with.

There was still more confusion to be had. Out in the Pacific Ocean, Western Samoa had decided to change its time zone which

---

1. *Sydney Morning Herald,* 31st October 1891

had the effect of altering the International Date Line. By doing this, the country ended up with two July the fourths in 1892. This meant that for the first one, today was tomorrow, while for the second one, today was yesterday.

Also defying time was Timothy the tortoise. Timothy, who was actually female, had spent time 'serving' in the British navy as a mascot and had 'retired' to live on the estate of the Earl of Devon. Timothy was thought to be aged in her early fifties in 1892 which isn't all that remarkable; what is remarkable is that she lived on till 2004. You would think that would entitle the old girl to a world record; however Tui Malila the tortoise holds that. She died in 1965 – some 189 years after she was given to the King of Tonga by Captain Cook. So Timothy was but a spring … chicken.

Moving on from elderly reptiles, Alfred Deakin was back in the news in 1892. Deakin's day job was working as a barrister and he had scored the defence counsel gig for an English-born gas fitter named Frederick Deeming. Frederick was being tried for the murder of his second wife, who had been found buried under the floor of a property they had once shared. While Deeming was being investigated and located, English authorities had been called to a town that Deeming had previously lived in. It seems that no-one had seen the first Mrs Deeming - or the children - for a while. The police checked some former residences and sure enough, the family were found under the floorboards in one of them. If Deeming received an acquittal in Australia, he would be shipped back to England for a chat with Scotland Yard. Deakin was on a hiding to nothing, really – so he went for the insanity plea. The jury didn't. Deeming was found guilty and hanged in May. Interestingly, as Deeming lived in London at the relevant time, some people to this day believe he was Jack the Ripper.

There were other murmurings from the old country in early 1892 as correspondents wrote of tension and rumours within the financial world. The concern was over a depression in value of American stocks, political trouble in Greece and the economic difficulties being experienced by Italy, Spain and Portugal and they say that history never repeats. At the time, Australia had its own problems as the numerous claims on insurance companies arising from the influenza epidemic were lowering their stock value. Also the trade deficit was alarming; there was a 14% increase in imports and a 6% decrease in exports. However, the Bank of Australasia said things were jolly as they posted a half-year profit of £94,000 or around seven million dollars today.

It's believed that in early 1892, an unemployed man was making a speech to quite a crowd at Queen Victoria's statue in Sydney. On top of his bitter ramblings, he told the people that workers, by depositing their money into banks, merely created wealth for the capitalists. This allowed the capitalists to lend that money out at exorbitant rates and get rich on the profits. The man went on to say that he had heard that the Savings Bank of NSW had 'gone bung'. And with that, the proverbial butterfly flapped its wings in the rainforest.

The 'news' travelled like a February bushfire and the people marched down to the bank's branch in Barrack-street. An estimated three thousand people gathered outside, clambering the stone steps, beating each other out of the way. They wanted their money and they wanted it in gold. The police were called into action and they would only allow a dozen people in at any one time. The branch stayed open till 10pm to deal with the crowd. It is quoted that £50,000 ($4,000,000) was withdrawn that day.

In times of crisis, people need some reassurance from the powers-that-be, so Premier George Dibbs stood up to make a speech in parliament. He claimed that the Savings Bank of NSW 'was as sound an institution as any bank in the world'. Oh George, where were your spin doctors? Four months after his statement, the New Oriental Bank Corporation of London was wound up, the private bank of Messrs J Barker & Co was suspended and a run on the Mercantile Bank of Australia saw it shut its doors temporarily. Within a year, eleven Australian banks had stopped trading or collapsed. But the Savings Bank of NSW survived and lived on till the 1930s when it was gobbled up by the Commonwealth Bank.

In September of 1892, there was another marriage in the O'Brien family. Frank, eldest living son of John O'Brien and Ellen Cunningham, married Ellen McAuliffe in Sydney. As mentioned, Ellen's family had left Ireland to try their luck in America before settling in Sydney. It was a truly international family; Ellen's elder siblings had been born in Ireland while Ellen and the younger children were born in North

America – most certificates state that Ellen was born in Barrie, Canada but the US Census of 1871 has her listed as being born across the border in New York State. Frank and Ellen were my great-grandparents. Four months after their marriage, another wedding was held down the road in Paddington. Richard Carroll and Sarah O'Shea, both from fine (and large) Tipperary families, tied the knot and became another set of great-grandparents for me.

They began their marriages in troubled times. The world's fiscal situation had fizzled as the United States was in the grip of a depression. New companies had been established to build railway lines across the great expanse of America and these companies needed money. They borrowed heavily from the banks but after a time of rising costs, found they couldn't meet their repayments. The banks, who had previously been rubbing their hands with glee, were now on shaky ground. The people got wind of the potential crisis and flocked in to withdraw their money – before the outlaws did, anyway. Banks collapsed like houses of cards and the railway companies followed suit. Unemployment worsened and people were tossed into the street because they couldn't pay their mortgages. Parts of the nation soon resembled ghost towns; empty houses and rusting railway tracks were all that was left for posterity.

Yet, as broke as the Yanks were, they still managed to hold the World Fair of 1893 in Chicago. 600 acres of land had been set aside for dazzling displays of the latest innovations, inventions and thingamabobs. Over twenty million people visited the fair that was meticulously run by its director, Charles H. Wacker. At the fair, some of the earliest known cinematic devices were exhibited; a projector called a zoopraxiscope was unveiled by its inventor, Eadweard Muybridge (and no, that's not a spelling mistake) while the Electrochyscope of Ottomar Anschutz was also premiered. Elsewhere, there was a moving walkway to transport people back and forth or if they wanted to go up and down, a chap called George Ferris had created a new novelty – an eighty-metre high spinning metal wheel with compartments in it. Norway had sent over a Viking ship for people to gawk at, Mr Milton Hershey was selling his new chocolate products for people to nibble on and new music was played by a young musician named Scott Joplin.

The American judicial system was also kept busy in 1893 and not just with bankruptcies. The United States Supreme Court spent sixteen days deliberating on whether the tomato was a fruit or a vegetable – for the record, they decided vegetable. Meanwhile, in a court in Massachusetts, a jury acquitted a thirty-two year old woman named Lizzie Bordern of murder. She had been accused of hacking her father and stepmother to death with an axe.

Back in Australia, the fledgling city of Brisbane had been hit by three back-to-back cyclones and the resulting heavy rains flooded the Brisbane River. Thirty-five people were killed including seven miners, trapped underground in a collapsed shaft of the Ipswich colliery. Hundreds of people were left homeless.

The calendar flipped over to a new year and there were happier times in Sydney. Steam-powered trams had begun running to Bondi Beach and many took advantage of a day by the sea. Most would take a picnic and stroll along the sand while the more daring would remove their shoes and paddle in the ocean. That was far as they could go; it was illegal to swim at the beach between the hours of 8am and 8pm as the baring of flesh was considered indecent and immoral.

If they wanted more than a wash of their tootsies, they could take a saunter round the rocks to nearby Tamarama where the fabulous Bondi Aquarium was located. All sorts of aquatic life were on show with tanks full of bream, whiting, lobsters and sharks. There was a seal pond, where the frolicking mammals were watched by a solitary, and presumably bored, penguin. But if the beasties of the seas weren't your thing, there was a switchback railway (an early roller-coaster), concerts and fireworks on a Wednesday night.

This, of course, was all very nice if you had some leisure time. The Randwick Labour League met in 1894 to discuss a proposal to the government. They wanted all government clothing to be manufactured in government workshops and not by private contractors. They felt that this would stop the practice of women working 72 hours a week for a take-home pay of five shillings, or around $18 today. Also NSW omnibus drivers were worried about their new rosters; they would be working 365 days a year with only an eight hour break each day. For this they would be paid the grand sum of 36 shillings (or $125) a week. Yet, the *Herald* was more worried that the 'white man' was missing out on work on the Queensland cane-fields. It declared that 'white labour should prove its superiority so the South Sea savages will go without being pushed out'.

If the people could get time off, they could enjoy the public holidays that we enjoy today – although they celebrated the Queen's birthday at a different time. Today we have a day off in early June for Elizabeth II's birthday, even though her actual birthday is in April. What we are honouring in June is the birthday of her grandfather, George V; no-one ever got round to changing the public holiday date. In 1894, they commemorated Queen Victoria's birthday in late May, which actually was when she blew the candles out on her cake – if she did, or could still do, that sort of thing.

Needless to say, on that public holiday there was plenty to see and do. The Crystal Maze at the Strand Arcade had a number of mechanical novelties and the Government Printing Office Dramatic and Musical Society were performing 'East Lynne' at the Royal Standard Theatre. Away from the city, the Moore Park Zoological Gardens had performing elephants (named Jessie and Toby) and a featured show of 'The Wild Man in the Woods' – which was just an orang-utan in a cage. The Port Jackson Steamship Company sailed steamers to Manly while there was a 'first-class programme of amusements' arranged for the Sir Joseph Banks pleasure grounds at Botany. There was horse-racing at Randwick, holiday sessions at the Darlinghurst Skating Rink and a game of Australian football, between West Sydney and East Sydney, played at the Royal Agricultural Ground. At the famed Bondi Aquarium, you could see Abd-el-Murad, Egyptian juggler and necromancer; the 'world's greatest acrobats' and Miss Phoebe Levy, skating in costume. At the not-so-famed Coogee Place Aquarium, well, they had a Bavarian brass band and a sheep with six legs.

It wasn't just Sydney having all the fun, though. In Melbourne, there was horse racing at Flemington, a military parade through the city, a twenty-four hour bicycle race, a tug-of-war competition at Richmond, an Australian Rules match between Geelong and Melbourne and to top it off – a concert at the Town Hall starring Mesdames DeVere-Sapio and Camilla Urso. Adelaide partied, too: horse racing at Gawler, a fifty mile bicycle race, an Australian Rules match between South Adelaide and Port Adelaide and a chess tournament.

Away from all the knees-ups was the New South Wales parliament, discussing and debating the Children's Protection Amendment Bill. They were bothered that some unscrupulous adults were making money from children. The first thing they wanted to implement was the prevention of children selling newspapers in the street. The big topics, however, were that they wanted to lower the figure paid in advance to adopt a child and to have all still-births registered. They believed there was a 'large number of children being murdered and stowed away in backyards and other places and explained as a still-birth' or if the child escaped being murdered by their birth parents, they were sold for adoption and murdered by adopted parents.

To demonstrate: in September, a woman named Jane Harrison was charged under the new Act. She had received a child named Roy without registering the adoption. The child had originally been adopted by a Mrs Rooke, who passed it on to Mrs Griffin who in turn gave it to Mrs Harrison. Jane testified that after three weeks she gave the child to a woman who said she was his grandmother. Roy's birth mother testified that she paid £8 ($560) to Mrs Rooke to adopt the child for life. Mrs Rooke sold the child on for £3. Jane Harrison ended up paying £1. What is recorded in this case is that Mrs Rooke was jailed for two years for her part. What is not recorded is the sentences for the other women or the whereabouts of little Roy.

Thankfully not every parent treated their child as an item of commerce. In 1895, Frank and Ellen O'Brien and Richard and Sarah Carroll brought new life into the world with the birth of William O'Brien and Frances Carroll. With the population of Sydney and its surrounds being 422,000, it is an even money bet that the Carroll's and the O'Brien's didn't know each other from a bar of soap but they lived only three kilometres apart – Kippax-street, Surry Hills for the O'B's and Wentworth-street, Paddington for the Carroll's. The families would get to know each other in around twenty-five-years, when William and Frances married. Those of you with prescient abilities will already know that William and Frances were my grandparents. In my grandmother's memoir, she described her house at Wentworth-street as 'a terrace house with two bedrooms upstairs and a front room, dining room and kitchen downstairs, but … you had to go to the bottom of the yard for the lavatory, which was covered in honeysuckle vine.'

The genetic jigsaw puzzle that is me was nearing completion. Another part was slotted in from a place distant from these shores. In the grimy, dirty, smoky shipyard town of Port Glasgow, Scotland, a young man named Robert Craig married his sweetheart, Martha Freeburn. In this hard and cold environment, tuberculosis and consumption were the diseases *du jour* and the Craig's, and hundreds of other couples, lost several children to the maladies. But one daughter would grow strong and end up forging a link between Scotland and Armidale in New South Wales, some 17,000 kilometres away.

In 1895, politicians were a dull lot – though, I suppose, little has changed. But there was one colony's Premier who had a bit of life in him and in whose exploits would have made juicy reading – Charles Kingston, the South Australian leader. Three years previously, a fellow member of the Legislative Council had called him a coward and a bully. Kingston then promptly challenged him to a duel. The offending politician became a little nervous and told the coppers who in turn, told him not to show up on the day and they would handle it. Sure enough, Kingston arrived at the designated time with a loaded pistol. He was arrested and placed on the equivalent of a twelve-month good behaviour bond – which, amazingly, he was still serving when he became Premier.

In July of '95, he was walking to Government House when he was attacked from behind by a man brandishing a whip. Kingston was carrying an umbrella but he dropped it and, with blood streaming down his face, he wrestled with his attacker. They were eventually separated and Kingston took the whip away; he intended to 'have it mounted and preserved as a memento of one of the most interesting episodes of my life'. He certainly had some interesting episodes and he certainly had some mementos. When he died in 1908, he had no living children from his marriage but it is thought he fathered as many as six illegitimate kids. Kingston was exhumed in 2008 for DNA testing and the tests proved positive, finalising the story of one little girl. She had grown up in an orphanage in the nineteenth century as neither Kingston or her mother wanted anything to do with her.

The writer, Mark Twain, didn't like duels. He once said that: 'I thoroughly disapprove of duels. If a man should challenge me, I would take him kindly and forgivingly by the hand and lead him to a quiet place and kill him'. Twain arrived in Australia in 1895 for a lecture tour and drew crowds like Lady Gaga does today. A man of quick wit, it didn't take him long for a wry observation when he was in New South Wales: 'God made the harbour … but Satan made Sydney'. He also tried some poetry when he composed a ditty to a creature that fascinated him – the platypus:

> 'Come forth from thy oozy couch
> Oh ornithorhynchus, dear
> And great with cordial cheer
> The stranger that longs to hear
> From thy own lips the 'tail' of thy origin all unknown,
> Thy misplaced bone where flesh should be
> And flesh where there should be bone.'[2]

He wasn't known for his poetry. You can see why.

So if God made the harbour, who was going to make the harbour crossing? For decades, people had to rely on leaking punts and chugging steamers if they wanted to go to North Sydney. As far back as Governor Macquarie's time, engineers had been scratching their heads and dreaming up ways to provide a crossing. One chap had come up with the idea of a floating bridge – the idea was popular for a while until someone asked how you got a ship through it. In the early 1880's, as Alan Roberts mentions, Premiers Henry Parkes and George Dibbs had looked at building a bridge across the harbour but they received little support. Indeed, Parkes had several radical ideas for Sydney's transport. Back then, the suburban trains stopped at Redfern and if you wished to travel further into the city, you caught an omnibus or you walked. Many folk wanted the trains to continue on to Circular Quay. Parkes thought that was unnecessary but decreed that Sydney did need a Central Station … which he wanted at The Rocks.

Jumping ahead to 1895 and the brains trusts had been thinking about the harbour crossing again. The Engineer-in-Chief of the Railway Construction Branch thought he had it sorted and presented an eleven-point plan to fix the transport problems. Apart from the electrification of Sydney's steam tramway, he suggested a subaqueous tunnel to be

---

2. *The Mercury,* 2nd November 1895

constructed between Milson's Point, North Sydney and either Dawes Point or Fort Macquarie (Bennelong Point). This would give a rail link between Redfern and North Sydney. In his scheme, trains would run through the tunnel to Milson's Point where they would be raised up to ground level by large lifts and then they could carry on to the North Shore line. He estimated the cost of this tunnel to be £372,611 or about 26 million dollars today.

The Royal Commission on City and Suburban Railways had other ideas and they suggested a bridge between Dawes Point and Milson's Point. This bridge would have a double line of rails and two footpaths. It would start from Princes-street in The Rocks and finish in the grounds of a hotel in North Sydney. They stated that the bridge could have a central supporting pier in the harbour and would have a clearance of 160ft (49m) above the water – interestingly, today's Harbour Bridge has a maximum clearance of 161ft. It was estimated that the bridge would cost £745,000 ($52,000,000). But a Mr Howarth considered this a tad pricey and said that an underwater viaduct, consisting of tubes anchored to the Port Jackson bedrock and decorated with white enamelled bricks and tiles, was the best idea for the crossing. His plan would cost only £185,000 or around 13 million dollars today. None of these plans ever got off the ground – or below the water. When we did get round to building a harbour tunnel, it cost over 500 million dollars.

Michael O'Brien

16. I WOULD FLY AWAY FROM ALL EARTH'S LIGHT

It was hot in January of 1897. Bloody hot. People who had recently arrived in the country must have thought they had sailed straight to hell. The continent was enveloped in a heat wave and hundreds of people didn't survive. In Bourke, temperatures reached 47º. The managers of Rookwood Necropolis hired extra staff just to dig graves – demand had outstripped supply. On the fifteenth of January, seventy people were buried, causing chaos at the cemetery and the Mortuary Station. Waverly Cemetery on the coast recorded double the average weekly amount of interments and it was estimated that over a million rabbits died at Wilcannia.

> 'Families walked the streets the whole night in negligible clothing. Many went into the Darling River and stayed there for hours up to their necks, but the water was lukewarm … When a man gets heat apoplexy he becomes unnormal [sic]. He sheds his clothes at intervals until he is naked, all the while walking around in circles. That is why many of the victims … were found entangled in rabbit-proof fences. Or rather, what was discovered were their skeletons.'[1]

---

1. *Barrier Miner,* 8th February 1929

In April, away from the heat, the first modern Olympic Games were held in Greece. Fourteen countries were represented with the participation of 246 athletes ... but 169 of them were Greek. The gymnastics and weightlifting events were held outdoors in the middle of the stadium while the swimming events were held in the sea off the coast of Greece. And how many athletes did we send? Believe it or not, just the one – Edwin Flack was his name. Now Flack was a Victorian and even though Australia wasn't a federated nation, he was considered to be representing the whole country, not just Victoria. And he did us proud – he won gold in the 800m and the 1500m running events and competed in the singles and doubles at tennis. He also took part in the marathon, even though he had never run that distance. He was leading until near the end when he collapsed with exhaustion. Edwin was helped to his feet by a spectator who he then punched, while in a state of delirium. Aussie, Aussie, Aussie, oi, oi, oi.

In the same month as the Olympics, a new Governor was appointed in Queensland. He was Charles Wallace Alexander Napier Cochrane-Baillie and while that name doesn't ring a bell, he was also the second Baron Lamington. Now, legend has it that his chef, while working on some leftovers, created a small sponge cake which he coated with chocolate and sprinkled with coconut. Ah, now what shall we call it? Legend also has it that the Baron wasn't overly impressed with this creation, referring to them as 'bloody poofy woolly biscuits'.

Down below in New South Wales, the newspaper reported on the twenty-first of April that the former premier, Sir Henry Parkes, was ill and had been confined to bed in his home at Annandale. Dr Maurice O'Connor was the physician in charge and he stated – 'He would be probably ill for weeks and it would be most likely months before he recovered'. Politicians and administrators flocked to Annandale to visit Sir Henry; he would have made a small fortune if he sold tickets which, in retrospect, wouldn't have gone astray. Piling through the front door were the current Premier, Mr Reid; the former Premier, Mr Dibbs; the Railway Commissioners; the Minister for Works; the Inspector General of Police; the Clerk of the Legislative Assembly; the Director of the Botanic Gardens; the Secretary of the Public Service Board; the Mayor of Manly and the Consul for Sweden (probably because he had nothing to do).

The following day, Dr O'Connor advised: 'Sir Henry was better and was certainly progressing favourably'. On the 24th of April, the doctor stated that: 'There was considerable improvement in his condition and while he hadn't passed the critical stage, there was no cause for immediate alarm'. On the 25th of April, O'Connor mentioned, 'His condition continues to improve and he is making gradual progress'.

Two days later, Sir Henry Parkes died.

Sir Henry didn't live to see his dream of a Commonwealth of Australia realised. He also didn't live in a state of financial security – he died in relative poverty. During his eighty years, he had married three times and fathered seventeen children, although not many of them survived to adulthood. Upon his retirement from politics, he had been granted a public trust fund which gave him an annual income but the fund had been eroded by the 1893 GFC. According to his future biographer, Charles Lyne, shopkeepers had threatened to stop Sir Henry's weekly supplies and that he 'absolutely did not know what to do to make ends meet'. He had sold off most of his books, papers, letters and artworks to provide for his family. Upon his death, some of the surviving members of his family were up you-know-where creek – under the original arrangement of the trust fund, the remaining money was to be divided among the children of his first marriage. The children of his second marriage and his third wife, who was looking after them, received nothing.

> 'I shall have to face the world alone with five young children,' said Lady Parkes, with tears in her eyes, to a **Herald** reporter yesterday afternoon. 'They are all very young ... the eldest being 12 and the youngest three years and eight months, and it will be many years before they will be able to earn their own living.'[2]

Later in the year, Britain decreed that their armed forces needed to earn a living so they declared war on Zanzibar, now part of Tanzania. Hostilities commenced at 9am with the Royal Navy shelling the island. At 9.40am, Zanzibar surrendered. To this day, it remains the shortest war in world history. The Brits continued their World

---

2. *Sydney Morning Herald,* 28th April 1896

Domination Tour in 1897 when they attacked Benin City (Nigeria) and overthrew the King, Ovonramwen Nogbaisi. Queen Victoria (yep, still going) celebrated all this new real estate by commemorating her sixtieth year as British monarch with an open-air service outside St Paul's Cathedral.

As Britain bombarded the bejeezus out of places for their conquests, a Swedish gentleman had a novel way for his. Salomon August Andree chose to lead an expedition to the North Pole. He planned on doing it in an unusual fashion – he was going to fly there in a hydrogen-filled balloon. He and two other men took off in 1897 with a basket filled with provisions and a cage filled with communication devices i.e. carrier pigeons.

It was the last time anyone would see them for thirty-three years.

Their bodies were eventually found by another expedition in 1930. Diaries found with the dead bodies indicated that the balloon crashed after two days and the men faced a cold and arduous walk back to civilization. The men didn't survive but the film in their cameras did and around two hundred photos were developed of the ill-fated expedition.

1897 was the year that a freak cyclone hit Port Darwin and it was estimated that 10-12 inches of rain fell in one night while strong winds wiped out whatever were in their paths. The railway line was washed away, the telegraph line had no hope and the majority of buildings were destroyed or badly damaged. Nearly every private dwelling was levelled or at least rendered roofless. The boats in the harbour were either sunk or blown to buggery. Numerous people were unaccounted for and one correspondent wrote – 'It was impossible to describe the state of ruin and devastation'. During the aftermath, some local carpenters walked around the ruins of the town and offered their services for repairs. They were charging £5 ($350) an hour.

While Port Darwin cleaned up, most of the country was suffering from the heat again and the beverage retailers swooped with advertising:

> 'During the hot weather, try Wolfe's Schapps and Iced Ginger Beer. It stimulates the organs of the body to healthy action'.

Or this one:

> 'Ain't it 'ot?
> Just the weather for
> Iced Victorian Lager Bier
> On draught or in gold top bottles
> At the leading Clubs and Hotels of our City.'

Many considered that a fantastic idea and partook of a cold one or twelve. But the wowsers were also out in force and in March, a F.B. Boyce wrote a lengthy letter to the *Herald*, full of detailed calculations and condemnation. Boyce had estimated that, for the ten years between 1887 and 1896, the colony had spent £45,000,000 (or 3 billion dollars today) on beer, wine and spirits:

> 'Although there is a great improvement [in social ills] we still have much lunacy and immorality through drink. Have we not nearly two coroner's inquests a week over the dupes of alcohol? Yet these are not a tenth of the drink-related deaths. Have we not 75 per cent of the cases in our Divorce Courts traceable to the same strange power? Have we not about 20,000 convictions for drunkenness every year? Are not our 58 gaols mainly needed by the victims of alcohol?'[3]

G.D. Clark joined the bandwagon in recommending that everyone got on the wagon. He or she claimed that New South Wales, in 1895, had 3,238 licensed public houses which equated to an average of one pub for every 391 residents. For purposes of comparison, if that ratio remained the same in the year 2010, there would be 18,670 pubs in NSW. Clark waffled on: non-drinkers, being children and 'a large proportion of women', made up four-fifths of the population so therefore, 'the quantity of alcohol consumed annually by habitual drinkers must be enormous and that many of them are in a chronic state of drunken stupidity'. Clark didn't stop there:

---

3. *Sydney Morning Herald,* 20th March 1897

> 'When the churches, instead of dodging around the tail end of the liquor fiend, make a bold attempt to grip the monster by the throat, its last dying cry will soon be heard and the dawn of a brighter national life will begin.'[4]

Dramatic stuff, yes, but the warnings were falling on deaf ears and were probably too late for some:

> 'Mr Rush will give away to the poor of Surry Hills, Tuesday night, at the rear of the Austral Hotel, TWO CASKS OF BEER, in honour of Her Majesty's record reign. No person intoxicated will be supplied. Heads of poor families may send vessels'.[5]

Morgan and Smith, Merchants, of 311 Kent-street, weren't helping the cause with their year-long advertising campaign:

> 'Good looks are more closely connected with good beer than most people are aware of. You cannot be good-looking unless you are healthy and you cannot be healthy if you drink adulterated beer. Franz Josef Pilsener Lager is what you call a pure, wholesome, palatable beer – pure enough for your children to drink.'[6]

So, there you have it – you and your children will be pissed but at least you will be attractive.

For the ones who could drag themselves away from the booze, there were other things to be doing. Many attended the opening ceremony of the Queen Victoria Market Building – the one now referred to as the QVB. The structure, situated in the block bordered by George, Druitt, York and Market Streets, was (and still is) an impressive display of modern Romanesque architecture. It had four hydraulic cart-lifts, each capable of holding a loaded cart and horse while there were four passenger elevators

---

4. *Sydney Morning Herald,* 9th August 1897
5. *Sydney Morning Herald,* 21st June 1897
6. *Sydney Morning Herald,* 20th January 1897

to lift the people. The original plan was to have a produce market in the basement while the other floors would host a coffee palace, shops, art galleries and a small concert hall. During the construction, contractors used 4,500,000 bricks, 3,000 tons of iron, 55,418 square yards of plastering, 6,050 square yards of tiling and 6,382 square yards of glass. The QVMB cost £252,230 or about $17,600,000 in modern money – which is probably the annual rental of a shop in there today.

The Premier couldn't attend the opening in July so the ribbon-cutting was left to the Mayor of Sydney. In a lengthy speech, Mayor Matthew Harris was heard to say:

> 'Ladies and Gentlemen, we have invited you here today to take part in the opening of this magnificent pile of building … We have not yet imbibed the enthusiasm of our American cousins for lofty structures, but then they have, as we all know, an insatiable desire to outdo creation.'[7]

The basement was offered to fruit and vegetable growers on a three month rent-free basis but few took up the offer. But upstairs, the shops filled rapidly and some of the first tenants included: Thomas Bergin, tobacconist; Frame & Co, hatters; Thomas Dowling, shoes; R.E. Blanchard, books; S. Rowley, sewing machine importer; M. Cohen, toys and novelties; P. Offer, printer and supplier of rubber stamps; S.M. Hewitt, fancy glass and chinaware; Pattinson's Drug Stores; Quong Tart Tea Emporium and Madame Satanella, the palm reader. The advertisements of the time for the new complex proudly declared: PRICES THE LOWEST IN THE CITY.

While Sydney's people had the thrill of the Queen Victoria Market Building, over in Queen Victoria's England, London's people had the thrill of the adventures of Louis de Rougemont. In 1898, *Wide World Magazine* serialised the story of a dashing voyager who, after surviving a shipwreck, had spent thirty years in the wilderness of Northern Australia. He was also invited to lecture at the British Association for the Advancement of Science. He told them of how he lived with the Aboriginals and was revered as a god by them. He told of riding giant

---

7. *Sydney Morning Herald,* 22nd July 1898

turtles and witnessing flying wombats. Many considered him the modern Robinson Crusoe and London was fascinated by his exploits.

There was a problem, though – it was all bullshit.

Louis de Rougemont was actually a man named Henri Grin who had worked as a dishwasher, photographer, real estate salesman and a butler for the governor of Western Australia. In 1892, he had married a lady named Eliza in Sydney and they had seven children. Grin abandoned his family, made his way to England and embarked on an enormous con job, creating the de Rougemont legend. It started to come apart when some experts smelled a rat; he couldn't speak any Aboriginal words nor could he identify the location of his travels on a map. Then, another newspaper managed to track down Eliza who blew the whistle on the adventurer.[8] Suddenly, the fifteen minutes of fame were over and the castaway was cast away.

Of course, newspapers weren't the only way of spreading the news of fake Australian adventurers; there was another method but in Sydney's 1899, it was struggling to attract users. The telephone system had begun operating in 1880 in Australia yet the Postmaster General was amazed. He advised in January that there were telephone bureaux set up at the GPO and in over 20 suburbs around Sydney but hardly anyone was using them.

> 'As is well known, a person desirous of communicating with any member of the telephone exchange has simply to go to a bureau, place sixpence in the slot, when he will be entitled to three minutes conversation.'[9]

Possibly, therein lays the problem. Looking at the part that reads "communicating with any member of the telephone exchange", the fact that there were only 8,321 on the subscribers list of which 659 were residential customers and 647 were from the country and you can see there weren't a lot of people who you could give a quick ring. Also, there were complaints that for subscribers whose telephone number exceeded the numeral 3000, or if you wanted to call someone with one of those numbers, the service slowed dramatically

---

8. Biographical information from B.G. Andrews, *Australian Dictionary of Biography*
9. *Sydney Morning Herald,* 31st January 1899

Yet, even though there were only 8,932 telephones in Sydney and the Postmaster General was saying that hardly anyone used them, the average number of calls per day exceeded 70,000. Later in the year, it was decided, for the sake of public convenience, that telephone officials would listen in to your call and if they decided it was an 'ordinary and unimportant conversation', you would be cut off after five minutes. The 'frivolous and unnecessary use of the telephone' was to be curtailed. And businesses advised you to use the telephone wisely as well; the following advertisement by the NSW Fresh Food & Ice Co Ltd appeared quite regularly:

> 'We have three telephone numbers for the head office of the company – 244, 1002 and 2334. Many of the calls are on 244. It is suggested customers might avail themselves of the other numbers and so relieve the congestion of 244.'

Maybe some congestion was caused by people spending a sixpence and discussing the war in Africa. British forces, always up for some argy-bargy, were fighting a load of rebellious farmers and settlers from the South African Republic and the Orange Free State. These rebels were known as Boers and the argy-bargy developed into the Boer War. Technically, it was the second Boer War as the first Boer War had been fought nineteen years earlier, but no-one ever mentions that war. The British were taking this current one seriously and called on Australia for help. Over 16,000 Australians served in Africa with the bulk of our forces being mounted units.

The Sydney Meat Preserving Company stated that their factory at Rookwood had been busy canning meat for the troops in South Africa. They disclosed that an average of 4,000 sheep per day had been tinned and the 'works were capable of treating much larger quantities than this, but sheep are not coming forward in sufficient numbers to warrant greater efforts'.

Well, you can hardly blame the sheep.

There was another kind of food that was popular at the time and it had no difficulty in beating its chest with pride. Arnott's Milk Arrowroot Biscuits were marketed at the younger crowd and described in regular advertising campaigns as a 'complete food, meeting all the requirements of infant life - strengthening, fattening, health giving –

from the youngest infant to the oldest child – suitable also for the aged'. And if little Johnny or Nellie wanted one of these biscuits, they even came with serving instructions:

> 'For very young children, rub the biscuits very lightly on a clean nutmeg grater, or crush very fine and sieve through a sieve; mix carefully with boiling water, stirring well, and give through feeding-bottle or by spoon. As there is milk in them, it is advisable not to add it. For older children, pour boiling water on biscuits as they are and give by spoon. A good way is to put a saucer over the cup or basin in which the biscuits are placed to soak, until they swell out, leaving no water.'

It's possible the nation's parliamentary members were nibbling away at bickies while they debated the Commonwealth issue. Nineteen years after Sir Henry Parkes had put forward the proposal of a federated Australia (and was laughed at and told to piss off), the pollies were edging closer to the concept. There were some doubters; leaders of the smaller states were concerned that New South Wales and Victoria would dominate everything while other members remarked that the federated United States had just about wiped itself out with a civil war. Still, the Commonwealth of Australia looked like going ahead and with a draft constitution penned by a gentleman named Andrew Clark, a referendum was held to see what the voters thought – and they thought 'Yes'. So the politicians grabbed some more bickies and sat down to write a proposal to the Queen.

Her representative in New South Wales was the governor; the man who held that position in 1899 would be the last governor of the New South Wales colony, as opposed to it being a state of Australia. His name was William Lygon, the 7th Earl Beauchamp. In his earlier days as governor, he had become quite popular as he visited everywhere and seemingly would turn up for the opening of an envelope. Upon his later return to England, he became very unpopular – especially with his wife. After twenty-nine years of marriage and having fathered seven children, he announced that he preferred the company of men … if you know what I mean. He would end up in America, having been stripped of his titles.

The 1800s were coming to an end and it was time for another New Year's Eve party. The League of New South Wheelmen planned to go out with a bang as they planned a Night Cycle Carnival to be held at the Sydney Cricket Ground. The ground would be 'brilliantly lighted with the latest luminant [sic], acetylene gas' and the highlight of the show was a five-mile international scratch race. The King-street Opera House was hosting 'Hamilton's Colossal Spectacle of the Boer War', supported by Mr Walter Bell's 'specially selected' vaudeville company that included Salina the Marvellous English Dancer, Mr Miller Fraser the Scottish tenor and the lady juggler, Miss Vidi Providi. But not everyone saw the need for a celebration, as seen by what one correspondent wrote to the paper:

> 'Seeing the old year out and the new year in generally means our fair city is turned for the time being into a kind of pandemonium. The custom may be though innocent but none the less is idiotic … The times are serious and demand seriousness and it would be a cheering testimony to the profession of certain sterling quantities of heart and brain which are claimed as characteristics of our race if this year, the youth of Sydney were found abstaining from a demonstration very ill-suited to the circumstances and conditions of the day.'[10]

Others thought 'bollocks to that' and combined the troubles of the times by indulging in the favourite activity of the times, thereby ensuring themselves of their own troubling times:

> 'FOSTERS BASS ALE AND GUINESS STOUT
> WERE SUPPLIED TO ALL THE AUSTRALIAN
> TROOPSHIPS
> TRY THE NEW SHIPMENT
> PERFECT CONDITION'

---

10. *Sydney Morning Herald,* 30th December 1899

Time has no divisions to mark its passage. There is never a thunderstorm or blare of trumpets to announce the beginnings of a new month or year. Even when a new century begins, it is only we mortals who ring bells and fire off pistols.

           Thomas Mann
        The Magic Mountain, 1924

Michael O'Brien

17. MCM

The year 1900. The last year of the nineteenth century for people of the western world. It was also the year 6650 on the Assyrian calendar, 1307 for the Bengalis, 2444 for Buddhists, 1262 for the Burmese, 1892 for Ethiopians, 5660 for Hebrews, 1317 for the Islamic, 4233 for the Koreans and the Japanese were celebrating year 33 of the Meiji period.

> 'The birth of the new year took place under a thickly-veiled sky in this part of the continent. Long before the good old year passed away the streets of the city were noisy with the tramp of people marching in companies, and for the most part armed with trumpets, whenceforth [sic] came blasts at intervals. As the city clocks sounded the death knell of 1899, signal guns were fired from on board the shipping, rockets were sent up from all parts of the city and bands of music played through the streets, while the bright lustre in the sky told of the burning of scores of bonfires. At the quay, the steamers' sirens announced the birth of 1900 and the shipping joined in the general festival by a brilliant illumination.'[1]

Not everyone was enamoured with the noise, though:

---

1. *Sydney Morning Herald,* 1st January 1900

'Bands of youth paraded the thoroughfares blowing tin trumpets, twirling rattles or making the night hideous by means of other musical instruments of torture.'[2]

And some people had to work:

'The Fire Brigade received numerous calls to large fires, which proved to be bonfires on the street. When extinguishing the fun, the firemen were sometimes subjected to a fusillade of blue metal and flour bags. The firemen occasionally retaliated by washing the crowd with a hose.'[3]

And then there were the people who didn't celebrate at all:

'Passing through the parks, other thoughts took the place of holiday ones, these being suggested by figures lying on benches, and in the grass, their sole canopy the firmament, their only protection from the night, the more or less ragged clothes they wore. Little in common had they with the jostling crowds passing without the gates and bearing the goodies of life wherewith to begin a happy new year.'[4]

As most of the people in Sydney celebrated, they had no idea that there was an underlying menace in the city and it was about to rear its ugly head – or heads, really.

'Cork-tipped Tally Ho Cigarettes
are absolutely clean.
No impurity can soil your lips. 3d a packet.'

---

2. Ibid.
3. Ibid.
4. Ibid.

The advertisement above was a regular feature in the newspapers of the time. It was ironic that Tally Ho cigarettes were considered to be 'absolutely clean', because the very city they were sold in, wasn't. As January and February progressed, so did a frightening outbreak of bubonic plague.

A person who contracts the plague is guaranteed an unpleasant time. Swellings called buboes occur on the body and blood poisoning sets in. The person will also suffer nausea, fever, muscle pain and seizures. The disease has a high fatality percentage. The plague was spread in Sydney by fleas that had been carried in by rats that had stowed away on ships – the ships that were docking at Darling Harbour. Rats don't mind a bit of filth. In Sydney, they found plenty of it. Parts of the city were in a slum-like state as unemployment, high rents, overcrowding of dwellings and faulty or non-existent sanitation all added up to create one heck of a disgusting environment – but not if you were a rat. They wallowed in the filth, their fleas moved on and suddenly it was discovered that Sydney had an epidemic hot-spot.

Hell had opened its doors. Most of the plague victims were living or working in an area bordered by Darling Harbour, Erskine Street to the south, Kent Street to the west and the Gas Works at Millers Point to the north. The victims (both living and dead) were despatched to the Quarantine Station on North Head. The epidemic area was quarantined itself and the government stepped in with a radical plan. One thousand men were employed, inoculated and divided into two groups. Half of them were sent into the area to clean, and to drive the rats towards the waters of Darling Harbour. They would set traps for the vermin; the rats that were caught and killed were then burned in an incinerator in Bathurst Street.

The other 500 men were required to reside in the area and disinfect everything. The work commenced in March; just after the Minister of Works suggested that they should burn barrels of tar in Sussex Street to purify the area and have fire engines on standby as the burning tar might set fire to the housing. Residents of the area (the ones who hadn't been dragged away in one state or the other) were given a choice: stay and help clean or be shipped off to North Head for an indefinite stay.

> 'To pass along the streets, one might see barrels of limewash [sic], great watering cans filled with water boiling from the addition of sulphuric acid and giving off steam as it boils, mud coming up from some underground apartment and men filling the same into drays … Many of the yards have now the family oven or cooking stove standing exposed to wind and weather, because the wooden shed which sheltered it has been thrown into the street and burned … Moored to the wharfs are large pontoons or punts, more than half-filled with soil, manure, old tins, scraps of rusty iron, pieces of what appear to be skins of animals, and a hundred other forms of garbage.'[5]

Next time you are at Darling Harbour, sipping an over-priced caramel latte and nibbling on a focaccia – picture that scene.

While the great clean-up progressed, the numbers contacting the disease reduced but other areas of Sydney were affected and being inspected. The health officials moved onto Glebe, where the O'Brien family had lived, and found similar, if not more worrying problems. The district medical officer was there in May:

> 'He states that structurally speaking, the area is about the worst that had been opened up in the city … One cottage he mentions is in a low-lying position; its floor is rotten, the boards are loose and sunken, and beneath it was found a large quantity of stagnant water, the presence of which is caused by the height of the street and the back yard. This dwelling is not connected with the sewers, but a cesspit is on the premises, the soakage from which must find its way beneath the floor of the dwelling.'[6]

The plague outbreak is thought to have finished by the end of July of 1900. Over 300 people contacted the disease; 103 of them died. It is estimated that some 40,000 rats were killed and incinerated.

---

5. *Sydney Morning Herald,* 30th March 1900
6. *Sydney Morning Herald,* 22nd May 1900

'The plague will have no place in your thoughts if you make for Attwater's Bulli Family Hotel.'[7]

There was one woman who lived through the plague, the overpowering stench, the plumes of smoke from burning houses and burning rats, the sheer terror and panic of the people. But three months after the plague, heart disease claimed the life of Ellen Cunningham. She died on the 13th October in the Sydney Hospital. She was 51. She remained loyal to John O'Brien till the very end; her death certificate and burial were registered in the name of Ellen O'Brien. They couldn't have married officially; he was still married – on paper – to Mary. The informant for Ellen's death was her daughter, Kate; she was now married to an engineer named David Waddell and they lived at Harris Street, Pyrmont. As for John, he is not recorded as deceased – but God only knows where he actually was.

Two weeks before Ellen's death, Queen Victoria (yeah, I know, crazy, she was still going) proclaimed that as of the first of January, 1901, the six colonies of Australia would be united in a Federal Commonwealth under the name of the Commonwealth of Australia. Now it was time to panic, panic, panic and get everything ready. In December of 1900, the first Governor-General of Australia, the Queen's representative, was a chap called John Adrian Louis Hope, although better known as Lord Hopetoun. One of his roles was to appoint a Prime Minister; this is normally easy as you give it to the leader of the majority party at a federal election. However the federal election wasn't going to be held until March 1901, so Lord Hopetoun had to appoint an interim Prime Minister until the vote. All you trivia buffs are sitting there thinking, well, this is an easy one – the first <u>appointed</u> Prime Minister of Australia was Edmund Barton.

And you would be wrong.

As Lord Hopetoun had no majority party to pick from, he decided that the Premier of the most populous state should be appointed interim Prime Minister. This fell to the NSW Premier, William Lyne. Lord Hopetoun offered him the job and he accepted. William Lyne was the first person to be appointed Prime Minister of Australia. There was a small problem, though: Lyne was a staunch opponent

---

7. *Sydney Morning Herald,* 3rd July 1900

of Federation and consequently, he didn't have many friends in politics. He had about as much chance of being the next Archbishop of Canterbury as he had of fellow parliamentary members voting for anything he said. After a while, and maybe a little sulk, he returned the appointment to the GG. Lord Hopetoun then tossed it over to the barrister and cricket umpire, Edmund Barton, who would then go on to be Australia's first elected Prime Minister. He would also become the first Australian Prime Minister to receive a nickname when *The Bulletin* referred to him as "Toby Tosspot". His first cabinet would include Alfred Deakin; Charles Kingston, the loveable philanderer from South Australia and James Dickson. Dickson made the record books by becoming the first federal minister to die in office – unfortunately, ten days after he started.

Of course, every federated nation needs a federal capital – ah, but where to put it? One man, who had 'Sir' in front of his name so should have known better, suggested that the capital be shared by Sydney and Melbourne over alternate ten year periods but the politicians made him have a little lie down after saying that. The constitution agreed to by the state premiers decreed that the capital would be situated in New South Wales but had to be at least 160kms away from Sydney – and this was decided before the plague. Bombala, Orange, Yass, Albury, Tamworth, Armidale and Tumut were all suggested and toured by the pollies. Then Dalgety took the inside running and favouritism.

While the pollies swanned around in the selected towns, being wined, dined and generally schmoozed, the people were thinking up names for the yet-to-be-decided capital. The quills scratched furiously as letters poured into the newspapers. Someone suggested "Hopetoun". "Bartonia" was another. "Bankstoun" (as opposed to Bankstown) was a third. Then there was "Australopis" and "Kookaburra" and "Woolgold" and my personal favourite – Cooeeton". Some said the capital should be named after Cook or Philip or Parkes or Flinders. The people were in a creative frenzy; even Rudyard Kipling was inspired to write a poem – part of which follows:

> So it was done in the presence,
> in the hall of our thousand years

> In the face of five free nations
> that have no peer but their peers.
> And the young Queen out of the Southland
> kneeled down at the old Queen's knee
> And asked for a mother's blessing
> on the excellent years to be.

Another great lyricist who may have written something had he not had the misfortune of dying in November of 1900 was Arthur Sullivan, one half of Gilbert & Sullivan. The pair had delighted audiences with their light and breezy operettas before their partnership fizzled out over an argument on the price of a carpet. A famous writer also left the world at the end of 1900 after he had just published a work under the name of 'C.33'; this was his prison number from the time he spent in confinement for homosexual activities. His real name was Oscar Wilde.

But if anyone was going to literally kneel at the old Queen's knee, they had to hurry because the news out of England was that she wasn't well. However, she was in better shape than her counterpart in Italy, King Humbert II, who had been shot dead by a radical named Angelo Bresci. This followed an incident earlier in the year, when an assassination attempt was made on the Prince of Wales; Jean-Baptiste Sipido, angered by the Boer War, fired several bullets at the Prince, but he couldn't hit the side of a barn, let alone a prince. These were restless times.

On the first of January 1901, the people of Sydney weren't restless – they were ecstatic. Over a quarter of a million people flocked through the streets and on to a reclaimed swamp, freshly named Centennial Park. They were there for the ceremony of Federation and they listened politely as Lord Hopetoun read out the Queen's proclamation. Then they watched as the Governor-General swore in Barton's ministry and bingo! – the Commonwealth of Australia was official.

A choir of 15,000 children sang its heart out as the people rushed to the next activity – a parade through the streets of Sydney. A group of shearers led the parade, followed by Boer War troops and brass bands. The party lasted well into the night as the words 'colony' and 'colonial' were struck out of the national vocabulary.

Three weeks after the shindig was over, the *Sydney Morning Herald* reported that Queen Victoria was in poor health and that while her condition was grave, it was not entirely without hope. The Queen died the day that story was printed. Victoria was 82 and remarkably, had reigned for 64 years, having first sat on the throne when she was 18. She spent the last forty years of her life wearing black mourning clothes (in honour of her beloved husband, Prince Albert) and she had reduced her ceremonial duties dramatically. She outlived Albert, four of their children and a cabinet full of prime ministers. Shortly after her death, her son, the man who had previously avoided being assassinated, took over and became the seventh English king to bear the name of Edward.

Elsewhere, in a great moment of nomenclature, a motor vehicle was given a name, purely to please a politician. Gottlieb Daimler had developed a high-performance (at the time) motor car, which had four cylinders in a 5.9 litre engine and was capable of reaching speeds of 90kmh. Daimler gave the motor car to the Consul-General of the Austro-Hungarian Empire and chose to name it after the Consul-General's daughter. Her name was Mercedes.

Across the sea from Europe, amongst the murk and the soot and the thick black clouds from the Port Glasgow shipyards in Scotland, a wee lassie was born to Robert and Martha Craig. Robert made his living as an iron dresser; his days full of cleaning sand and impurities from the cast iron moulds. The girl was their fifth child and she was christened Annie McFettridge Craig; Robert's mother's maiden name was Annie McFettridge. The parents were hoping for some good fortune; in 1899, two of their four children died within three weeks of each other. This time they were blessed and Annie went on to become my grandmother.

Back in Sydney, if you were shopping in Sydney's Haymarket area on the 10th July, 1901. If they were though, you would have witnessed one of the most terrifying events ever to occur in Sydney; Anthony Hordern's Emporium, the biggest retail shop in Australia, had caught fire. As staff and customers ran screaming into the streets, the fire consumed the building and each floor of the complex collapsed into a pile of rubble below. Fire brigades valiantly fought the inferno as hundreds of people gathered to watch. Then someone saw something that would be forever etched on the memories of the witnesses – there was a man clinging to the roof. The floors had disappeared below him and the flames were reaching higher, licking at his feet. The man's name was Harry Clegg.

> 'The crowd, which by this time had worked itself into a feverish state of excitement, shouted to cheer the spirits of the man who, to all appearances, seemed doomed. In the meantime, the firemen moved an escape ladder to what they thought would prove to be a more advantageous angle from which to reach the man. Clegg, it is thought, witnessed the removal of the escape ladder and must have wrongly come to the conclusion that the firemen ... had abandoned the idea of rescue and had deserted him ... He removed his hat from his head and waved it to the people below. He was next seen to cast his eyes heavenward as if engaged in prayer. He then, to the horror of all who were looking at him, extended his arms and dropped feet first from the parapet.'[8]

Harry Clegg may have also seen several men who were occupied in assembling a kind of tarpaulin or net for him to jump into and mistakenly thought that it was ready. The fall was eight storeys and he landed in a crumpled heap in the street. Several women fainted, men averted their eyes and Harry was quickly rushed off to Sydney Hospital. Upon arrival there, he was pronounced dead. He was twenty-two years old, lived at home with his parents and played with the Ashfield brass band. Several days later, his funeral was given full military honours and an estimated 10,000 people lined the streets as the procession moved to Waverley Cemetery.

You would think that the fire ruined the Hordern's business but the retail juggernaut had other ideas. The day after the fire, they published an advertisement in the paper:

> 'Anthony Hordern's Only Universal Providers. We are burnt out. The stocks of goods which filled our store and made the Haymarket the most delightful resort

---

8. *Sydney Morning Herald,* 11th July 1901

in the city are a heap of ashes ... Nothing but charred walls and burning embers remains ... Let nothing you dismay ... another half a million pounds worth of stock ... uninjured by fire and ready for sale ... business has been temporarily transferred to the Exhibition Building, Prince Alfred Park."[9]

Ten days after the fire, workmen clearing up the mess in the Haymarket found a charred pair of boots in the basement. The boots were laced up and closer study revealed they contained the burned remains of human feet.

As Australian society embraced new technologies and moved with the times, Australian criminals found they had to adapt as well but they used old bushranging techniques to rob new targets. Early on a Sunday morning in August, in Patrick O'Brien's old town of Hawthorn, Victoria, four armed and masked men boarded a horse-powered tram and robbed the driver and passengers. "Pull up your horses," called out one robber as he rammed a revolver into the driver's cheek, "or I'll spill your brains on the floor." Another member of the gang, apparently with a dry sense of humour, walked up the carriage saying – "Fares, please", as he relieved people of money and jewellery. The bandits then took off with over £20 ($1,400) of cash and valuables.

They weren't the only daring men with guns. The world was shocked to hear in September that the President of the United States, William McKinley, had been shot by a Polish anarchist named Leon Czolgosz. Once again, the doctors toddled out to waiting reporters and stated that the President's condition was favourable ... and of course, he died eight days later. The Polish anarchist wasn't far behind him, being executed in October.

There was death at Gostwyck in September as well, when Susan Kingdom succumbed to cardiac failure and 'senile decay'. She was 79 years old and was laid to rest with George at the Old Uralla Cemetery. The matriarch had survived two children with her marriage with John Elliott and one child from her union with George. There's no elaborate headstone for her and George; matter of fact, there's nothing to indicate

---

9. *Sydney Morning Herald*, 11th July 1901 – same day the fire was reported.

where they lay. Today, Old Uralla Cemetery is a quiet little resting place, where bodies and secrets lie undisturbed. It is tucked away several blocks from the main road, behind houses and a school. The only noises you hear are the bleating of sheep on a nearby property and the bleating of tourists scrambling to see Thunderbolt's grave.

The Australian parliament had opened earlier in the year in the Exhibition Building in Melbourne. The King's son, the Duke of York, attended while crowds filled the streets, waving hats, hankies and umbrellas. Australia was now responsible for its own military and naval forces as well as telegraphic and postal services – and some of these services haven't improved since that time. Australia in 1901 had a population of nearly four million and a national debt of nearly £200,000,000 – or 14 billion dollars in today's moolah.

So, it was time for the politicians to proclaim a few things and show the people that they were actually doing something. Late in the year, the Governor-General signed off on the Immigration Restrictions Act, which led to what is known as the White Australia Policy. Shortly afterwards, the right to vote was given to all people over the age of twenty-one – providing they weren't Asian, African or even Aboriginal. While they were doing this, the new President of the United States, Theodore Roosevelt, angered many Americans by inviting a black man to dinner at the White House. It seemed there were no grey areas in the former colonies of Britain.

After a few months of Australian parliament, the flag was unfurled for the first time and allowed to flap in the Melbourne breeze. During the previous year, the government held a contest and invited people to submit a design for the new national flag, with the winner receiving a handsome cash prize. Some 32,000 entries were submitted from around the world and they finally decided on the one we have today. And politicians being politicians … it took another fifty years before the flag's dimensions were agreed upon.

18. Dry Old Arguments

Early on the morning of the 27th January, 1902, Lieutenant Handcock and another man from the Australian forces fighting in the Boer War, were taken outside, tied to a chair and shot dead by a firing squad. The men had been fighting with the Bushveldt Carbineers and they had been convicted of murdering unarmed Boer prisoners. While Handcock's name misses the eye whenever history's pages are turned over, the other man was etched in legend. He was Lieutenant Harry 'Breaker' Morant.

Like a lot of stories, there are a lot of stories within. It had been claimed that Handcock and Morant had murdered a Boer and robbed the corpse of money; another colleague stated that the pair were forty miles away when this man was killed. That didn't bother an English journalist who wrote that 'the Carbineers were a mixed scallywag body and the murder and looting of surrendered Dutchmen and natives required exemplary punishment for the credit of Great Britain' – (because the British were very circumspect on who they murdered). The most popular theory was that the two men were outraged when they found the mutilated body of a comrade and had acted out a plan to avenge his death. Handcock and Morant were brought before a British court-martial on the 26th February, found guilty and taken out and shot the next morning.

'Breaker' Morant was a well-respected horseman and had received accolades for his poetry. On the morning of his execution, he refused a blindfold and called out – "Be sure and make a good job of it". Handcock was a veterinarian and left behind a wife and three children.

The first his wife heard about the execution was when she read about it in the paper.

A short time after their deaths, the war in Africa came to an end when the Boers surrendered to the British forces led by Horatio Herbert Kitchener. In all, Australia had 251 men killed in action, 267 died of disease and 882 were wounded.

Back in New South Wales, it was a dire time and it called for drastic measures. The big problem was rain – or rather, a lack thereof. The state was suffering from the worst drought ever recorded. The government took the unusual step of proclaiming a type of public holiday for the 26th of February; it was set aside as a day of 'humiliation and prayer for rain'. Special church services were held throughout the city while Randwick and Newcastle horse races were cancelled - so they must have been serious. Also cancelled were the matinees of Mr Harry Rickard's New Tivoli Vaudeville Company (which included the 'frantic excitement of a great novelty – the American Netball game, with ten young ladies!') and J.C. Williamson's production of 'Ben Hur' at Her Majesty's Theatre.

Meanwhile, in Melbourne, the cricket match between England and Victoria had play abandoned – due to rain.

As the state dried up in February and March, it was reported that King Edward VII had travelled to Cowes to commence his Easter yachting cruise. In honour, the warships at Portsmouth fired 21 guns. None of them hit him.

Less than a month after the day of prayer, J.C. Williamson may have been praying for rain again as Her Majesty's Theatre burned down and 'Ben Hur' was cancelled permanently. Luckily, the theatre was empty at the time of the fire. Unluckily, a bakery at the rear of the theatre wasn't. A young woman named Bella Pye had previously evacuated the bakery and was standing on the street with hundreds of others, watching the fire. Apparently she then remembered that she had left some jewellery inside the bakery and hurried back in to collect it. She didn't return. They found her body under a collapsed wall, with a small gold brooch held tightly in her right hand.

Most people in NSW were scouring the skies for clouds but some scoured their brains for new ideas to relieve the anguish of the drought. In early April, Roberto Pullen, who was an Australian residing in New

York City, wrote to the newspaper and said that the time had arrived for 'serious consideration of a system of street tunnel construction, for transport and essential services, in Sydney and the new Federal capital'. It still took some time for mail to get here; a week before his letter was published, three Park Avenue mansions were destroyed when a subway roof caved in.

The year, and the drought, continued. In Cobar, they were in serious trouble and described themselves as being in a 'water famine'. The water from the local tank had been declared unfit for human consumption so they had to import water into the town. Every day, a train brought 10,000 gallons (about 45,000 litres) of water, which was sold off at the railway station. In Corowa, people were carting water from the rapidly diminishing river and had to hand-feed their stock, while farmers in Scone were forced to move their cattle towards the coast and feed them on roasted prickly pear.

While the waters didn't flow, the effects of the drought did. The number of unemployed men had increased as a number of mines closed and while some farmers employed people to cut scrub, the work was phasing out. The government were forced into action and the Head of Works had come up with some plans, God love him. He proposed that single unemployed men should be sent to various rivers to pan for gold as the water levels were low. He also suggested that the workforce employed on construction projects such as Central Railway Station and La Perouse cemetery be swapped at regular intervals so that everyone had a turn for some wages. Men were also needed for the continual cleansing of the wharfs and foreshores of Darling Harbour.

While there was the issue of people not having any money, even if they did they couldn't afford to buy food. New South Wales was confronted with the prospect of a beef and mutton famine; prices were high and getting higher, while some of the sheep that were brought into market were only considered fit for boiling down. Flour had risen by £3 a ton, wheat by two shillings a bushel, potatoes had doubled in price, hay was £3 a ton dearer and butter had risen seven pence a pound. The O'Brien family in Sydney, along with most other families, would have struggled to make ends meet.

In May, a member of parliament in the Central West area received the following letter:

'To your kind enquiries as to myself and the drought, I can only say that things have never worn such a gloomy aspect. I do not expect to have 1000 sheep alive by the end of May. I have sold my cattle at 30s [around $100] a head and all the horses I can dispense with at £5. Tomorrow I am starting to cut the throats of all the weakest of the sheep and thus make sure of the pelts. A cheerful outlook after nearly 40 years in happy Australia, but a man must endeavour to keep a stiff upper lip, particularly as he knows if he is to go to the devil, he will go in good company and the track will not be a lonely one.'[1]

In May, the future of the Moore Park Zoological Gardens was in doubt when numerous animals were found dead – not from the drought, but from the dreaded bubonic plague. The gardens were shut down indefinitely as the death toll included three guinea pigs, a porcupine, a condor, a coypu rat, an antelope and Mr Joseph Benson, a zoo attendant. When the deaths slowed in June, an Indian gentleman offered to sell some animals to the directors of the beleaguered zoo. He had a male snow leopard on sale for £200 ($14,000) and for double that sum, he was offering two Tibetan wild asses. The directors declined the purchase. The zoo was shifted to Mosman in 1916 and renamed Taronga. The old Moore Park site became a home for a different sort of animal – it is the location for Sydney Boys and Sydney Girls high schools.

If you think we had it bad, and we did, spare a thought for the townspeople of St Pierre, on the West Indian island of Martinique. A volcano erupted in early May and destroyed the town. Buildings were flattened and people were killed by toxic fumes. Out of the 30,000 people who lived there, only one man survived. He was locked up in the prison, serving time for drunkenness; I wonder if he woke up, looked out the barred window and thought – What the bloody hell did I do last night?

Two months later, the Wollongong area of New South Wales had its own disaster when uncovered lights in a Mount Kembla colliery ignited

---

1. *Sydney Morning Herald,* 6th May 1902

gases and caused an enormous explosion. The blast blew the roof off the engine house and was heard ten kilometres away. Sadly, over 80 miners were killed in the explosion.

In Melbourne, the folks welcomed back the Dame Joan Sutherland of the time, Nellie Melba. The shows of her concert tour were sold out and people were desperate for tickets; police were brought in to clear the crowds for the trams. Two years earlier, Nellie had attracted some criticism when she performed in a concert in Germany, which was raising money for wounded Boers. She hadn't been on our shores for sixteen years as she had sailed to Europe to further her career, but Nellie still called Australia home – that's if any Australians were in earshot, anyway. In her Melbourne shows, she sang songs from her Greatest Hits package, received several encores and lots of money. However, she didn't sing any of the popular tunes of the day, such as 'In The Good Old Summer Time' or 'Bill Bailey, Won't You Please Come Home'.

If wandering warbling women weren't your thing and sitting down in a quiet corner and reading a book about animals was, 1902 was the year for you. The shelves were crammed with new releases: Beatrix Potter's *The Tale of Peter Rabbit*, Rudyard Kipling's *Just So Stories* and Sir Arthur Conan Doyle's *The Hound of the Baskervilles* had arrived. If you wanted a book that was darker and more disturbing, Joseph Conrad's *Heart of Darkness* was published. Maybe you wanted to read some science fiction about something that would surely never happen, you could have picked up a copy of H.G. Wells's *The First Man on the Moon*.

On a warm day in November, Mr William Gocher walked into the surf at Manly Beach, wearing a neck-to-knee costume. He was promptly arrested for swimming in daylight hours. Manly council had continued to ban daylight swimming as there were no change sheds and 'appropriate costumes were scarce'. Today, only the material in the appropriate costumes is scarce and Manly Beach is covered with uncovered people, airing their differences.

In the month of April, 1903, the organisers of the Royal Agricultural Show, the forerunner to the Royal Easter Show, were delighted as they reported record attendances and takings. It was the most successful yet when overall receipts hit £6,798 or around $475,000 in today's money – in 2020, this amount would only buy you a family pass and a showbag. As they did not have showbags then, they had to stay true to the agricultural theme. For instance, on Wednesday, 15th April, the crowds were treated to the horse-riding prowess of Mrs C Elliott. She was crowned champion of the high jump, riding a horse named Skylark, and then she hopped on a horse named Rattler and won second prize. I presume there were other entrants but they missed out on the silverware. After watching Mrs Elliott, the people could then stroll around the exhibits: the Knowles Automobile Company displayed several 'handsome gasoline runabouts' and the engineering company, R.A. Hervey, showed off their Bayley's grist mills, flexible metallic tubing and lawn mowers.

After the punters marvelled at Mr James Stephen winning first prize for his Australian-made fishing line, they could have plonked themselves down on a bench in Messrs Griffiths Brothers for a cup of tea, coffee or cocoa. And if they preferred to keep moving, they could order their hot drinks as a takeaway – the container being a tin billy.

The population of Australia now had two targets they could vent their spleen at: federal politicians and state politicians. In Serbia though, they displayed their displeasure at rulers a trifle more demonstratively. King Alexander I had decreed that if his marriage was childless, the heir to the throne would be his brother-in-law. Not in a million years, said the Serbian parliament as they favoured a distant relation of the King's. No-one could agree so a group of army officers, allegedly under the control of the Prime Minister, decided to sort out the matter. They stormed the Royal Palace, shot the King and Queen, disembowelled them and threw their remains out of the window and into a pile of manure. Next!

A less violent but similarly ruthless display was shown by the New Zealand rugby union team as they played the first ever test match with Australia. New Zealand won 22-3 and pretty much every game since.

"Anyone can see it is going to be gigantic," said the Minister for Works in August of 1903. What was he talking about? Was it a new retail complex? A harbour crossing? His superannuation package?

> 'The Minister for Works, Mr O'Sullivan, was facing the dawn from a plasterer's plank at the Central Railway Station. With his umbrella as a balancing rod, he had been performing prodigious feats on piers, girders, brick walls

and concrete superstructures. "Gigantic," he said again. He might have been referring to the cost but it transpired he was speaking architecturally. He was flushed with a pardonable pride and looked around with an air that suggested – 'Here am I, immortalised' or perhaps – 'All this is mine'. What most impressed others was that his lordly political mausoleum was appropriately built over a cemetery.'[2]

I take it that the journalist was neither a fan of Mr O'Sullivan or of Central Railway Station but nevertheless, a month later on a rainy day in September, the NSW Premier, Sir John See, stood on the reclaimed cemetery and laid the cornerstone of Sydney's new transport hub. A crystal casket, containing newspapers of the day and copies of building proposals, was placed beneath the stone. He cemented the stone in with a silver trowel and tapped it into place with a polished mallet. As he did, someone called out – "They have plenty of money to waste".

Then it was speech time and nearly everybody had a go. Mr O'Sullivan praised the Premier, saying – "He was the pilot who weathered the storm and the ship of the state was on an even keel", apparently forgetting he was on a railway station and not a dockyard. He then went on to describe the building to the guests while assuring them that the railway would ultimately go to the 'deep waters of Port Jackson' – this was possibly an answer to criticism from the state opposition leader, who had said – "The money would have been better spent in that direction [train-line to the harbour] then in being lavished on the present central station".

As the hours rolled on, so did the speeches and the guests wondered when lunch would be served. Starving and bored as they were, they had to admire the scope of the project. Some 300 to 400 men were employed and the construction needed, amongst other things, 3,900,000 bricks, 169,000 cubic feet of stone and 650 tons of steel girders. The finished station would have thirteen platforms with trains carrying people and goods to all parts of the state, so it was vital to the welfare of the economy.

---

2. *Sydney Morning Herald,* 17th August 1903

While state politicians patted themselves on the back over the size of their erection, federal politicians were still debating the location for the capital – and some of them still wanted it in Sydney. A meeting at the Protestant Hall in August had drawn a big crowd and they were spurred on by the rhetoric. One man stated – "A capital legislature, planted in the bush, cut off from contact with the mass of citizens, would become corrupt and sink into degeneracy. It would be safer for the Commonwealth to see the Federal capital in Melbourne or Brisbane than to establish a mushroom town in the bush". In October, the House of Representatives and the Senate both had a ballot for their preferred capital site. The vote in the House of Reps favoured Tumut; the Senate went for Bombala. Back to the drawing board, boys.

Towards the end of the year, another federal election was held. Edmund Barton had had enough and he went off to become a High Court judge. Alfred 'It'll Never Happen' Deakin took his place as PM. The election was unique in history, due to the presence of a woman. Vida Goldstein stood as a candidate for the Senate and became the first woman in the entire British Empire to contest a national parliamentary election. She then also became the first woman to contest a national parliamentary election and not get voted in. The year was also a prominent one for lords in the British Empire: Lord Esher formed a committee to investigate Boer War criticisms; former British PM, Lord Salisbury, died; Lord Hopetoun stood down as Australia's Governor-General while Lord Tennyson replaced him ... and Lord Cardigan won the Melbourne Cup.

Meanwhile, over in the U.S. of A., in a cowpat-coated paddock in North Carolina, two brothers named Orville and Wilbur Wright flew the first controlled and powered airplane and then flew into history. Admittedly, their first flight only covered 37 metres but look at what they started. The Wright Brothers were called 'lunatics' by various people who didn't believe in powered flight. These people were wrong. But across the ocean in England, a group of men and women were called 'lunatics' by various people - these people were probably right because the men and women were patients of the Colney Hatch Lunatic Asylum in London. Some of them were housed in a temporary wooden building which had previously earned the ire of the Commissioners of Lunacy, who had warned the building was a fire hazard. These

Commissioners were right, too; the building burned down in 1903 and 52 lives were lost.

On to 1904 and in April, John O'Brien's wife, Mary, after many years of struggle and abandonment, succumbed to senile decay. She was residing in Newington Asylum at the time of her death and had still been working as a needlewoman. Newington Asylum was on an estate that once was the home of John Blaxland, the elder brother of the Blue Mountains explorer. His house had been converted into an asylum for infirm and destitute women in 1886. While Mary's death was recorded by the matron, one of her sons [unnamed on record] turned up and tried to provide details for the death certificate. He thought his mother's age was 72 but he wasn't certain; he listed his siblings but he didn't know how old his sister was. Maybe it wasn't only her husband who had abandoned Mary.

Shortly after, an Australian Royal Commission announced that they were concerned. They stated that the population of Australia would be almost one million higher if it wasn't for a decline in the birth rate between 1864 and 1902. Well, don't blame my family, they did their bit. They were getting into it in New England, too; Henry and Mary Ann Kingdom presented the world with Herbert Harold Kingdom in June. He was their tenth child and also my grandfather.

Those newfangled things called automobiles were really starting to get some press. Earlier in the year, a bloke called Henry Ford had set a new speed record as he drove across a frozen lake at 91mph (150kmph). And in England, a car salesman named Charles Rolls and an electrical engineer called Henry Royce formed a new company to sell cars – I will let you work out what they called the company.

The new technology wasn't just cars though; in June, electric lighting brightened Sydney's streets for the first time with the power coming from Pyrmont power station. Sydney was a bit late with the innovation – the town of Young had full electric street lighting in 1888.

As bright as this new light was in Sydney, it couldn't penetrate some dark shadows within the city. It was mid 1904 when the bodies of 26-year-old Joseph Walker and 21-year-old Winifred Pownceby were found in a bed in the Lloyd Hotel on George Street. Both had a bullet wound to the head. On the dressing table next to the bed was a letter, simply addressed – 'To Whom It Concerns'. The letter read:

I am going to shoot Joe and myself. He is asleep and knows nothing about it. I told him last night that I was going to kill him but he would not believe it. He has been going with other women and I cannot stand it; so I decided if we cannot live together, we can die together… I will not let him go with other women and I have decided to kill him. I told him yesterday that I wanted him to send my brother a revolver and I got him to buy one and I will take this from him and shoot him with it.

Signed, Winnie Pownceby[3]

So this looked like a fairly simple case for the police and the coroner – a written confession with the handwriting identified as Winifred Pownceby's. But there was a teensy problem – Joseph Walker was holding the gun.

A woman testified at the subsequent inquest that she had been drinking with Mr Walker on the previous night and at one stage, he had stood and said he had to "see his girl". He left and returned with a young woman who was introduced as Miss Pownceby. The young woman then asked the witness – "What would you do if your boy was with another woman?" The witness answered that she would either leave him or shoot him. Miss Pownceby then said – "I will do that tonight". Eerily, Walker turned to the witness and said – "If you look in the morning papers tomorrow, you will read the account of this tragedy". The witness seemed to think at the time that Walker wasn't kidding.

Eventually the coroner's jury decided that the two had decided to die together and Mr Walker had shot Miss Pownceby and then himself. They had spent time deliberating on whether she had shot him, then put the gun in his hand and shot herself with it but this was deemed to be too difficult. The coroner accepted the finding but added that he had seen a sheaf of letters written by Miss Pownceby that had protested Walker's treatment of her and how she was going to take her own life. The coroner was convinced that something was missing or had been

---

3. *Sydney Morning Herald,* 6th June 1904

held back and until it had been brought forward, there would be an element of mystery in the case – the element has remained ever since.

But there was no mystery in the case involving Mrs Mary Harrison of Ballarat in Victoria. She had been having some issues with her 'drunken husband'. After she had gone to bed one night – curiously, the same night that Walker and Pownceby lay down for the last time – she heard a noise outside and got up to investigate. She saw a small column of smoke rising from beneath her house and she assumed that someone was trying to set fire to it. She found a box filled with smouldering rags and she hurried away to get a bucket of water. This move saved her life as the box then exploded and destroyed half the house. After the police spoke to the shaken woman, they decided they needed to talk with the husband. He was found in a room at the local pub and after some questioning, admitted to the cops that he had placed several sticks of gelignite under the house with the sole intention of 'blowing my wife to hell'.

Away from the disastrous domestic matters that so entertained the reading public, the federal politicians had sat down again to vote for the nation's capital. Previously the Senate and the House of Reps had favoured two different places but this time they agreed – the Australian Federal Capital would be at … Dalgety. That seemed to be the only thing they could agree on, though, because in 1904, Australia had two Governor-Generals, three Prime Ministers (Deakin, Chris Watson for four months then George Reid) while New South Wales had three Premiers. The second one, Thomas Waddell, only had the job for two months and was actually second choice for the role. After the resignation of Sir John See, the first choice of Premier was a gentleman by the name of Paddy Crick, but the Governor had refused to appoint him as Premier. Apparently, Crick's excessive drinking in parliamentary meetings had caused issues.

The Chamber of Manufacturers was also worried in 1904 and they were planning a campaign to promote locally-made goods to the Australian public. They said that Australian products were as good as imports but it had been shown that people would not buy goods if they were marked 'Made in Australia'. Today, that mark is hard to find.

In August, the third modern Olympic Games were held in America and the Americans won every event but two. For once in Olympic history, it was the marathon that supplied all the excitement. It was discovered that the winning American athlete had accepted a lift from a passing truck during the race and he was disqualified. The race was then handed to Thomas Hicks, who ran the marathon while being refreshed with doses of brandy and strychnine.

Towards the end of the year, the Japanese Consul in Australia, Mr Iwasaki, was at a luncheon and was asked about the Russian-Japanese War in Manchuria. He told everyone not to worry as 'Japan had never been an aggressive race and the Japanese were essentially a peace-loving people'. Two days later, the non-aggressive and peaceful Japanese destroyed the entire Russian naval fleet near Korea.

As the world's calendar flipped a page onto 1905, the poor old Russians were not having a good time. After surrendering their Korean fort to those Japanese peace-lovers, they fought a land battle over Manchuria and lost 200,000 men. It wasn't much better at home; thousands of Russian workers marched in a rally in St Petersburg only to find themselves facing a wall of soldiers, who then opened fire and killed over 500 people. And you weren't even safe if you were a member of the royalty. The Czar's uncle, Grand Duke Sergei, was riding in his carriage one morning when a package was thrown into his lap. He didn't have time to unwrap it as the package was a nail bomb and it exploded. Parts of the royal carriage were found 200 metres away; parts of Grand Duke Sergei were never found.

Back home, Paddy Crick had packed a few hip flasks and undertook a 6500km tour in the west of the state. He was viewing the condition of the country that was suffering from drought, rabbit plague and sandstorms. At one particular station, he was shown a fence that was nearly buried by sand. This fence was built on top of another fence that had already been buried. The sand wasn't being held by the vegetation because the vegetation had been eaten by rabbits.

In other parts of the state, it was mice that were causing havoc. In Singleton, people were reporting that as soon as night fell, the mice attacked. They would swarm all over a household, eating and destroying food, chewing on clothing and rope and stripping wallpaper off. They would climb onto a bed, gnaw at the sheets and bite the hands and faces of people. Babies and small children had to be watched carefully.

In Sydney, the rats were back (that's if they ever left) and Darling Harbour was infested again. The government offered a reward for the capture of rodents in the metropolitan area. They had set up incinerators near Central Station and they told the press that the officers in charge were 'busily engaged during the greater portion of the day, receiving rats and mice from men, women and children'. The catchers would score a penny for each mouse and four pence for a rat. For some people, this was their only source of income.

The authorities were concerned because some of the rats were affected by bubonic plague. The plague broke out again in Sydney but to a lesser extent than in 1900. However, cases were now being reported in Newcastle, Grafton and as far north as Brisbane. Quarantine stations were set up, whole-scale cleaning and scrubbing resumed and hundreds of rodents were barbequed. The human death toll on the eastern seaboard wasn't as high as it was five years ago but the disease caused the same mass panic and paranoia. Still, there's always someone worse off than you. It was reported in early 1905 that the country of India was plague-ridden and between the years of 1896 and 1904, three million people had died from the disease. Shortly after the article was published, India was rocked by an earthquake and another 20,000 souls were lost.

Away from the critters, over in South Africa they were digging the earth in search of diamonds. A large one was found in early 1905 and taken to the mine manager's office. He took one look, thought it was too good to be true, announced that it was only a crystal and threw it out the window. Luckily for him, it was retrieved. It was indeed a diamond and it weighed over 3000 carats. Christened the Cullinan Diamond, it was given to King Edward VII for his birthday. A special ship was chartered to carry the jewel with British detectives guarding it. But if anyone had tried to rob the ship, they would have been disappointed. The ship was a ruse – the real diamond was posted to England. Upon its eventual arrival, it was chopped up and the largest bits now reside in the Imperial Crown and the Sceptre with the Cross. How much was the Cullinan Diamond worth? In 2012, a diamond weighing one percent of the Cullinan's original weight sold for ten million US dollars. And remember – in 1905, they mailed it.

In this year, most nations of the British Empire agreed that they would celebrate May the twenty-fourth as Empire Day. The date was chosen as it was the late Queen Victoria's birthday. The Australian government joined the party as they wished to reassure the people who were concerned that Federation would eventually end all connections with Britain. The day would be filled with parades, marches, speeches and fireworks. But in these early days of Federation, there were early rumblings of republicanism. There were some who believed that to follow in the footsteps of the British Empire was to accept Asian slave trading, amongst other ideologies. It's not that these people didn't want slaves in Australia – they didn't want Asians in Australia.

> 'The BULLETIN, therefore, in all seriousness, urges those Australian parents who are Australians first – who are earnest in the belief that the one sure duty of the people holding this lonely outpost in the Asiatic seas is to keep it free, and clean, and white.'[4]

The weekly newspaper, *The Bulletin,* was a radical rag that didn't mind expressing an opinion or two. It was against the creation of Empire Day, totally against the use of 'non-white' labour and it only saw one colour when it came to Australian citizenry. To give you an idea, here's what they wrote in 1900:

> 'Shutting out the Asiatic does him no injury save the passive injury of leaving him as he is, and as Australia isn't responsible for him being as he is, to leave him so is no wrong.
>
> There is nothing the coloured man does which the white man can't do as well. He fills no want whatever. Nobody felt the need for him before he came, or will feel it when he is gone. He is an unhealthy and artificial habit, like opium.
>
> The BULLETIN moves these resolutions:
>
> 1). That under Federal law it shall be absolutely illegal for any black, brown or yellow man to settle in this country, whether he is a British subject or not.

---

4. *The Bulletin* quoted in *The Citizen's Bargain: A Documentary History of Australian Views Since 1890,* J. Walter and M. MacLeod, University of New South Wales Press, Sydney

2). A heavy import duty to be put on sugar, in order that it may be able to compete with white labour against the nigger-grown sugar of other lands.

3). If these necessary measures lead to an increase in the prices of sugar, the circumstance is not regrettable. The nation which will abandon its status as a white race and become a mottled hybrid to make its sugar … cheaper, doesn't deserve to have any sugar and may the Lord have mercy on its soul.'[5]

Thankfully, they wouldn't be able to publish anything like that today. Yet, ninety-six years after *The Bulletin* purged out that bile, a fish-and-chip shop proprietor, who had won a parliamentary seat in a federal election, stood up in the House of Representatives and gave her maiden speech. Her name was Pauline Hanson and in her utterings, she happened to say:

'I and most Australians want our Immigration policy radically reviewed and that of multiculturalism abolished. I believe we are in danger of being swamped by Asians.'[6]

I firmly believe in free speech but, really, some people should be charged for it.

---

5. Ibid.
6. *House of Representatives Official Hansard,* 10th September 1996

Michael O'Brien

19. Terra Not-So-Firma

In 1906, the planet Earth and Mother Nature made a furious statement to mankind - anything you can build, we can break better … and quicker. They started with an earthquake off the coast of Ecuador which recorded a magnitude of 8.8 and left 500 dead. That was followed by a typhoon at Tahiti which killed 10,000 before they turned their attention to Italy. Mount Vesuvius erupted and rivers of lava poured down from the summit, wiping out villages, towns and around 100 people. Eleven days later, an earthquake rocked the western coast of America, centring on the city of San Francisco. It struck with a force of 7.8 and left 3000 dead and hundreds of thousands homeless. Most of the dead were killed by the subsequent fires or by falling debris. The living spent the night in parks, huddled up in the cold while police patrolled the wreckage-strewn streets and shot looters on sight. And to top it all off, another earthquake struck in Chile in August, registering 8.2. The city of Valparaiso was flattened and 20,000 people were killed.

In Australia, away from all the moving and shaking, a retail mover and shaker was buying up some choice real estate in Sydney in an apparent quest for CBD domination. Hordern Brothers snapped up blocks of land on the corners of Elizabeth, Market and Castlereagh streets for £38,500 or about 2.7 million dollars in current money – you would need to add some zeroes to the figure for that purchase today. The parcel of land complemented their land on the corners of George, Pitt and Goulburn streets where, in the previous year, they had opened the largest retail emporium in the southern hemisphere. Known as the Palace Emporium, it was six storeys high and had a total floor space of 15 acres on 3.5 acres of land. The building used 10,000,000 bricks, 400 miles of timber, 50,000 bags of cement, 8000 sheets of corrugated iron, 1430 windows and 15 miles of brass tubing for its pneumatic cash conveyance railway. Inside, showcases were constructed from Tasmanian blackbutt with beech panels and fittings were carved from polished marble.

But like many other examples of Sydney's architectural heritage, the Palace Emporium is gone. The building was demolished in 1986 and the location remained a hole in the ground for twenty years, until the soulless and concrete World Square complex was completed. This is apparently called 'progress'.

Around the world, some more buildings were opened for the first time. In May, an organisation known as Our Dumb Friends League opened a hospital in London. This was not a place for sick politicians, but an animal hospital. Today, the organisation is known as the Blue Cross and it specialises in the treatment of pets whose owners cannot afford private veterinarian's fees, i.e. most of the population.

In July, a 23-year old man named Donald John McLeod was quite fond of animals – in particular, horses. He was an unregistered bookmaker and one Saturday he took his place at Flemington races in Victoria. His day started badly as he took numerous bets on the first two races and he faced large payouts on both. Therein lay the problem – he started with only £2 in his bag. He refunded people's bets with a promise to pay the winnings on Monday. But punters like their money and they complained vigorously. He was sworn at and pushed and shoved until he became frightened and ran for the exit.

> 'The crowd streamed after him like a wedge, the fastest runners in front. McLeod's white hat and white face could be seen darting across the flat. Then the points of the wedge reached him and as he went down the rest of the crowd surged round him and he was lost sight of in a mass of whirling fists and kicking feet.'[1]

Two mounted constable arrived and drove the crowd away. Unfortunately, it was too late – Mr McLeod was dead.

---

1. *The Argus,* 16th July 1906

Up in Sydney, the Labour Council had produced a report on the growing problem of sweating – and they weren't referring to people's armpits. The report stated that various factories, warehouses, millinery establishments and 'high-priced' luncheon and tea rooms were acting like sweat shops. The complaints had been flying in. A Drummoyne girl had worked at a drapery for twelve months for no pay as she was an apprentice. After the year finished, she asked for wages and was fired. Then there was a shop assistant who was being paid 5s ($35) a week and she was suffering from feet problems due to the constant standing. If she had a day off due to the pain, she was docked 10d ($7). Or there was the 16-year old girl who worked for six months without wages while still having to pay her fares to work and buy her lunch – which she had to eat in the street. At the end of six months, she was told she was unsuitable and was sacked.

The Labour Council investigated further and found more little shops of horrors – fourteen-year old girls making cardboard boxes at piece-work rates; dairy employees working 102 hours a week for £1 with board and lodging, including inedible meals; women in jam factories working 54 hours a week for 9 shillings; nightwatchmen working 84 hours a week for £2; people working in luncheon rooms for 12s per 72 hour week and having to have their lunch break in a damp basement.

The report concluded:

> 'Our hospitals and asylums open wide their doors to receive the maimed and broken victims of the sweater, stricken down before their time and cast aside as useless and unwanted, while our cemeteries are being filled with the pulseless victims of the rapacity and greed of those to whom human life is but a cheap and easily acquired commodity.'[2]

While the *Herald* printed the findings of the Labour Council, it sure didn't agree with them. An editorial described elements of the report as 'fudge' and went on to blather:

---

2. *Sydney Morning Herald,* 13th July 1906

'There is nothing of abjectness or misery about these young Australians, rather there is a brisk alertness as of persons who know their value and expect it to be acknowledged. There are, of course, many who believe growing girls would be better engaged, for their own sake and for the country's sake, in domestic work.'[3]

Back down in Melbourne, certain groups also had ideas for women in the workforce. In September, at the Central Methodist Mission, the Reverend A.R. Edgar announced he had 27,000 signatories on a petition against barmaids. The Mission was supported by the Melbourne branch of the Women's Christian Temperance Union. The Union had a membership of 67; the population of Melbourne was 530,000. But parliamentarians debated the petition and came up with a compromise. No female under the age of 21 could be employed as a barmaid – unless they already were employed, or they were the publican's wife or daughter.

Not long after, the Victorian government shut down another form of employment. They made an amendment to the Victorian Police Offences Act which effectively made fortune telling an offence. 'Any person professing to tell fortunes or using subtle craft or device, palmistry or otherwise, would be fined £25 [$1750] or face six months prison'. I wonder if anyone saw that legislation coming.

One event that appears to have been unforeseen was the death of my great-grandfather, Henry Kingdom, in Armidale. He was only 48 when heart disease claimed his life. Henry left behind his wife and eleven children; the youngest was Clarence, who had been born only five weeks earlier. Mary Ann Kingdom was probably distraught from the loss of her husband and an uncertain and bleak future.

The year came to a close not long after the release of the world's first feature film – and, surprise, surprise, it didn't come from Hollywood. The Australian-made film, *The Story of the Kelly Gang*, was written and directed by Charles Tait and cost £1000 ($70,000) to make. It was a box office success, taking over £25,000 ($1,750,000) but it wasn't popular in parts of Victoria – it was banned from several towns as they

---

3. Ibid.

considered the film glorified criminals. The original film ran for over an hour but today only seventeen minutes of it remain intact.

The new year of 1907 brought another first to Australia as the newly-formed Bondi Surf Bathers Life Saving Club undertook their first rescue. In January, several proud but nervous members plunged into the briny depths and rescued two proud but drowning schoolboys. In future years, the lifesavers would tell their story over and over again – one of the schoolboys was the young Charles Kingsford Smith.

Away from the ocean, in the European country of Romania, an aide to the king marched up to his Highness, King Carol I, and told him the peasants were revolting. "I know," he replied. The peasants were looking at a grim outlook as wealthy landowners had bought up all the real estate and left the common folk without anywhere to live, no employment and short of food. The peasants reacted and they reacted violently; with pitchforks and flaming torches in hand, they burned down buildings and killed landowners. The king sent out the army that reacted even more violently as they had a licence to kill. When the rebellion was finally quashed, the king had all the relevant paperwork destroyed; the actual death toll is unknown but it is believed to be 11,000.

So that's what you do with a bunch of unhappy underclass types – shoot them. Later in the year, thousands of miners and their families marched to a school in the north of Chile and set up camp. They were there to protest their working conditions. The Chilean army arrived and told the people they had one hour to disperse. Up yours, said the miners. Have it your way, said the army. Sixty minutes later, the soldiers unleashed a hail of fire from their machine guns. Over two thousand men, women and children were killed.

Meanwhile, as the masses were being slaughtered, King Edward VII and Queen Alexandra were planning to tour Ireland in July and everyone in the Emerald Isle was running around, making sure things were fine. That's when somebody popped into Dublin Castle to dust off the Crown Jewels of Ireland and discovered they were … well, missing. Oh dear. The jewels had been placed in a safe and the keys were held by the Officer of Arms and his staff. It was known that the Officer of Arms enjoyed a tipple on his nights of duty and regularly fell asleep. He, at a later tribunal, denied any wrong-doing and suggested they should blame his second-in-charge. Remarkably, no-one was charged with the theft and even more remarkably, at the time of writing this, the Crown Jewels of Ireland remain missing.

While the Irish were unprepared, a former British military hero, Sir Robert Baden-Powell, was unimpressed. Since his return from the Boer War, the youth of the country had weakened. He said, "I have seen thousands of boys and men … hunched up, miserable specimens, smoking endless cigarettes, many of them betting". It does seem like he was talking about a Saturday afternoon at a modern-day TAB but he was referring to British youth. So he formed the Boy Scouts movement and strapping young lads would stamp out their Salmon & Gluckstein's Life Boat Navy Cut cigarettes and be taught skills such as woodcraft, fire-making and tracking. They would camp overnight in forests; donning their winter woollies to avoid freezing in the night air as various insects nibbled away at them. In July of 1907, twenty boys were selected to make up the first-ever troop and they were dragged off, kicking and screaming, into the woods.

In November, the President of the Federal Court of Conciliation and Arbitration established a basic wage figure for Australian workers. He decreed that a family of five could exist quite comfortably on £2 2s a week – that's about $147 today. That would buy you bugger-all in 2020 – so how much bang for your buck could you get in 1907? Let's have a look at prices of goods and services from a November issue of the *Herald*:

(For ease of comparison, £2 2s = 42 shillings, while one shilling would have the value of around $3-50 today.)

REAL ESTATE FOR SALE:
5 room brick cottage in Pymble – £650;
Double-fronted cottage, Berry St, North Sydney – £650;
5 shops in George St, City – £5750;
Land in Moss Vale – £4 an acre;

RENTAL PROPERTIES:
4 room stone cottage in Balmain – 9 shillings a week;
6 room house in Surry Hills – 15s a week;
Furnished house in Manly – £2 2s a week;
7 room house in Milson's Point – 25s a week;

EVERYDAY NEEDS:
Prime butter – 10 pence (d) a pound (around .45 of a kg);
Bodalla cheese – 6½d a pound;
Middle bacon – 8d a pound;
Northern River eggs (some very rough) – 5d a dozen;
Navel oranges – 20s a case;
French crab apples – 10s a case;
Lemons – 8s a case;
Bag of coconuts – 10s 6d;
Fijian bananas – 14s 6d a case;
Large box of American pears – 18s;
Large cabbage – 4s;
Quarter-case of inferior tomatoes – 2s;
Large pumpkin – 6s;
Parsley – 1s a bunch;
Victorian turnips – £2 15s a ton;
Tasmanian redskin potatoes – £9 a ton;
Brown Spanish onions – £12 a ton;
Victorian straw – £2 10s a ton;
Old hens – 2s 6d;
Extra heavy gobblers – 15s;
Muscovy ducks – 4s 6d;
South Australian port – 2s 6d a bottle;
Large bottle of Moet & Chandon champagne – 11s;
Small bottle of NSW claret – sixpence.

NOT-SO-EVERYDAY NEEDS:
Shares in BHP – £4 17s, with a dividend of 2s 6d;
3 course dinner at the Central Railway Station Café – 1s;
Hire purchase of a piano from F. Aengenheyster & Co, on George Street – 5s a week;
2-seater Renault from the General Motor Co on Pitt Street – starting at £75;
Phaeton from Square & Compass Saleyards, Haymarket – £10;
Brown mare – £15;
Ladies real ebony-backed hairbrush with genuine French bristles

from Angus & Coote – 3s 6d;
Train ticket to Woy Woy – 2s 6d;
Large family box of Bile Beans for Biliousness – 2s 9d;
Cooking stoves from £2 7s;
Men's serge tennis and cricketing trousers from 7s 6d;
Panama hat – 12s 6d;
Boy's Crash Conway suit – 6s 6d;
White blouses from 2s 6d;
Muslin blouses – 5s 6d;
Ladies black Sicilian skirts – 13s 11d;
Elbow-length suede gloves – 5s 6d;
Coloured underskirts – 6s 6d;
Paper picnic boxes – 1s;
Jerda billy cans – 2s;
14 packets of garden seeds – 2s;
Book of 'Picturesque NSW' – 1s;
Ferry to Watson's Bay – 8d, return;
P&O Steamer to London from £38.

So, in summary, if you wanted a buy a house and you were on the basic wage, all you needed to do is put away a shilling a week for 260 years and you would have enough to buy a cottage in North Sydney. Alternatively, you could rent the place at Balmain, wear cricketing trousers, have 4 dinners a week at the Railway Café and spend the rest of the week eating bacon, Bodalla cheese, rough eggs, dodgy tomatoes, a tenth of a case of oranges and a couple of crab apples. That way, you could still buy a ticket to Woy Woy on your day off and get plastered on NSW claret. You would have to do all this by yourself, though – your wife and children would be in the Destitute Asylum.

Before we move onto 1908, it is worth looking at a testimony from the advertisement for an item off our shopping list – the charmingly-named Bile Beans for Biliousness:

'After taking a few doses, I began to feel an improvement and thus encouraged I persevered with the Beans, taking in all three boxes and I am now thoroughly cured and can do my housework with pleasure.'[4]

Australia's coat of arms was unveiled in May of 1908 to roars of indifference but King Eddie sent his approval. The original design featured a seven-point star, the words "Advance Australia" and a kangaroo and an emu supporting a shield that was emblazoned with the Cross of St George. The kangaroo on the original looks as if he is leaning on a bar and ordering a schooner while the emu appears to be performing *Riverdance*. The design proved to be very unpopular and was replaced four years later with the one we use today. The emu is less of a contortionist but Skippy is still propping up the bar.

As we are looking at federal matters, let's see how the national capital at Dalgety was progressing. Brilliantly … but it wasn't going to be Dalgety anymore. The MPs had changed their minds again; it seems that Dalgety was considered too close to Melbourne and too far away from Sydney. So, the lads got out their yardsticks and plumped for an area of land in the Yass/Queanbeyan region. This area had been settled by Europeans in the early 1820s when a chap named Joshua Moore built a property there and named it 'Canberry'. In 1908, the area was known as Canberra. This is believed to have derived from the word 'kambera' which meant 'meeting place' in the local Aboriginal language. Others said that the word meant 'place of winds'. However, some said these theories were a load of horse-feathers – they claimed the name derived from the word 'nganbra' from the same language. That word translates to 'the hollow between a woman's breasts'. They all could be right – today, Canberra is a meeting place of tits with lots of wind.

For those New South Welshman bored with the debates on the Federal capital, there was a new form of entertainment to be enjoyed. The New South Wales rugby league premiership kicked off in 1908. Initially, there were nine teams: Balmain, Cumberland, Eastern Suburbs, Glebe, Newcastle, Newtown, North Sydney, South Sydney and the Western Suburbs. Souths beat Easts in the final to win the first trophy while Glebe, known as the 'Dirty Reds', finished third. The Cumberland side only played eight games – losing seven

---

4. *Sydney Morning Herald,* 8th November 1907

of them – and were unable to field a full team for their matches, sometimes 'borrowing' players from other sides. They disbanded at the end of the season.

In Victoria, they also had a new form of entertainment – club swinging. This is not to be confused with 'swinger's clubs' (which they may have enjoyed also) but rather a strange form of gymnastics. It involves a person holding a wooden club in each hand and whirling them about their head and body in a variety of patterns and movements. At the Melbourne Waxworks in June, a new record for continuous club swinging was set by an unemployed sewerage worker named Mick Bourke. He commenced his swinging at 6.00am on a Thursday and didn't stop until 11.14pm on the Saturday, 65 hours and 14 minutes later. Mr Bourke was carried away after his record, suffering from faintness, exhaustion and severely swollen wrists. But he didn't stay the toast of the town for long – a week later, he appeared in court on a charge of deserting his wife. Mrs Bourke testified that she hadn't seen or heard from him in twelve months until she read about his club swinging record. Mr Bourke testified that he received no financial reward for the feat and due to ill-health, he hadn't been employed for a year. The judge was suitably unimpressed with his story and ordered the club swinger to pay his wife 15s a week.

Another trial in Melbourne which caught everybody's attention was the manslaughter charges laid upon two train drivers. Two months earlier, a Melbourne-bound train from Bendigo slammed into the back of the Ballarat mail train at the inappropriately-named Sunshine railway station. The accident happened late at night so it wasn't until early the next morning that medical personnel arrived – by train. 44 people were killed in the crash and with over 400 injured, the medicos had their hands full. Bystanders were allowed to clamber through the wreckage, in search of their loved ones. More trains were despatched to collect the dead and transport the injured to hospital. Both train drivers and the station master were charged with manslaughter; the station master's charges were dropped and the drivers were found 'not guilty'.

In a rare moment, the government did something useful. In June they passed the Old Age and Invalid Pension Bill. This meant that Australian senior citizens, who mostly had worked their arse off ever since they stopped wearing nappies, would receive a pension. This figure was 10 shillings (about $35) a week for singles and 17s 6d for couples. Please refer back several pages to see what that wouldn't buy you.

Worldwide, other governments were busy with bills too. The French passed a bill to grant automatic divorce to a couple after they had been legally separated for three years. The Germans passed their Naval Bill, which allowed them to increase the size of their battle fleet. This move brought some concern from around the globe.

But for now, it was time for the countries of the world (well, some of them) to get together and participate in another Olympic Games. This time, the extravaganza was held in London but unfortunately, once again there was controversy with the winner of the marathon. Dorando Pietri was the first runner to enter the stadium for the finishing lap; the trouble was, he was knackered. Upon entry, he ran in the wrong direction for a while before realising his goof. He turned his worn-out body around, started off again – and fell over. He received medical attention and a helping hand from kind officials but that act of kindness disqualified him and ended his dream of a gold medal. For the record, Australia won four medals. There was a gold in rugby (obviously, New Zealand didn't show up); there was a silver to Snowy Baker in boxing and a silver and bronze were awarded to a swimmer named Frank Beaurepaire.

It was also the year a great sporting career came to an end when the legendary English cricketer, Dr W.G. Grace, padded up for the last time. Understandable, really – he was sixty years old. The bulky batsman with a bulky beard started playing in 1865 and during his career, he had scored over 50,000 runs in first-class cricket and took nearly 3000 wickets. While he was known for his batting, he also had a reputation for bending the rules. There is one anecdote of a match he played in; while batting, he was clean-bowled by a young bowler. He turned, picked up the bails, put them back on the stumps, swivelled back to face the bowler and said – "They have come here to see me, not you, now play on". Four days before Dr Grace's last match, a boy was born in Australia who would go on to be fairly well-known in world cricket – his name was Donald George Bradman.

Over in the U.S of A. the Wright Brothers were in the news again. Orville, who five years earlier had demonstrated that motorised air flight was possible, went a step further and demonstrated that dying in an airplane crash was also possible. He was showing off a craft to US War Department officials in a bid to excite them with its capabilities. But a propeller snapped in mid-air, caused structural chaos and the plane crashed to the ground. Orville's passenger, who was sitting in the front and thereby having a stunning view of the plummet, was a man named Thomas Selfridge. He entered history books (and presumably a fair bit of the earth) as the first person to die in an air crash. Orville survived, but he was badly injured and carted off to hospital. Meanwhile, Orville's brother, Wilbur, managed to keep his airplane in the air over France for more than an hour – and as an added bonus, he didn't kill his passenger. While Orville and his plane were being put back together, Wilbur won a $100,000 contract with a French company.

On to 1909 and it was the seventieth anniversary of Mathew and Catherine O'Brien leading their family off the ship and onto the dusty shore of Sydney Cove. Ten years later, George Kingdom, the other ancestor I've been concentrating on, stepped onto the same dusty shore – probably a bit more gingerly though, as he was manacled in chains. Mathew and George's families had gone forth and multiplied; some of them did so with gusto. A quick calculation showed that between the O'Brien/Kingdom/Elliott patriarchs, they had 133 grandchildren. Now, while 25 of these grandchildren didn't live past the age of fourteen, it is still an astonishing figure, and when you add the fact that the surviving children had children who also had children etc. – my family tree is a Californian redwood. And then, after your calculations are complete, consider I have only mentioned four of my great-great-grandparents – there are twelve more.

With scores of the little darlings running around your feet, you might have thought a calming drop of booze would help to keep you sane. In Australia, obtaining the calming drop was simple, as long as you weren't stuck in a small pocket of wowsers. But elsewhere, buying booze was difficult. In New Zealand, brewers had decided to totally ban barmaids and then moved to ban women from buying alcohol. In certain states of America, it did not matter what sex you were – if you wanted an alcoholic drink, you were not going to get one … legally. The Prohibition Movement was in full swing and it wanted a nationwide ban on alcohol. In Ohio, 57 out of 66 counties closed their bars, while 315 towns in New York State shut their saloons.

Strangely, in Tennessee, the state whose name adorns many a bottle of whiskey today, it was a crime to manufacture liquor. Many took the law on and brewed moonshine and rotgut in backyard stills. They then loaded their hooch into cars and sped across the countryside, dodging coppers along the way. After Prohibition died out, the drivers of the cars still wanted to race and outrun the opposition so they formed a regular competition. This turned out to be the birth of the American institution they call NASCAR.

Still in America, Commander Robert E. Peary announced to the press that he had reached the North Pole in April and he was the first man to ever have done that. Hurrah, said the people. Pig's arse, said Frederick Cook, another adventurer – I did it a year ago. Bollocks, replied Peary – I was told by Eskimos that you had turned back early. Horse feathers, replied Cook, and so the debate raged on. Cook stated that he had three boxes of supporting evidence but they had been left behind in Greenland and couldn't be found. His claim was later dismissed by an investigating commission and Peary was declared the first to have reached the Pole. Cook never recovered from the slight and was later jailed for defrauding potential oil investors while Peary went on to fame and fortune. In modern times, it is believed by many scientists and adventurers that neither of them actually reached the North Pole.

In early July, the *SS Waratah,* a passenger ship of 9000 tons, set out from Melbourne to sail to London. Towards the end of that month, it was at the South African port of Durban, picking up and dropping off passengers. The ship sailed out of Durban with 211 people on board – and into oblivion. The *Waratah* and its passengers were never seen again. Many theories for its disappearance have been offered: a freak wave; an explosion; a whirlpool and there was also one gentleman who disembarked at Durban, saying that he didn't sail on because he had visions of a man holding a blood-covered sword. Whatever the reasons for the demise, not a single bolt, rivet or personal belonging has ever been found. One man dedicated twenty-two years of his life to look for the wreck. He eventually stopped and said that he had no idea of where it was.

The Kingdom and O'Brien grandchildren might have found the end of 1909 a trifle uncomfortable. In early November, coal miners went on strike in Newcastle for higher wages and better conditions.

Three weeks later, they hadn't got them; they hadn't gone back to work and NSW was running out of coal – the lifeblood to many industries. Public transport services had to be cut, factories shut down, people were sacked, ships without fuel stayed anchored in Sydney Harbour and prices of everyday goods skyrocketed. The state of New South Wales was slowly grinding to a halt. In a scenario that Joseph Heller would have appreciated, the miners refused to work until there were negotiations and the mining companies refused to negotiate until the miners went back to work. The state government declared they would confiscate the coal and arrest the miners – this didn't appear to scare them as the strike lasted for four-and-a-half months.

There's nothing like consistency in politics and in 1909, that's what Australia had – nothing like consistency. The craftsmen who made the nameplates for parliamentary office doors were as busy as a three-legged cat in a sandbox. Every state but Victoria had two different governors that year – this included the Governor of Queensland moving to New South Wales and the Tasmanian Governor taking over in Western Australia. South Australia and Victoria both had two premiers for the year while Tasmania had four of them in 1909 – one bloke lasted a week while another had two different reigns. Australia had two Prime Ministers – one of them, Alfred Deakin, was having his third (and what proved to be final) bash at the job. The good ship Australia, girt by sea, was sailing along with too many captains and not enough crew. The captains wished to sail in different directions; some wanted to float off alone and others were comfortable drifting in the wake of the mother ship of England. None of them, however, could see the danger on the not-so-distant horizon.

Michael O'Brien

20. THE CALM BEFORE THE STORM

Bertie wasn't feeling well. He smoked twenty cigarettes and twelve cigars a day – behind his back, some people called him "Chain-smoking Charlie". He had sailed to France for a holiday but while there, he developed bronchitis. He stayed there for a month which attracted criticism; the people hadn't been told of his illness and wondered why he was still in France. You see, Bertie – who was called that only by his family – was King Edward VII.

He eventually returned to England but refused to rest. He started to suffer from heart problems. On the 6th of May, 1910, he was told that one of his beloved horses had won a race. He replied, "I am very glad". Feeling faint, he went to bed and slept. He didn't wake up. King Edward VII's reign was over. While his reign was quite short in comparison to his mother's, Edward VII had held the record as the longest-serving heir apparent to the throne, until modern-day Prince Charles broke the record in 2011.

So the King was dead; long live the King – Edward's second son, George, was in the house. George V, as he would now be known, led the funeral procession a fortnight later. It marched through London from Buckingham Palace to Windsor Castle and had one of the largest number of world royalty members ever seen together in one place. There were kings, queens, dukes, grand dukes, archdukes, duchesses, princes, crown princes, hereditary princes, princesses, highnesses, royal highnesses, serene highnesses and imperial highnesses. What's even more amazing is that a good portion of them were related to Edward, as his nephew, niece, cousin, second cousin, son-in-law or brother-in-law or combination thereof. Perhaps a couple of chaps at the back of the procession felt a little left out: Prince Mohammed Ali of Egypt and Prince Fushimi Sadanaru of Japan weren't related. It was nice of them to come, though.

However, the Royal Departure wasn't the first newsworthy event of the year. A man named Syd Day hit the headlines early in the year when he set an Australian time record for driving a car between Sydney and Melbourne. His time was 20 hours and 10 minutes. Syd, driving a 25-horsepower Vinot, was accompanied by a mechanic and beat the previous record by an hour – he also beat the mail train by five hours. His time might have been quicker had it not been for a tyre puncture, a gas generator change and troubles with railway gates. Syd also mentioned that if the roads weren't so cut up by wheat traffic, he would have had an easier drive.

Dunlop Motor Tyres were quick to jump on the bandwagon … or the Vinot, in this case … and placed an advertisement in the newspapers, virtually claiming the success of the drive was due to their tyres. The British Imperial Oil Company weren't far behind; they declared the vehicle was powered by their new fuel called 'Shell'. Meanwhile, the car's manufacturer, French company Vinot-Deguingand, said nothing. Less than a month later, Syd's record was beaten by twenty-three minutes by a driver using a different car with different tyres.

There was excitement in the USA with the release of the first film to be made in the area of Southern California called Hollywood. The film, 'In Old California', was produced by D.W. Griffiths and featured actors telling the story of a Spanish maiden's liaison with a governor of California. Around a hundred years after the film was released, an actor who had been the governor of California was trying not to tell the story of his liaison with a Guatemalan maid.

In another story that belonged in a Hollywood film, a Chief Inspector from Scotland Yard clambered up the gangplank of a ship in Canadian waters and arrested two of the passengers. They were listed on the ship's manifest as 'Mr Robinson and son' but the ship's captain had seen through that subterfuge and contacted authorities. The two passengers were in fact, Dr Hawley Harvey Crippen and his mistress, Ethel Le Neve. They had disappeared from London, shortly after the dismembered body of Crippen's wife was found under the cellar floor of their home. The flight of the fugitive lovers only lasted three weeks as eagle-eyed members of the public spotted them everywhere they went. Dr Crippen only lasted a few more months as the judge at his trial sent him off to see the hangman.

Crippen maintained his innocence all along and therefore didn't play the 'mental illness' card at his trial. He might as well have – according to one expert, England was full of nutters. Dr Lyttelton Forbes Onslow, a criminal lunacy expert, announced that lunacy in England was increasing at an enormous rate. "In 1859," he said, "there was one lunatic in every 536 persons but in 1910, it was one in 277. We are gradually approaching, with the decadence of youth, a near proximity to a nation of madmen." Dr Onslow had made announcements before this one. In 1888, he announced that he knew who Jack the Ripper was. His suspect was a Canadian who talked to himself, kept revolvers in a chest of drawers and told his landlord that prostitutes should be drowned. The police investigated the Canadian and ruled him out quickly. They then turned their attention to Dr Onslow, as he appeared to have a peculiar interest in the case.

From English lunatics to the Australian government; the lads in power stated they were going to build a railway line between Kalgoorlie in Western Australia and Port Augusta in South Australia. They also stated that this engineering feat would be a trifle easier if the states could agree on a uniform rail gauge. In 1910, if you wished to travel interstate by train, you would have to get off at the border and hop on a different train as the state's railway lines weren't compatible.

The Prime Minister who was – hang on, who are we up to, I've lost count … oh yes – Andrew Fisher said that the railway line would cost £4,000,000 ($280,000,000). In the year's federal budget, he had also set aside £2,800,000 for defence, £2,000,000 for old age pensions and £45,000 for the development of the federal capital. He proposed to introduce a penny postage stamp to help pay for all of this. By my calculation, he would have needed to sell only 884 million stamps to cover those costs.

Mr Fisher apparently needed someone from the NSW Railways on his finance team – the choo-choos were absolutely rolling in it. A report at the end of the financial year advised that NSW trains had carried

53,644,271 passengers, earning £6,671,283 (about $460,000,000) and the profit was £568,167 or nearly 40 million dollars today. The trams were going along nicely too with 201,151,021 passengers and a profit of £45,879 ($3,200,000). Staff employed on the networks (which included Frank O'Brien, my great-grandfather) totalled 26,604 and the wage bill for the year was £173,000. That averages out to about 6.5 pounds each or about $455, so I guess not everyone was making a pot of money.

But if you do have a pot of money, why not spend it? Mr Hutchinson, Chief Engineer for Railway and Tramway Construction, delivered a proposal in August to the Public Works Committee. The proposal was for a harbour railway tunnel. His plan consisted of a tunnel starting near Central Station, heading north-east in a curve and going under Elizabeth, Hunter and Phillip streets, then under Macquarie Street, Government House, the Tarpeian Way (edge of the Botanical Gardens), then sneak under the tramcar shed at Fort Macquarie (where the Opera House is today), then go under the harbour to Kirribilli before turning west to meet up with Milson's Point railway station. The depth of the tunnel below the city would range between 44ft and 94ft (13-28 metres) and there would be a minimum of 40ft (12 metres) of water above the top of the tunnel in the harbour. This bizarre little plan had a total estimated cost of £1,038,070 or around 72 million dollars in current money.

If you were a surveyor or a cartographer in Australia, you would have been quite busy. The Federal Government had nabbed a chunk of land off New South Wales – this was the land around the proposed site of Canberra. They christened this land the Australian Capital Territory – very imaginative. Then they took possession of the northern section of South Australia and they called it, also rather imaginatively, the Northern Territory. Mind you, that name beat off several creative suggestions such as 'Kingsland', 'Centralia' and 'Territoria'. Actually, back in 1846 the area was known as 'North Australia' and included most of what we now know as Queensland within its boundaries. It had been set aside as a penal colony but that idea didn't get off the ground.

You have to feel sorry for poor old South Australia. In the 1830's they had agreed on a border line with the colony of Victoria; it was the 141st degree of longitude east of Greenwich. That all sounds very straightforward but it turns out that when the cartographers mapped it out, they stuffed their calculations slightly and missed the line of longitude by 3.3kms. This error gave Victoria more land. For the next seventy years, the two colonies fought over this land, known as the 'Disputed Territory'. South Australia wanted the land back or they wanted money as they argued that Victoria had been selling and leasing South Australian land. In 1911, they took Victoria to court, seeking compensation for lost revenue. South Australia lost the case. Three years later, still spitting chips, they took the matter to the High Court of England. They won the case and received a payout of over £200,000.

In June of 1911, it was reported that a man had joined the unemployment ranks of New South Wales. This was not an earth-shattering event in itself but it is worth mentioning because the man was the Public Executioner. He had resigned as the last seven death sentences handed out by judges had been commuted to time in prison. The executioner was paid £100 ($7000) per annum plus ten quid for each execution but lately the poor man was hanging around while no-one else was. What became of him after his resignation is unknown but his CV must have been interesting.

Speaking of hanging, in France there was something that was supposed to be hanging but wasn't. Way back in the early 1500's, a chap named Leonardo da Vinci painted a portrait of a woman. She is believed to be Lisa Del Giocondo, the wife of a Florentine merchant – though some scholars argue (mainly because they've nothing better to do) that the portrait was of Leonardo's mother. Whoever the lady is, her picture is referred to as the *Mona Lisa* and it has been hanging on a wall in the Louvre since the French Revolution. But on the 21st of August, 1911, it wasn't. Guards walking past noticed she wasn't there but thought the painting had been taken away for some photographs. This proved to be an incorrect assumption. The most famous painting in the world was gone. Utter chaos and panic reigned supreme as countless people, including Pablo Picasso, were questioned over the theft.

But no-one spoke to Vincenzo Peruggia, an employee of the Louvre – which is a shame really, because he had hidden in a broom closet, waited until the museum closed then stuck the painting under his arm and walked out. An Italian patriot, he had wanted to return the painting to Italy but wasn't sure how to go about it. So he kept the painting in his apartment – for two years – while the world went crazy looking for it.

One day he tried to sell it to a gallery in Florence, as eBay hadn't been invented yet. The gallery alerted the authorities, the *Mona Lisa* went back on the wall and Peruggia went behind some walls for six months.

In other criminal matters, King George V was dealing with a snaky journalist. French journalist, Edward Mylius, had just published a story that claimed the king was a bigamist. George V had married Princess Mary in 1893 – she was previously engaged to his brother, but he thwarted the marriage plans by dying. Mylius claimed, before that date, Georgie-porgie had kissed the girls and made them cry – in particular, another lass named Mary, who was the daughter of an Admiral in Malta. The King was disgusted with the article and took an unusual step for a royal – he sued Mylius for libel, with the help of England's Home Secretary, Winston Churchill. King George couldn't testify in the case; it is against English law for the person who wears the crown to give evidence for the Crown, as it is their court, really. But he had Richard Muir as his prosecutor who was fresh from helping despatch Dr Crippen to the gallows, so Monsieur Mylius didn't stand a chance. He not only lost the case, he spent the next year in prison for libel.

Returning home, there were murmurings from manufacturers in Sydney that they wanted their employees to work their allotted hours between Monday and Friday and have Saturday off. They found that the work done on a Saturday was inconsequential and wasn't worth the expense and the bother of opening up the factory. You would have thought this would have pleased all concerned, but no. The Eight-Hour Committee (remembering them as the organisation that dear great-great-grandfather O'Brien stole money from) were not enamoured with the idea. They believed that the hours worked during the week would be lengthened and employees would be pressured into finishing everything by Friday afternoon. However, industry wanted it and one union had already taken the Saturday holiday concept to the NSW Wages Board. The union, the sadly now defunct Straw Hat Makers Employees Union, had allowed for an increase of hours on weekdays in return for a full Saturday holiday. The union claimed 44 hours as the basis of a week's work, making straw hats.

These discussions took place at the end of 1911 so it was a chance to have a look at the newspaper of Saturday, December 30, 1911 and discover what the people could do if they had the day off. Highlights include:

Shopping at Lassetter's on George-street for ladies' patent glace Lily Brayton pump sole shoes (13s 6d or about $45) or English made Russian calf ox shoes at 18s 6d;

Buy some men's Zephyr fashion shirts in 'Fancy Stripes' (blue, green or pink) for 3s 9d ($14);

Attend the 25% off fabric remnant sale at David Jones;

Enjoy a Hawkesbury River excursion to Cowan Bay for 2 shillings, return (about 7 bucks);

Catch a train from Circular Quay to Randwick racecourse for 1s 6d (return);

Family bathing at Rose Bay Crystal Baths;

Have a picnic at Clontarf with 'luncheon and refreshments at city rates and free hot and cold water';

Go to the Adelphi Theatre for a performance by Redford and Winchester ('America's foremost comedy-juggling duo) and a show by the Famous Pony Ballet;

Buy a ticket at the Standard Theatre, Castlereagh-street, for Miss Rita Carlyle in "The Girl Who Knew A Bit" and Mr John Cosgrove as "The Widow O'Brien";

View some land for sale: acre blocks at Greenacre for £30 ($2100), lots at Lindfield at 30s ($105) a foot, Rose Bay at 40s ($140) a foot, blocks at Burraneer Bay for £15 ($1050) or if you were seriously cashed up, the old Dixon's Tobacco Factory on the corner of Elizabeth- and Park-streets in the city was on sale for £90,000 or around $6,500,000 today;

Purchase a car from Mr Phizackerley of Elizabeth-street, who was the agent for the 4-cylinder, 4-seater Hupmobile which boasted four doors and a windshield. It would set you back only £295 (about $20,000) or maybe you could buy a 4-cylinder, water-cooled Metz Runabout for £210 ($14,200) from Brown and Hellicar of Pitt-street;

Have your dandruff and blackheads cleared up by Madame Patey of Bligh-street or have your teeth 'painlessly extracted' for 2s 6d (around $8.50) by Charles Harris of King-street or pop next door and see Miss Maude Maddocks for the removal of your moles and superfluous hair';

Or you could sit in the pub and get pissed.

Preserving heritage is vital to preserve the soul of a city and its people. Sydney in 1911 was 123 years old. It had a constantly changing landscape as traces of the original colony were swept away for the modern technology and architecture. In December of 1911, workmen were laying electric cable in Liverpool-street, when one of them struck the ground with his pick and was surprised to hear a hollow sound. Underneath three inches of soil and a slab of wood, they found a well. It was deep and had roughly hewn bricks put together with no mortar. Many locals were asked about the well but no-one had known of its existence. Historians flocked to the scene; they believed the well was a source of water supply from the earliest days of Sydney's history. They welcomed the chance to drain the well and investigate it further. The workmen and their supervisor were far from fascinated from the discovery; they filled it full of dirt and covered it over before any examination could take place. The well remains lost today.

1912 arrived with a wind of discontent blowing it along. The dramas started with dissent in the hallways of Australian cricket. Our team had just been comprehensively flogged by the English in the previous series and the Australian Cricket Board felt it was time for change. They announced that they, and not the players, would select future team managers. Several senior players, including the captain, Clem Hill, threatened to withdraw from the next series. The selection committee met in February and things turned nasty. One selector, Peter McAlister, was drawn into heated words with Clem Hill and was heard to shout out – "You're the worst captain I have ever seen!" Hill asked McAlister to withdraw the remark, but the selector carried on with the insults. That's when the Australian captain chose to smack McAlister in the chops. The pair exchanged blows for some time before the blood-spattered selector was prone on the ground with Hill standing over him. Hill dusted himself off and then resigned from the captaincy. Clem Hill had played 49 tests for Australia and scored 3412 runs; McAlister's career lasted for 8 tests and he barely troubled the scorers with his total of 252 runs. In future years, Hill had a grandstand at Adelaide Oval named after him and was inducted into the Australian Cricket Hall of Fame. McAlister didn't and wasn't.

Up in sunny Queensland, the discontent continued when several tramway employees were sacked as they wore union badges on their uniform and refused to take them off. This led to some unpleasantness and the trade unions of Brisbane called a general strike. The unions arranged a protest march but the Police Commissioner wasn't having a bar of it. However, 15,000 people marched into the city to have their voices heard. The coppers were waiting, armed with batons. The Commissioner ordered his men to surge into the crowd and they bashed men, women and children at will. The only joy the people had was when a woman stabbed her hat pin into the rear end of the Commissioner's horse. Even though he went flying and fell to the ground, he didn't end up as bruised as some did that day. Queensland authorities have remained unimpressed with protests ever since; there was a joke doing the rounds when Bjelke-Peterson was premier – Why does the Queensland calendar only have eleven months? Because there's no March.

Still with March and a Norwegian fellow named Roald Engelbregt Gravning Amundsen arrived in Hobart, quite pleased with himself. He was the leader of the first expedition to reach the South Pole. Amundsen, along with four other men, four sledges and 52 dogs had left their base camp in October 1911 and reached the Pole in less than two months. They returned to the base camp with the same amount of men and sledges, but with considerably less dogs – supermarkets are scarce on Antarctica and sometimes you have to make do. Everybody celebrated their great achievement – well, maybe not everybody, as the other South Pole expedition, led by Captain Robert Falcon Scott, was in trouble. Scott had started in an unofficial race with Amundsen and had come second. On the journey back to their base camp, Scott's party had run out of supplies. The men were suffering from snow-blindness and they were exhausted. The dogs were also exhausted – if you know what I mean. The month of March rolled on; Amundsen and his men received accolades while Scott and his men slowly died.

Then there was controversy in Australia over the contentious matter of mixed seaside bathing. The Reverend Goyen of the Presbyterian Church was warning bathers to stay away from the 'viper of promiscuous hoodlums to be found on some beaches' but he added that 'there was no evil in families or good friends bathing together'. Hah, said Catholic Archbishop Carr, and opined that 'mixed bathing was an abomination and it showed contempt for women and brutalised men'.

Life in the Past Lane

But the Prime Minister waded into the discussion pool and disagreed; he said that he 'had seen no signs of hideous immorality at the beach and a dose of cold water was not conducive to moral lapses'.

While they were all debating, a passenger ship named *Titanic* struck an iceberg as she sailed to New York. This was a supposedly unsinkable ship yet she sank like a stone and over 1500 people perished. There was over 2000 people on board for the ship's maiden voyage but the lifeboats only had a capacity for 1178 people. The enormous liner cost around £1,250,000 or 87 million dollars today; the hull and the cargo were insured for £2,350,000 or 164 million. For a bit of perspective, James Cameron's movie of the event took over 1 billion dollars at the box office.

And how did a local newspaper report the tragedy? The full story appeared in the 17th April edition of the *Sydney Morning Herald*. The news of the disaster was summarised on the front page but in this 24-page newspaper, the whole story did not appear until page 19. It followed the classifieds, amusements, positions vacant, real estate, Herald's Page for Women, legal notices, rural news, businesses for sale, law reports, sport and the kennel and poultry news. The *Titanic* story appeared next to an item about a stray bullock in Dubbo, which apparently had seen its reflection in a shop window and charged at it, smashing the glass.

But after the dreadful disaster, people's hearts went on, and they turned their attention to the event that unites the world – the Olympic Games. Actually, in 1912 they didn't unite that much of the world as only 28 nations and 2400 competitors took part. Nevertheless, they descended on Stockholm, Sweden, for the Games and 14 sports were featured – including new events in cycling, fencing, football and the tug-of-war. The Stockholm Games also featured some fairly spectator-*un*friendly activities – art competitions. Yes, that's right: gold medals were handed out for literature, music, painting and sculpture.

Once again, the marathon grabbed attention for all the wrong reasons. Before the race, Portuguese competitor Francisco Lazaro had covered his body with wax to prevent sunburn; unfortunately, this act blocked his body's normal perspiration. Lazaro collapsed at the 30km mark and was probably dead before he hit the ground. As for the Japanese runner, Kanakuri Shizo, well, while he was running he had stopped at a roadside party to quench his thirst. He must have been enjoying himself because he stayed at the party, then caught a train to Stockholm and sailed home the next day. In the 1960s, he was invited back to Sweden to complete his run. He did so - his unofficial time for the marathon was 54 years, 8 months, 6 days, 8 hours and 32 minutes.

Back in Australian political matters, the Federal Government felt the country needed to increase its population – as long as the increase was with white people. It introduced a baby bonus. The payment of £5 ($350) would be received by mothers – irrespective of marital status, however they had to be of European descent and Aborigines need not apply. No doubt that wherever my ancestor John O'Brien was, he would have been cranky. If they had brought that plan in earlier, he would have been 75 quid better off.

On the 12th March 1913, Lady Denman, the wife of the Governor-general, stood on a hill located in the new Australian Capital Territory. She looked down upon a throng of people standing on a pile of uninspiring dirt and weeds and proclaimed that from this day on, the pile of uninspiring dirt and weeds would be known as 'Canberra'. The people clapped and cheered and looked around for the free sandwiches.

Previously, over one hundred entries had been received in an internationally advertised city design competition and the Federal government had awarded first prize to an American named Walter Burley Griffin. He was destined to spend the next seven years fighting changes to his design and be involved in a Royal Commission that discovered he was being given incorrect information.

Before Lady Denman made the announcement, she actually had no idea what she was going to announce. No-one but the members of the Federal cabinet knew what the capital of Australia was going to be called. In fact, the parliamentarians were still debating how to pronounce 'Canberra'. They decided that whatever way it sounded when it came out of Lady Denman's mouth would be the official pronunciation. As she made her way to the official dais, she was handed a small case with a card enclosed. This card had the magic word written on it. She made the proclamation, the politicians smiled and the Governor-general sat back and sneezed his head off. Days before, the wattle had been declared Australia's national flower – and the poor old Governor-general was allergic to it.

Back in the land of ice and snow, the bodies of most of Scott's Antarctic team were found. As that sad discovery happened, the leader of an Australian Antarctic Expedition crawled, barely alive, into his base camp. His name was Douglas Mawson and he, along with two others, had set out four months ago to explore the frozen continent's coastline. The trouble started soon after their departure when one of the men fell into a crevasse with his sledge and most of the expedition's food. The second man weakened and died on the return journey. Mawson survived on scraps of dog meat and slowly continued moving. At one stage, he was forced to tape the soles of his feet back on before donning his boots.

There must be an easier way to make a quid and in 1913, the Australian government did just that – in a way. The first Commonwealth bank note, the 10 shilling, was launched. Ten shillings was half a quid back then and the basic wage of Australia was eight shillings a day. In today's monetary value, ten shillings was worth around $35 … however, if you have one of the original uncirculated notes today, it would be worth around $370,000. In another great moment for future collectors, the government, after two years of deliberation (well, come on, they were busy with the pronunciation of 'Canberra'), approved the issue of an Australian postal stamp. The stamp, featuring a kangaroo, was quickly put into production. Less than a week later, the Postmaster-general decreed that it was the 'laughing stock of the civilised world' and quickly pulled it out of production.

So how were people earning those ten-shilling notes? Even though the population of Australia was nearly five million, a perusal of the classifieds shows that there was a range of jobs available:

-Lady required for beef and ham counter, Elizabeth Street.

-Rockchoppers required, H. Longworth's, Haymarket.

-Lady-like person, about 26, to mind glove and feather shop in Ashfield.

-Elderly man required, understands National gas engine and boiler, Waitara.

-Good blue metal sprawlers at Minnamurra Quarry.

-Respectable girls for fruit peeling at Annandale.

-Wanted, respectable boys at Annandale.

-Coat and knicker [sic] machinist, H.J.Goeby & Co, off Elizabeth Steet.

-Erecting engineer required by well-known firm.

-A generally useful man, must be sober and able to milk, needed at Hornsby.

-Wanted: six young ladies. Must be good swimmers and divers. Apply stage door, Her Majesty's, Friday. Applicants to bring bathing suits.

The year dragged on and soon it was time to stop your rock-chopping, blue metal spreading or theatre-swimming and prepare for the Christmas/New Year holidays. The Railways announced discounted interstate holiday fares for 1913, but they may have left some people scratching their heads on the platform:

> 'Tickets issued at 2d and 1d per mile will have a coupon attached which will require to be exchanged for a single ticket for the return journey within one calendar month from date of issue. Tickets issued at 1¾d and ½d per mile on December 31 and January 1 will be available for return until Friday January 2. Tickets issued at Single Fare and Quarter Rate for distances not exceeding 20 miles will be available for return within six weeks from date of issue. Tickets issued in the Down direction (from Sydney and intermediate stations) will be available for return by any train. Tickets issued in the Up direction (to Sydney and intermediate stations) will not be available for return by the Express or Mail trains.'[1]

There were some who may have decided that this was all too complicated so they would stay home and read the newspaper. If they bought a copy of the *Sydney Morning Herald* on the last day of the year, they may have noticed this article tucked away:

---

1. *Sydney Morning Herald,* 31st December 1913

>'*The Daily Chronicle* comments on the "growing alarm that is being felt in Australia as to the cost of military training, including evidence that the expenditure per head is double that of Germany. Australia, being a land of high prices, must be prepared to find her army dear also. Nevertheless, having regard to her geographical isolation and her youthfulness as a community, the burden of non-productive expenditure is decidedly excessive."'[2]

Seven months later, the leader of the Australian Labor Party, Andrew Fisher, would stand up and say that Australians would defend Great Britain to 'our last man and our last shilling', if it became involved in war with Germany.

Now, it is time to talk about cost.

---

2. Ibid.

The sea was hell and the shore was hell
With mine, entanglement, shrapnel and shell
But they stormed the heights as Australians should
And they fought and they died as we knew they would

"Song of the Dardenelles"
Henry Lawson

21. WHAT IS IT GOOD FOR?

The year started peacefully enough. In Melbourne, a new variety store was opened by the brothers George and J. S. Coles. They employed six staff in their shop and hoped that their low prices would attract customers. They boasted that they 'sold nothing over a shilling'. As apparently our last shilling was to be used to defend Great Britain, this would be useful. But what was Andrew Fisher talking about?

There have been hundreds of books written about World War One and this is not one of them. What follows is a simplification of the events that led to the catastrophe of 1914-18. In June of 1914, the heir to the Austro-Hungarian throne, Archduke Franz Ferdinand, and his lovely wife, the Duchess of Hohenberg, were sitting comfortably in a car as it drove through the streets of Sarajevo in Bosnia. Suddenly a package was thrown into their car. The Archduke picked it up and tossed it back into the street. The package exploded and injured people in the following car. He was far from pleased by this Bosnian souvenir and complained about it at the next stop. Sometime later, as the regal car slowed at an intersection, a man stepped out of the crowd, raised a pistol and fired twice. He was a good shot. The Duchess was killed instantly, the Archduke died shortly afterwards.

During the next month, Austrian authorities told Serbian authorities that they wished to investigate the killings. The Austrians smelled a rat and they believed the rat to be named Serbia. They gave them 48 hours to reply to their request. Germany stuck its nose in and said they fully supported Serbia. Great Britain, who already had enough trouble of its own with the Ulster uprising in Ireland, said they would mediate the situation. Germany said – 'Bull-scheisse, you will'. Austria said – 'Doesn't matter anyway, because we declare war'.

Russia cranked up its army as did France. Germany invaded Belgium with a view of taking France. England declared war on Germany. Russia attacked Prussia. Austria attacked Poland. The British Empire turned to its dominions and asked for help. Canada, Australia, New Zealand and the Barotse tribe of Rhodesia pledged support.

Australia had been quick to respond. Prime Minister Joseph Cook declared – 'Our duty is quite clear. We must gird our loins and remember that we are Britons.' In Victoria, they quickly girded their loins and guarded their lines. There was a German steamer in Port Phillip Bay and sensing trouble, the captain had ordered it to sneak quietly out to sea. However, the lads at the Point Nepean Fort had other ideas and fired a cannon across the ship's bows. The ship turned around and the crew were detained. Around Australia, German shops and clubs were raided as over a thousand Germans suddenly applied for Australian citizenship. Australia also took over the German-held section of New Guinea while New Zealand did the same with Western Samoa. It was all too much girding for Prime Minister Cook; he resigned and Andrew 'Last Shilling' Fisher became the Australian leader.

Field Marshall Sir John French, commander of the British Expeditionary Force, was heard to say that the war would be over by Christmas – but he didn't say which year. Christmas had passed in 1914 and January of 1915 was progressing when a train full of picnicking families departed for a journey to Silverton in western NSW. The sun was shining and it was a beautiful day to enjoy some sandwiches and take your mind off the war. The train passed two men sitting in a dilapidated ice-cream cart that was pulled by a dilapidated horse. The picnickers on the train smiled and waved. The two men smiled and waved back. They then produced a Turkish flag and two rifles and commenced firing upon the train.

In the matter of minutes, four people were dead and seven injured. The two men (who weren't actually Turkish, but Afghan and Indian) took off. They were pursued by anyone who could find a gun. The Turkish sympathisers must have realised that this was going to end badly. They took shelter in a rocky outcrop but carloads and cartloads of pursuers kept arriving. Soon, the outcrop was charged by the townspeople. They found one man dead and the other wasn't far from joining him.

Like the people of Broken Hill that day, Australians rushed to volunteer for active service. Thousands of men (and in some cases boys) turned up at recruiting offices. Thousands of families waved goodbye to loved ones as they marched from their homes, towards the unknown. Thousands of families were affected by the First World War and the O'Brien's and Kingdom's were amongst them. The following is some of the stories from the two families. I have made every effort to trace WW1 participants but it is possible that I have missed some. What I have found from military records and the odd surviving letter depicts the life of a soldier and the lives of the people waiting at home.

Charles Kingdom was a grandson of George and Susan Kingdom. The 21-year-old farmer joined the 53rd Battalion in 1915. He remained unscathed until the September of 1918 when he was hospitalised with a gunshot wound to the right wrist. In November of 1918, the following telegram was sent to the family:

CORPORAL CHARLES KINGDOM ILL PROGRESS REPORT EXPECTED.

Strangely, on the same day, this was sent to the family:

NOW REPORTED CORPORAL CHARLES KINGDOM ADMITTED TWENTY NINTH OCTOBER SUTTON MILITARY HOSPITAL SALISBURY ENGLAND PNEUMONIA SERIOUSLY ILL.

Charles eventually recovered and returned to Australia in 1919.

Walter Kingdom was another grandson of George and Susan and my grandfather's brother. He was also a 21-year-old farmhand but he joined the 13th Battalion in 1916. Less than a year later, he was admitted to hospital suffering from a shell wound to the head. Another telegram was sent to Armidale:

REPORTED PRIVATE WALTER KINGDOM ADMITTED INFIRMARY RED CROSS HOSPITAL

WINBORNE ENGLAND NINETEENTH AUGUST GUNSHOT WOUND CRANIUM SEVERE.

Thirteen days after that telegram, this was sent:

PRIVATE WALTER KINGDOM PROGRESSING FAVOURABLY.

Two months later, a doctor wrote on Walter's chart: 'Mental condition low. Hardly responding. Complains of headaches.' By December of 1917: 'He says he feels well.' Walter re-joined his unit in France in February of 1918. In September he was back in hospital, having been shot in the leg. He returned home safely.

James Cameron was yet another of the Kingdom grandchildren – his mother was Fanny Cameron, the first born. James was a 25-year-old grazier and he joined the infantry in October of 1914. In May of 1915, he was despatched to a place called Gallipoli. In August, he was hit by shrapnel from a hand grenade explosion and received a compound fracture of the tibia. He was shipped to England and admitted to London's Hampstead Hospital on the 30th of August. The medical report states that 'no anti-tetanus serum was given'.

James died seven days later. He was buried in Hampstead Cemetery.

In May of 1920, a major from the Australian Imperial Force Base Records Office wrote to James's mother. He advised her that the inscription she had chosen for her son's gravestone was too long. It exceeded 66 letters and she would have to submit a shorter inscription. She wrote back and asked for them to write – 'Sleep on beloved, sleep, and take thy rest'. She added that she hoped that inscription would meet with the major's approval.

Lance-corporal Andrew Elliott was a grandson of Susan Kingdom from her marriage with John Elliott. He was a 23-year-old policeman and he joined the 1st Field Ambulance in September of 1914. By August of 1916, he was serving in France. The following is a letter written by a Sergeant N. Clifton, on behalf of the Red Cross:

> 'On the evening of 18/8/16, L/Col Elliott was sent with seven others to the Regimental Aid Post situated slightly to the right

of Pozieres village. The place had been shelled very heavy all that day but unfortunately the men had to go up. On arriving at the post, they sat on the steps of a deep German dugout. A shell exploded right in the mouth of the dugout, killing the four men at the top and leaving unscathed the four men further down. I saw the bodies next morning and had them buried in a shell hole about 10 yards from the trench.'

Andrew's personal effects were sent to his family. They consisted of a belt, a cap comforter, a bible and a stone.

Sydney Augustus O'Brien (known as Gus) was a son of John O'Brien and Ellen Cunningham. He joined the 31st Battalion in 1915 when he was 33 years old. Gus was reported missing on 17/8/1916. He was then reported as not missing, but wounded, two weeks later. He was discharged as medically unfit in 1917 and sent home.

Clarence Frank Kennedy's grandmother was Ellen Kennedy, John O'Brien's sister. At the age of 30, he joined the 2nd Battalion in 1914. In May of 1915, a telegram arrived at his father's house:

REGRET REPORTED SON CORPORAL CF
KENNEDY WOUNDED WILL ADVISE UPON
RECEIPT FURTHER PARTICULARS.

Four months later, a doctor wrote on Clarence's medical chart:

'He was invalided from the Gallipoli Peninsula suffering from purulent conjunctivitis and loss of vision caused partly by sand irritation and partly as the result of shell shock. He was also suffering from neurasthenia. He is still nervous and occasionally has tremors. His vision is recovering but is still defective and is unable to go about at night.'

Two and a half years after that report, Clarence was declared medically unfit and sent home.

Andrew John McArthur Waddell was another grandson of John and Ellen. He was a locomotive engine cleaner and at the age of 18, he enlisted. In 1916, he joined the 9th Field Ambulance and within a year found himself in France. The following is a letter written to the Red Cross by a Private Curry:

> *'I was wounded along with Waddell by the same shell during the advance on Messines on June 7. We had just bought a case down and were standing outside the dressing station when a shell landed close to us. Waddell's leg was blown right off and he died in a few minutes.'*

Andrew was buried at Pont D'Achelles. His personal effects were sent home to his mother. They consisted of a safety razor, strop, letters, two handkerchiefs, electric torch, pipe, mirror, French dictionary, badge and a cigarette holder.

Sydney John Green had married Eileen O'Brien, a grand-daughter of John and Ellen. They had been married for just over two years when he enlisted in the AIF. He was badly wounded in action and spent a long time recovering in England. During his recovery, he wrote to his family. The following sections of the letter testify to the ANZAC character:

> *'The Second Division got busy with them 18 pounders, just at the rear of us, and opened up on him* [German forces]. *They had dragged their guns out of the pits, right up to within 400 yards of where we had Fritzy* [Germans] *held up and gave him some lively time for a while then knocked off. That was the signal for us to charge and charge we did but it is a saying that Fritzy doesn't like the cold steel and it is a fact. Of course he was demoralised; the 18 pounders and the Lewis guns, not to mention rifle fire, had put the wind up him and he squibbed it. As we went out, he went off – any that showed fight got hurt, but to see the Fritzys coming out of shell holes without rifle or equipment, holding their hands up and crying "Mercy" was too funny for words.'*

A few days later:

> *'All was going well when I falls ace over diamonds into a shell hole just outside his line. This was the beginning of the*

end for me for as I was getting out, I felt such a kick in the arm that it made me look to see if it was still there. It was there alright so I got back into the hole and had a look at it and decided to go back and get it dressed. I did get back but how I really don't know.'

After he was treated by First Aid, he was sent to the Dressing Station:

'I left for the dressing station quite happy and had almost reached it when I feels something hit me a whack in the back and I spins around like a top then hits Mother Earth with a thud, then I hear a bang of an unusual size and reckons it must have been a shell that hit me in the back but no, I never stopped it at all, for it killed 5 others just behind me; four stretcher bearers and the case they were carrying.'

Sydney was rescued by another group of stretcher bearers. Their efforts in dressing his wounds saved his life. After several operations to remove shrapnel, he was told that an artery had been cut and he was lucky to be still alive.

Lastly, we will look at the story of Bombardier Leopold Bede O'Brien – a son of John and Ellen's. His records remained quite elusive to me for years until a chance discovery. It seems Leopold didn't like his birth name, so he spent his life being called Edward O'Brien. Edward joined the AIF in 1916, declaring his age as 38 (a couple of years off) and that he was single. However, on his application that part has been crossed out and a wife named Margaret is recorded (there is no official record of any wife for him – nor does her name appear anywhere else ever again). He was sent to England for training in 1917. During that period, he faced a court-martial hearing at Perham Down. The charges were being drunk on active service and using insubordinate language to a superior officer. From a witness statement:

'The accused returned to No 7 camp at about 9.15pm on 7/4/17. In my opinion he was mad with drink. He was in No 5 hut and before lights out Bomber Winslow and I

covered him with this blankets when he was lying down. Some ten minutes later he got up and started hitting the wall with his bare hands. He was walking around the hut in a very drunken state and accidentally rolled against the table on which were placed plates and bowls. The table was upset and a number of plates and bowls were broken. The accused was then arrested.'

Next witness statement from Sergeant Fugger:

'Private O'Brien was placed in the guard room. About 1 am he kicked the wall of the cell. He asked for some blankets and I gave him 6 of them. Just after doing so he called me a motherless bastard. In my opinion he was very drunk.'

Edward pleaded guilty to all the charges. He mentioned in his defence that he wasn't used to drink, so he had become very drunk and had no control of his actions. Edward received seven day's detention as punishment.

Edward was posted to France and appeared again in official documentation around twelve months later. But this was for a different reason. From the Major-General Commanding 1st Australian Division:

'In the operations near Harhicourt from 18th to 21st September 1918, Private O'Brien showed great courage and devotion to duty. On 18th Sept. as a Lewis gunner he performed most valuable work getting forward with his gun and providing covering fire for the remainder of the platoon, while enemy points of resistance were being attacked, during periods of exploitation after barrage had ceased. On 21st Sept, he again performed most valuable work with his gun, inflicting many casualties on the enemy who could be seen moving about after the objective had been captured and showed good choice of position for his gun. Throughout he set a fine example of courage and initiative and greatly assisted in the taking and consolidation of the objectives assigned to his platoon.'

Edward was awarded the Military Medal.

When the war finished in 1918, he was discharged. In 1919, he re-enlisted to assist with transport operations. In 1920, he appeared in an English court, charged with assault. He was sentenced to one month's imprisonment in Pentonville Prison. After his release, he was sent home.

The war lasted four years. In those years, soldiers heard whistling shells and wondered did they have their name on them? Postmen at home delivered telegrams that did have their name on them. There were vacant seats around dinner tables; mothers and fathers wept quietly in the kitchen, maybe touching the bible or the cigarette case or the razor that fell out of the envelope. Children played outside and didn't really understand why their brother wasn't coming home.

Then there were the ones that did come home. They weren't the same person that smiled and walked out of the door years ago. Some hated loud noises and the night-time and the dreams and the memories. Some sat in silence; some raged and screamed. But some came home, kissed their mums and wives/girlfriends and carried on as if they had just been down to the corner store and had a big adventure along the way.

We should be proud of all of them.

Michael O'Brien

22. Bless You

'It is mingled feelings that each of us faces this bright New Year. Will it remain as bright as it promises? Can we reasonably hope that 1919 will be an epochal date in the history of the world? The commencement of a continuous reign of peace the world over – with goodwill between men?'

So read the advertisement for Farmer's Summer Cash Bonus Sale (hundreds of bargains in every department!) in the newspaper of January 1, 1919. There's nothing like some retail therapy to lift your spirits. F. Lassetter & Co., Universal Providers in George-street (open Thursday mornings at 8:20) joined the philosophical shopkeepers:

'The year 1919 has been ushered in pure and unsullied. Henceforth may the peoples of the earth keep it so and realise their duty to their fellow creatures.'

Which was, no doubt, to spend money in their store. Other retailers pitched to the public differently:

'Wassiamull, Assomull + Co, leading Indian silk store – the friends you forget at Xmas can be remembered for New Year.'

'Barracluff's Ostrich Farm, South Head: There is a lot of difference between a tail feather of a Tomtit and a gorgeous feather of a Barracluff Ostrich.'

'The Paget Manufacturing Co of Regent-street: Insist on Shi-noleum for your linoleums.'

'You all want peace. Get Alligator Corn Cure in a box. Nuff said.'[1]

The folks at home needed some good news. The First World War had killed more than nine million people with over 60,000 of them being Australian. If that wasn't bad enough, the world was experiencing an influenza pandemic. The pandemic, which started in 1918, was systematically wiping people out and making the death toll of the war seem an inconsequential figure. Some fifty million died during this time with 10,000 dying in Australia. The population of the Great Southern Land was taking a hammering.

Australia had turned its attention from fighting Germans to fighting germs. North Head Quarantine Station, situated at the picturesque entrance to Sydney Harbour, was working overtime. It had processed fifty incoming ships since October 1918 and thousands of people had been checked. Over 600 people from these ships stayed on as patients; 43 of them did not make it any further onto Australian soil.

The government decreed that if you were going outside, you must wear a mask. Retail and pub staff also had to wear a mask. To go without a mask, you risked catching influenza and you risked losing some money. There were fines for failing to wear one on a train or tram. On February 25th, the *Herald* reported that one Eileen Leigh, 19, was fined 20s for not wearing a mask on an Oxford-street tram; Sydney Jones, 18, was fined 30s for walking along Oxford-street without one while Frank Roberts, 37, and James Clarke, 28, for the same offence in Elizabeth-street.

The shops made special notice of the precautions they were taking. William's Pharmacy and Factory in George-street advised that their entire staff had been inoculated and were wearing masks. Each mask was sprinkled with 'garrolised menthol' which was a compound containing menthol, camphor, eucalyptol, phenol and formalin. Nock & Kirby's Department Store advertised that their George-street store was sprayed

---

1. *Sydney Morning Herald,* various issues, January 1919

daily with formalin. As for Winns Ltd of Oxford-street – they were clever. They advertised that they had just purchased 20,000 yards of muslin – suitable for masks.

But even with these precautions, commerce was suffering. Shops were shutting earlier. J. C. Williamson's theatres closed indefinitely. The Easter Show was cancelled. Schools and churches closed. It is estimated that 40% of Sydney's population had influenza. The mortality rate was three in a thousand and much higher in the indigenous community. At the time, New South Wales had some 2,000 hospital beds; in a nine-month period, 25,000 people were admitted to hospital. Most of them were taken to temporary hospitals set up in private houses, churches and bowling clubs.[2]

The pandemic began easing off in March of 1919 – so, in Queensland, it was time for the people to march again. There was bad feeling in the air from the war, the Russian Revolution and the slaughter of the Tsar and his family. People were edgy about anything 'Russian'. Returned servicemen were struggling to find employment and the ones that did were constantly involved in strike actions, organised by radical trade unions. What bothered some people was that the symbolic colour of the trade union movement was red which matched the symbolic colour of the Russian Revolution. The state government, in an effort to cool things down, declared that flying a red flag was illegal and this was like waving a red rag to a bull to some folks.

Demonstrations were organised in Brisbane to protest this law. The organisers promised that they would not fly red flags ... but they didn't say anything about ribbons or hankies. The protestors marched to the Domain and listened to speeches and sang songs. Then, word passed around and eventually several thousand men agreed that they would pay the Brisbane base of the Russian Workers Association a visit. However, they found their way blocked by mounted police armed with rifles and bayonets. So it was on for young and old. By the end of the melee, some fifty men were injured and a police horse was dead.[3]

---

2. *An Australian Perspective of the 1918-19 influenza Pandemic*, Peter Curson and Kevin McCracken, *New South Wales Public Health Bulletin, 2006*
3. Information from *The Oxford Companion to Military History* – Peter Dennis, Jeffrey Grey, Evan Morris, Robin Prior, Oxford University Press, Melbourne 1995

Life in the Past Lane

If there was a positive outcome to the riot, it was to bring attention to the welfare of returned servicemen. Membership of the Returned Sailors and Soldiers Imperial League of Australia grew. Today that organisation's title has been shortened to the RSL. And just to end the military theme for 1919 – the Melbourne Cup was won by Artilleryman.

As 1919 prepared to shut its doors, a child was born in Dubbo. Although no-one knew it at the time, she was destined for infamy and an unwanted place in the record books. The sweet little country girl was named Marjorie Jean Maude Wright and she would grow up to become a sour city prostitute, who spent her nights robbing her clients. But one robbery went horribly wrong and her 73-year-old client was violently killed. Marjorie, who was calling herself Jean Lee, and her accomplices for the night were charged with murder and subsequently executed. In 1951, that little girl from Dubbo became the last woman to be hanged in Australia.

Christmas was here and the Australian people were treated to a present – a federal election. It was won by the Nationalist Party of Australia, led by Billy Hughes, and if anyone was befuddled on polling day, it's not surprising. Hughes was formerly the leader of the Labor Party before he created the National Labor Party which then merged with the Commonwealth Liberal Party to become the Nationalist Party of Australia. In the election, the Nationalist Party defeated the Labor Party, the Country Party (which went on to become the National Party) and several independent Nationalists. If you were a person who voted for a personality rather than a party, you would need to swing like an out-of-control pendulum if you wanted to vote for Hughes. During his time in politics, he represented six different parties and four different electorates. And he managed to annoy the American president, Woodrow Wilson. President Wilson referred to Hughes as a 'pestiferous varmint'.

Woodrow's fellow Americans awoke one in day in 1920 to the news that the star baseball player, Babe Ruth, had been traded by his team, Boston Red Sox, to the New York Yankees. The sum involved to complete the deal was $125,000 or about $8,500,000 today. This was a fair slug of moolah in 1920 but fades in comparison with today's sporting deals. In 2001, Jason Giambi also moved to the New York

Yankees; this time the player came from the Oakland Athletics and it cost $120,000,000 – admittedly for a seven-year deal. It's not just baseball though; in 2013 footballer Gareth Bale moved from Tottenham Hotspur to Real Madrid for $135,000,000.

These days, people say there's too much money in sport and maybe they were saying it back then too. Although, some of the players didn't agree. In 1920, eight Chicago White Sox players were indicted on charges of conspiring to fix games in the previous year. Two of them confessed; one of the players, named 'Shoeless' Joe Jackson, said that he had received $3000 from a gambling consortium. Perhaps he wanted to buy shoes.

In another sporting controversy that is echoed in current times, two members of Australia's Olympic team alleged that there was widespread use of drugs to boost athlete's performances. George Parker, who won silver in the 3000m walk in 1920, said it was obvious many competitors were 'fortified by drugs or stimulants. Yet the man who beat him to the gold in that race enjoyed another type of stimulation. Before the race, Italian Ugo Frigerio strolled out to the band in the middle of the field and handed the conductor some sheet music. He requested that it be played as he competed; Frigerio then took his place at the starting line and walked to victory.

Australia only sent a small team to the Olympics in Brussels and consequently came back with a small amount of medals. We won a silver in the 200m swimming relay and that chap named Frank Beaurepaire won bronze in the 1500m freestyle. Shortly after the Olympics, Frank wanted to earn some money, so he had the idea of starting a motor vehicle tyre business. It was a good idea.

Still on sport; international cricket tests had been postponed during the war but in 1920, they resumed. The old foes, Australia and England, united in war, divided in cricket. Australia had appointed a new captain, a Victorian by the name of Warwick Windridge Armstrong. He was nicknamed 'The Big Ship' – mainly due to the fact he was 6' 3" and 21 stone (or 130kg for the young'uns). He was a hard-hitting batsman, a wily leg-spinner and a dominating presence at the wicket. Like Dr Grace, anecdotes about him are delightful. During the Sydney test of the Ashes series, Australia were batting and losing wickets rapidly. A look around the dressing room found no sign of Armstrong. He was found in the Member's bar, fully padded up, drinking whisky, waiting for his turn to bat. He walked out and scored 158. Australia won the series 5-0. Obviously current fitness regimes are overrated.

So it wasn't a good year for the English cricket team nor was it a good year for the president of France. In May, he fell out of the window of the presidential train and wandered up the track in his nightshirt until he was found by a bemused farmer. Later in the year he excused himself from a cabinet meeting, proceeded to walk outside and stroll into a lake, fully clothed. Finally, after greeting the British ambassador while wearing his presidential sash … and nothing else … it was thought that he might have an issue or two. He resigned and was placed in an institution.

At home, the cricket team weren't the only English visitors to our shores. Prince Edward, the Prince of Wales and eldest son of King George V, toured Australia to thank the people for their war efforts. He visited here, there and everywhere. He delivered speeches, shook hands, waved at crowds, attended dinners – and nearly died in a train crash. In July, while touring Western Australia, he was travelling by train to his next town. The locomotive and the carriages that were carrying him and a group of parliamentary ministers, was derailed when they suddenly stopped due to a bull on the line. The Royal carriage rolled down an embankment and came to a rest in the dirt. From all accounts, rescuers found the prince sitting amidst the wreckage, smoking a cigar. 'Hurt?' he apparently said. 'Bless your heart, no, and I'm glad to say the whisky flask is not broken either'.

They really did breed them differently in those days.

The prince survived the train crash and continued his tour. In honour of the visit, 2000kms of existing linked roads between Sydney and Port Augusta was renamed the Prince's Highway. Then Randwick Hospital joined in and became Prince of Wales Hospital. The prince himself would go on to become King Edward VIII but his love for an American divorcee would cut his reign short.

But he was 16 years away from that and thousands of miles away from his home. In one speech in 1920, he was heard to say – 'And I am quite sure of one thing, that as Australia stands by the Empire, so will the Empire stand by Australia for all time.' Three cheers. For he's a jolly good fellow.

It turns out that the Empire wasn't going to stand by Australia financially. When the war finished, the Treaty of Versailles stated that Germany would have to pay compensation. The sum agreed on was today's equivalent of 22 billion pounds. (Germany finished paying the debt in 2010, some 91 years later. They probably would have finished sooner but that fellow, Adolf Hitler, stopped the payments for a few years.) Australia was expecting some of the reparation but Britain had other ideas. They said that since Britain had provided transport and maintenance for our forces, we actually owed them. Our indebtedness to the British government stood at £42,000,000 (over 2 billion today) and they wanted £8,000,000 of it repaid – pronto. Funnily enough, at the same time the British government owed Australian woolgrowers for their half of the profit actualised by Australian wool sold on by Britain. The figure owed? £30,000,000.

Money was too tight to mention in 1920. The NSW government statistician produced a report that compared the prices of food and groceries between July 1914 and January 1920. Meat prices had increased 76.3% while other food and grocery items had risen 61.2%. Since January 1919 only the prices of milk, potatoes, onions and cheese had lowered while everything else increased. The cost of living was hurting everyone. Even the Vatican's cardinals asked the Pope for an increase to their daily allowance. But even though times were tough and families struggled to put a meal on the table, one constancy remained; the statistician revealed that for the previous year, a sum of £10,251,000 was expended on intoxicating liquor in NSW.

The newspapers took to devoting space to handy household hints that would save money. Take this recipe from March:

> 'Take beef round, put through a mincer, form into round cakes, dust with flour then broil. Served with horseradish sauce and baked banana, they will provide quite a novelty at many tables.'[4]

The papers also recommended that you shop for bargains but warned of the dangers:

---

4. *Sydney Morning Herald,* 1st March 1920

'A latent spirit of avariciousness seems to come to the surface of some women's natures at sale time. They cannot see a thing without wanting it, and even if they have no intention of buying it, they examine it closely, debar intending purchasers from getting near it and in the end, return it to the sale basket, crumpled and soiled from handling.'[5]

1921 started with a shocking event in Melbourne which had everybody talking. A twelve-year-old girl named Alma Tirtschke had been asked by her grandmother to take some meat to her aunt's house in Collins-street. The next day her body was found in a lane near a place called Gun Alley. She had been raped and murdered. The owner of a nearby bar, The Australian Wine Saloon, was Colin Campbell Ross and suspicion fell upon him. Basic forensic investigation (remembering this was well before Gil Grissom) located a hair on the girl's body and this hair was thought to have belonged to Ross. He protested his innocence to no avail; he was arrested and charged. The following year he was found guilty and he was hanged. Seventy years later, the evidence was re-examined ... and disproved. In 2008, Colin Campbell Ross was granted a pardon. Though it is probably little consolation to him, he was the first (and only) Australian to receive a pardon after being judicially executed.

Another unwanted record setter was NSW politician Percy Brookfield. He was travelling in South Australia when he arrived at a railway station, only to find a Russian waving a gun and creating havoc. Brookfield stepped in with an attempt to disarm the Russian and was shot. Several hours later, Percy Brookfield became the first Australian politician to have been murdered in office.

I am lucky enough to be in possession of a memoir written by a lady who lived through these times. During the war years, she and her mother had travelled to England and Ireland to visit family. They were delayed there when war broke out as all available shipping was needed for the hostilities:

---
5. *Sydney Morning Herald,* 9th January 1920

> 'We met a nice chap going out to Egypt to re-join his regiment. He asked my mother if he could marry me. We corresponded for a long time after I arrived home. There was also a boy I was friendly with in Ireland and he was supposed to be coming to Australia. I eventually wrote and told him to stay where he was.'

Upon her return to Australia she founded a tennis club at Tempe, a suburb of Sydney named after a mansion that had been built on Cook's River. As a fund raiser, the club held a fancy dress ball. The young lady looked across a crowded room and saw a dashing young Naval man:

> 'He commenced seeing me after work. We went out for a year or so and then became engaged.'

Today, we see what might have happened (or rather what might not-of happened) if that young lady went off with the swooning digger or the love-struck Irishman. Basically – you wouldn't be reading this. The young lady was Frances Carroll; the naval man was William O'Brien – one set of my grandparents. You can't help wondering though, as to what happened to the other two suitors.

Nana came from a close Irish family – her father's sister married her mother's brother – or her aunt married her uncle. Poor old William came from an Irish family that was nuttier than a barrel of monkeys. Though his father, Frank, appears to have been fairly sensible, Frank's brothers spent time in His Majesty's prisons on various counts of drunkenness, assault and desertion. Cornelius even appears to have added assaulting a police officer to the mix. All, apart from Frank, appeared to be true sons of the father.

The big wedding day was set for March 5, 1921 at St Peter's and St Pauls' church at Tempe. Now what was available for a blushing bride? According to her memoir she made her own wedding dress but there is always the going-away outfit to think of:

> 'Accessories and going-away clothes. Lassetter's on George-street or Anthony Hordern's on Brickfield Hill.
> Two button washable suede gloves. 18s/6d.

Crepe de China blouse, pin tucked around the neck, Venetian embroidery on front – colours ivory, navy, black, pink and putty. 29s/6d.
Pale pink camisole with ribbon shoulder straps, trimmed front and back with Valenciennes lace. 21s.'

And of course, you have to look nice on the day:

'Modern treatments to regain and retain your appearance. Permanent individual removal from the face of superfluous hairs by refined amperage electrolysis. Permanent removal of warts and moles. Muscles, flesh and bleaching work on the face. Hair colouring using beautiful human colours and shades. Liquid shampooing. At Sister Vimard, two entire floors, 189 King-street.

L. T. Piver's Face Cream made in France. Supplied in tubes, in the following odours – Le Trefle, Azurea, Floramye and Pompeia.'

And don't forget:

'Why go without teeth? When a perfect set costs you so little. George and George sets of pretty teeth, which are equal to nature's own in size, shape and colour, costs only from £3/3. Each one is fitted with the famous 'Can't Fail' suction plate, which allows the wearer to laugh, speak, sing, chew and sleep with the perfect assurance that the teeth cannot wobble, drop or fall out.'

After the wedding and a short honeymoon in Katoomba, William and Frances lived with her parents in Tempe. However, Sydney was expanding and as the following classified boasted, now was the time to get on board:

'There's money in it. Experience has shown that Rickard Realty buyers in new townships have already made money.

Ever since our great Bankstown Station sale in 1909, shrewd investors have made big profits by securing the best sites in such subdivisions. On Saturday next investors of moderate means will have an exceptional opportunity at TOONGABBIE. On every hand, orchards, vegetable plantations, flower gardens and poultry runs abound and evidence the general prosperity and the fecundity of the soil.'

So with fecund dirt, wart removals, Pompeia odours and a poultry farm at Toongabbie, the future could gleam brightly for the O'Brien's. But for some other betrothed couples – the gleam was quite dull.

Earlier in the year, a wedding was timed for 7pm on a Saturday in Redfern. The party had arrived and were just preparing for the ceremony when two police detectives appeared. They questioned the bridegroom and then informed the bride that they would have to perform an unpleasant duty. They arrested the groom and took him away. Later that week the groom, Leslie James Grant aka James Henry Grant aka Harry Smith appeared in court on breaking and entering charges. His defence counsel advised the judge that the bride-to-be was still waiting to marry the defendant. A female voice was heard to call out across the courtroom – "I'll wait 40 years to marry him". But she only had to wait for three years – just until his hard-labour sentence was over.

It could have been worse. In Brisbane, a young bride with the enchanting name of Eleanor Bagslag collapsed at the altar. It was thought to be only a fainting fit so she was taken back home to recuperate. She died two hours later.

Sudden death also caused a problem in the NSW parliament later in the year. Up until the 5th of October, James Storey was Premier. Then unfortunately, he died on the 5th. His deputy, James Dooley, took over. But two months later, his party lost a no-confidence vote in parliament and Dooley was out. Nationalist Party leader George Fuller was instated. Seven hours later (yes, hours) Fuller also lost a no-confidence vote before anyone had the time to change the stationery and he was out. Dooley, who had started the day as Premier, had become leader of the Opposition by lunch, found himself Premier again at dinner time.

Life in the Past Lane

Another stationery department that was copping a workout was in Western Australia. The Governor there was Sir Francis Alexander Newdigate Newdegate. This is not a typo. Starting life as a Newdigate, he was required to adopt the other Newdegate under the terms of a family will. Even more interesting was Newdigate Newdegate's wife, Elizabeth Bagot. She was the daughter of the 3rd Baron Bagot of Bagot's Bromley. Baron Bagot of Bagot's Bromley was also Baronet Bagot of Blithfield. Bagot had earned his titles by having held the office of Gentleman of the Bedchamber to the Prince Consort. So Baron Bagot's bedchamber business brought Blithfield to the Bromley brood. Bloody brilliant, I say.

Bring on 1922.

Michael O'Brien

23. Irish Eyes Aren't Smiling

As of the 1st January, the British Empire covered one quarter of the world and ruled over one in four people. This did not include the Irish Free State; a place that today we simply call Ireland. The State was established after a war between the Royal Irish Constabulary and the British Army versus the Irish Republican Army. Both sides took great delight in blowing the blazes out of the other as the Republicans sought home rule away from England's clutches.

Two thousand people died before a truce was called. In 1921, Britain agreed to relinquish Ireland but the northern part wanted to stay with the Brits. So that relinquishment should have had the rebellious folks of the Free State cheering and singing songs. Alas, no. Shortly before the declaration, war broke out within the Irish Free State between the Irish Republican Army and the Irish National Army. It is believed over 4000 people died in this latest war – fighting in an area they had already won.

While Paddy and Mick were in a barney, a blizzard caused havoc in Washington, USA. It seems that many people took shelter from the ferocious conditions in Washington's new cinema, the Knickerbocker Theatre. While hundreds enjoyed the movie, the blizzard outside was dumping snow onto the theatre's flat roof. During the interval the roof collapsed and took the balcony seating with it. 98 people died and 133 were injured.

In a legal case that could be a movie script, a French second-hand dealer named Henri Landru was in court facing eleven charges of murder. He had been seeking female companionship and as eHarmony hadn't been invented yet, he listed himself in the lonely hearts column of the newspaper. Once he charmed the ladies and invited them back to his apartment, he murdered them and burnt their bodies in his oven. Eventually the gendarmes caught up with him and he was arrested. Landru was found guilty and sentenced to the guillotine. Le Rasoir National (The National Razor) had been eliminating French criminals (and the odd King) since 1792 and finally stopped in 1976. If you wish to know what Monsieur Landru looked like – just go to the Museum of Death in Hollywood - his severed head is on display.

1922 was the year that the state of Queensland abolished the death penalty. Previously there had been over 100 offences which could be punished by death. They included treason, murder, piracy, forgery, burglary, housebreaking, sacrilege and quite astonishingly, you could be sent to the gallows for cutting down trees in an avenue or garden.

But if you didn't chop down the jacaranda in the front yard, you could strive to reach the average life expectancy in Australia. This was 59 years, 1 month and 24 days if you were a chap and 63 years, 3 months and 22 days for the ladies. In November, there was a man in Sydney who didn't reach the average figure. He was an alcoholic, had spent time in prison for drunkenness and non-payment of child support and he was battling depression. He finally succumbed to a cerebral haemorrhage. Yet this rambling, shambling derelict, who didn't have two bob to rub together nor a pot to piss in, became the first person to be granted a NSW state funeral. Thousands of people, including the Prime Minister and the NSW Premier, lined the streets to watch the funeral procession. How did this derelict earn such an honour? Well, his name was Henry Lawson and he was one of the finest writers that Australia has ever produced.

Moving to a funeral that happened a long, long time before this one – Howard Carter and Lord Carnarvon became the first people to enter a particular Egyptian tomb in 3000 years. The tomb belonged to Pharaoh Tutankhamun. DNA tests performed in 2010 show that the young Pharaoh was the son of Pharaoh Akhenaten ... and Akhenaten's sister, who was also his wife. Tut then married his half-sister, Ankhesenpaaten – at least my family's not that bad.

The young Pharaoh's remains haven't had a moment's peace since being rested in peace. Numerous experts have scanned and probed, pushed and prodded. It is now thought that Tutankhamun died of malaria … or Kohler Disease. Or temporal lobe epilepsy. Or Marfan Syndrome. Or Wilson-Turner x-linked mental retardation syndrome, Frohlich Syndrome, Klinefelter Syndrome, Androgen Insensitivity Syndrome, Anomatase excess syndrome, Sagittal craniosynostosis syndrome, Antley-Bixler syndrome … oh, and one fellow thinks he was killed in a chariot race. Really? At the end of the day, and at the end of his days, he stopped breathing. It doesn't matter what was wrong with him – he isn't going to get any better.

To stop the year being described as a maudlin symphony because it finished on a sad note, there was a bright coda. Forty children in a Sydney home for the underprivileged were given a Christmas party by five businessmen. The men refused all publicity of their kindness and each one of them chose the name 'Mr Smith' when interviewed by the papers. The five men intended to continue their charitable work – to this day, the work is still going on under the banner of the Smith Family.

While these poor children enjoyed Christmas, they probably missed out on going to the following year's Agricultural Show. "The Show," trumpeted the *Herald* on March 27, "as the microcosm of our national life, is a call to all who have a love of their country." Very patriotic words (and probably not applied to modern times) but the star exhibit of the 1923 show was from New Zealand. The turnstiles revolved as 43,000 people paid admission to see Billy. Billy was aged 2, stood 3'9" high, 8'3" long and weighed 1158lb - he was a cross-bred Tamworth-Berkshire pig and his owners claimed he was the biggest pig in the world. Well, he certainly had a big appetite; his daily meals included 6 buckets of milk mixed with bran, two cases of apples and sixteen cabbages.

Billy wasn't up for any prizes, but some other porkers were. Five breeds were judged; Berkshire, Larger Yorkshire, Middle Yorkshire, Tamworth and Poland China. The Berkshire sow (under 6 months) was won by an entry from the Parramatta Mental Hospital while the larger Yorkshire section was won by a pig from the Gladesville Mental Hospital.

They do say you have to be mad to be a farmer.

Still on porcine matters, Sydney's pig sales were held with some 3000 sold. The market advised that prices remained unchanged for backfatters while porker's and baconer's values fluctuated. At Singleton, bacon was

1s to a pound, hams 1/½ a pound and eight pence would buy you a pig's head. At these markets, you could also stock up on horse hair, sheep and rabbit skins, Muscovy ducks, turkey roosters and pigeons.

There was a great (?) moment in science in 1923. French scientists claimed that smoking was beneficial as nicotine formed anti-bacterial chemicals. France was in the spotlight this year. The government had come to their own arrangements for reparation from World War 1 – they were going to take Germany's coal supply. They sent in troops to load the coal onto trucks – and any German miner who objected was shot on sight. The trouble is, Germany wasn't producing enough coal to supply its own population, let alone for the French. As the Allied powers were disagreeing over the reparation plan, Germany's currency was devaluing. In June, one British pound would buy you 620,000 German marks. A loaf of bread in Berlin cost 200 billion marks. Construction workers were paid three trillion marks … a day. New postage stamps were no longer printed – existing ones were over-stamped.

As the Bavarian dictatorship met in the Royal Palace to discuss the future, a former army corporal stood in the watching crowd. He pulled out a gun, fired a shot into the ceiling and announced that the national revolution had begun. Later he led a march through Munich to attract support. Upon reaching the palace, the demonstration was greeted by police. The ex-corporal escaped but was arrested the following day as he hid in a nearby village. Sentenced to five years for treason, he was told he would probably be paroled in six months. The ex-corporal's name was Adolf Hitler.

Across the water in England, British rugby league teams were attempting to sign players from the NSW competition. But they struggling to meet the economic demands – signing-on fees ranged from £500 to £1000 and players had to be found employment outside of the game and be paid travelling expenses. In 1923, Britain imposed an embargo on colonial players as clubs said the terms were impossible. In 2015, clubs could pay whatever they liked for a marquee Australian player as only £200,000 ($347,000) of the payment would count towards their salary cap.

So, English rugby league clubs cried poor but one English company was about to make money. After a hundred years of talking, Sydney's fixed harbour crossing was about to happen. The turning of the first sod occurred at Milson's Point on July 28 and construction began on the Sydney Harbour Bridge. Tenders for the construction had been sought worldwide; twenty were received but an English company won the day with a price of £4,217,721, 11s and ten pence. We made the final payment on that bill in 1988.

Over 400 buildings were destroyed on the North Shore with little or no compensation while Princes-street on the southern side was obliterated - its remains are buried under the Bradfield Highway. The bridge itself weighs 39,000 tonnes, is held together by 6,000,000 rivets and if you wish to give it a coat of paint, you will need to pop into Bunnings and order 30,000 litres. When it opened three years later, it would have cost you sixpence to cross it in a car or on a motorcycle – but you could ride your horse across for threepence.

As workers started on the bridge in 1923, some workers in Melbourne were downing tools. The police were on strike as they were displeased with the introduction of plain-clothed supervisory constables. The Victorian premier promised that here would be no punishment if they went back to work but they refused and 600 of them were fired. So what do the mice do if the cat is away? Hundreds of drunken people gathered in the heart of Melbourne and created chaos. People stood in front of trams and forced them to stop - the drivers were then dragged out and bashed. Shop windows were smashed and merchandise was stolen. Downtown, a lone clergyman stood with a raised bible and pleaded for calm – he was knocked over and stamped upon. The special constables turned up, but they were horrendously outnumbered. Thousands of people emptied the shops and escaped in cars. By the end of this night in November, several people were dead, 110 were injured and Melbourne's Bourke-street resembled a war zone.

The calendar flipped over to 1924 and it didn't take long for some politicians to show their true colours … about colours. On tour from England, a chap named Viscount Leverhulme kicked off with this statement – "If Australia's wonderful resources are to be developed, the introduction of native labour to perform the donkey work is essential. If careful selection is made, there would be no fear that the native would be ever more than a beast of burden." Australia's Prime Minister, Stanley Bruce, counteracted with - "We are determined that all labour shall be done by men of the white race. The real reason for excluding colour races from the continent is that their ethical standards are different to ours."

While in modern times, everyone is welcome in Australia (if they are not an asylum seeker or one of Johnny Depp's dogs), the White Australia Policy had reared its ugly head in the 1920's. It is also worth noting that since 1909 all aboriginals in NSW had been under the control of the Board for the Protection of Aborigines. In 1924, 1085 'full-bloods' were counted within the state – this was 151 less than the count in 1917.

Those wacky old federal politicians were busy in the first half of the year as they shifted from Melbourne to Canberra. Parliament meetings were held in an old homestead called Yarralumla House until their new home could be completed. The workmen building the new home were housed in sheds and tents – tents that caused controversy. The government had to deny that they had supplied the workmen with 'inferior' Japanese cotton tents to live in. Meanwhile, a plague of locusts infiltrated the area which caused crop damage and proved that there was more than one type of pest in the national capital.

In Nepal, there had been several attempts to climb Mount Everest – these had all ended in failure, disaster or both. Two men, George Mallory and Andrew Irvine, were part of a British expedition that were about to call it quits. The incredibly harsh conditions, the lack of oxygen, snow blindness and the cold had defeated them. Mallory and Irvine gave it one last go. They were spotted when they were only 200 metres from the summit, but a squall blew in and the support team lost sight of them. It was the last time they were seen alive.

75 years later, Mallory's body was found and given a Christian burial. He had suffered a broken leg and it appears he had fallen on his ice-pick. Apart from his missing colleague, there were two other items not present. The climbers had taken a camera with them (scientists today say that the film inside would still be developable) and Mallory always had a photo of his wife in his pocket. He had promised her that he would leave it on top of the mountain when he reached it.

Since 1924, experts (and some other people) have argued as to whether they made it to the top. If they did indeed reach the summit, that would have been 29 years before Tenzing Norgay and Edmund Hillary claimed success. We may never know if Mallory and Irvine made it but it's fun to hypothesize. And it's more fun to hypothesize about the climbing of the mountain then it is to climb the bloody mountain. Today it costs between $80,000 and $150,000 to make an attempt – this covers your guide, equipment, supplies and the licence fee. It does not provide a guarantee of success or a refund if you don't succeed. The weather and the conditions could drive you back or like 250 climbers before you, you could die. Still, as 200 bodies of these 250 climbers are still up there, you will not be lonely.

Climbing a sodding big mountain wasn't the only physical endeavour being undertaken in 1924 - the Olympics roadshow was on again. Australia won a grand total of three gold medals (swimming, high dive and hop, step and jump) which was the same tally as one American swimmer. His name was John Weissmuller and during his career he won five Olympic gold medals and set 67 world records. He would later ditch the swimming and go on to Hollywood where he made twelve films as Tarzan and thirteen as Jungle Jim. Weissmuller's last film was called 'Won Ton Ton, the Dog Who Saved Hollywood', which opened (and probably closed) in 1976.

Another Olympian of the time who would have a future link to Hollywood was the 400m gold medal winner, Eric Liddell. He might have won more races over his career but due to religious beliefs, he refused to run on a Sunday. Liddell's journey to the Olympics was told in a feature film, *Chariots of Fire*. But there was another athlete from 1924 who succeeded at the Games but shunned the spotlight. The Finnish runner Paavo Nurmi finished with five gold medals and went on to become a businessman, share trader and eventually one of Finland's richest men. Before he died, he declared that compared to science and art, sports were a waste of time.

Christmas approached and looking at the ever-expanding O'Brien and Kingdom families, perhaps their thoughts to shopping for presents. But where to go? In early December, a man aptly named Percy Christmas opened a new store in Sydney's Imperial Arcade. He claimed that "every man, woman and child needs a handy place where good things are cheap". The STUPENDOUS BARGAIN BASEMENT was originally called WALLWORTH'S BAZAAR but Percy discovered that the name WOOLWORTHS had not been registered in Australia. All

Mr Christmas's Christmases had come at once – he changed the name to Woolworths and the rest is history.

There was some serious advertising for the grand opening –

> 'Woolworths is where goods are so cheap, variety so vast and shopping so easy and pleasant, that Sydney will wonder how it has managed to get along without this Stupendous Bargain Basement. In a few days, shopping folk will have forgotten pre-Woolworth days with their hurry-scurry search for bargains from one end of the city to the other.'[1]

So what was on sale? Full breakfast-size cups and saucers – favourite white and gold pattern, sixpence; tumblers, 6 for 1/6; Lightning bread saws, 1/11; all-hair brooms, 2/9; good quality vests, 2/9; 2 pin tin kettles, 1s; 9" scrub brushes, 6d; 4oz jar of Vaseline (should be in every household for sunburn, sprains and skin diseases), 6d; enamel wash basins, 1/6; stainless knives, 1/9 and Fuji-silk bloomers at 6/9. And not only could you buy some of these exciting goods but – 'Assistants will wrap, give change and information'. What more could you want?

Well, I'll tell you. A visit to the Supply Stores, Limited, Pitt-street would present you with a display of women's xylonite hair brushes, 5/11; Jicky perfume, 7/11; Art Silk Ribbed Sports Hose, 3/6; embroidered 12 button length Lisle gloves, 3/11½ a pair; Gloria umbrellas, 7/11; Colgate's Cashmere Bouquet toilet soap, 1/7½ and leather collar boxes at 7/6.

Not floating your boat? How about the Hub, Limited, Pitt-street? Down to the toy basement for boats on wheels at 2/11; train sets with rails, 4/11; life-size tortoises, 2/6; whirling aeroplanes, 4d; clown and dog set, 4½d; cricket bats, 2/3; grey-painted toy horse on wheels, 2/11½; teddy bears at 2/11 or a bucket and spade for the beach would set you back 7½ pence.

For the discerning adult, a visit to Mark Foy's would see them perusing over copper jardinières, 12/6; brass dinner gongs, 24/9; oak crumb trays and brush, 6/9; French pearl necklets, 3/3½; curling tongs,

---

1. *Sydney Morning Herald*, 5th December 1924

1/0½; Tetlow's Pussy Willow talc powder at 2/6 or fancy boxes of powder with a lamb's wool puff at 2/11.

If that was all too hard, you might just want to sit down with a good book. Pop into Dymock's Book Arcade at 428 George-street and browse through the exhilarating titles on offer. *My Wanderings and Memories* by Lady Norah Bentinck, 19s; *Savage Life in Central Australia* by G. Horne and G. Aston, 22/6; *Head Hunters of the Amazon,* F.W. deGraaf, 10/; *New Friends in Old Chester,* Margaret Deland, 5/6; *The Lunatic Still at Large,* J. Storer Clousten, 5/6; *An Outpost Wooing,* Nora K. Strange, 5/6 and the classic *Selected Poems from the Indian Love Lyrics of Laurence Hope* was on offer at a bargain price of 6/6.

24. Hello Mother, Hello Father

'Gr - Gr – rr - r.'

An unusual way to start an advertisement, you would think.

'Don't let your starter Grr-owl out its Morning Hymn of Hate.'

It's getting stranger.

'Your engine needs a highly volatile motor spirit to enable it to start up at the first jump of a spark. You want to avoid the delay, the annoyance, the undue strain on the battery caused by that repeated Grr-Grr-Grr. When you use Plume, the highly volatile motor spirit, you start with a smile.'

Motor cars were Grr-owling and Australians were Grr-inning as the interest in these vehicles was Grr-owing. In fact, 1925 was the year that the International Motor Show opened in Melbourne's Exhibition Building. I imagine that very few of the Kingdom and O'Brien clans clambered for tickets but thousands of others did. And what were those thousands of others be looking at?

'The splendid new Peugeot Cabriolet is the ladies [sic] ideal car for visiting, shopping and golfing and has the record petrol consumption of not less than 60 miles per gallon. £290 complete.'

'The new Willys-Knight £450. Vibrationless. Absolutely.'

Or the 10/15 hp Fiat Standard single-seater at £445; a 14/40 hp 4cyl Sunbeam Colonial double-seater at £850; Pierce-Arrow 2 passenger Roadster touring car at £960; Oakland Six Australian 5 passenger tourer at £395 or a Ford Universal 5 passenger touring car at £192/10 might impress the neighbours when it sits in your driveway. And of course, your new car not only had to look good, it hard to run smoothly –

'Barnet Glass Balloon Tyres have been thoroughly tested by the Yellow Cab Service and they have been given such perfect service that the next entire shipment of 50 cabs arriving shortly in Melbourne are to be fitted with Barnet Glass Balloon Tyres.'

The excitement of the motor car led to more excitement which was reported in *The Age* of 1/5/1925 -

'In Australia, which is not a manufacturing country, the motor business has assumed large proportions. The turnover in this industry during 1924 was, including the local manufactures of tyres, accessories and bodies was £41,000,000. Although not yet a manufacturing country for chassis, Australia is competing with the world's best in all other phases of motor manufacture. Australian tyres are at least equal to imported ones. It also turns out springs, accumulators, electrical equipment and general accessories which have nothing to blush about when compared to similar articles from overseas. More cars mean greater production which in turn means cheaper cars, and we cannot have motor cars too cheap.'

The article went on to report that Ford had purchased land in Geelong with a view to establishing a factory. It was expected that it would provide a great deal of employment.

Nothing lasts forever.

1925 was the year that Adolf Hitler promised Bavarian authorities that his Nazi party would not use any force and only obtain political power through legal processes. Also, German, French and Belgian leaders signed an agreement that they would never go to war against each other again.

Again – nothing lasts forever.

There is one final event to mention in 1925 – the birth of a son to William and Frances O'Brien. My father had entered the world, a native of the thriving village of Tempe, New South Wales. He was baptised at St Peter's and St Paul's Church – his name, the same as his great-grandfather, was John.

1926 arrived with a spark as electrical appliances became more widespread. John Logie Baird demonstrated the invention he had been tinkering with in his back shed. The device was able to transmit moving pictures via a wireless signal. He called it 'television' and he predicted that one day every home could turn into a moving picture theatre.

It was also the year that Sydney's first electrical train clattered down the tracks in a journey between Central Station and Mortdale. The train had six carriages and was able to offer up to 80 more passenger seats than a steam locomotive. On paper, it was also faster than a steam locomotive - in reality, it couldn't run any faster as the existing steam trains were in the way.

Australian households were filling with the new electrical appliances which changed domestic life. Hecla Electronics boasted that over 100,000 electric fires were in use and the company had seen increases in the sales of kettles, grillers, cookers, hot water services and stoves. Electric irons were used in nearly every home and there were about 20,000 vacuum cleaners in use in Sydney.

> 'Lighten household duties by investing wisely in Electrical Aids. Apart from their labour-saving qualities, they are so clean, efficient and economical – if purchased at Anthony Hordern's.

> ELECTRICAL KETTLES - Price 45/-.
> RAPID HOT-WATER JUG Will boil water for tea in a few minutes - Price 37/6.
> HOT POINT ELECTRIC TOASTER – Will make delicious crisp toast right at your breakfast table – Price 45/-.
> HECLA ELECTRIC STOVE – The most efficient and economical medium for cooking, beautifully clean and dependable – Price £18/17/6.
> HECLA GEM GRILLER – Will boil, fry, grill and toast. A perfect boon for the busy housewife – Price 38/6.'[1]

In today's money, the busy housewife would be paying a lot for her perfect boon. The kettle and the toaster equate to around $151- each; the hot water jug $125-; the griller would be $129- and the stove comes in at around $1260-.

Then, some women in that year weren't satisfied with being just a busy housewife. The famed Russian ballerina Anna Pavlova toured Australia; American Gertrude Ederle became the first woman to swim the English Channel; Irish woman Violet Gibson attempted to shoot Benito Mussolini but only grazed his nose and Beryl Lucy Mills won the inaugural Miss Australia Quest.

From my research, it appears that my family never lived in the Eastern Suburbs with its lovely coastal beaches … and maybe that is just as well:

> 'Is it the reports of sharks which pay periodical visits to Coogee or are bathers becoming aware that more than a fair amount of sewage gets washed into this beautiful little bay?'[2]

And in a letter to the *Evening News* of February 27th:

---

1. *Sydney Morning Herald*, 12th January 1926
2. *Sunday Times*, 26th January 1926

'Visitors to our Queen City behold the vilest of all stenches – sewer gas. This blows full blast onto Bondi, wafted by the prevailing summer northeaster. The flotsam and jetsam pollute our beaches and they are covered with a heterogenous mass of filth.'

Oh dear. It's worth noting that at this time, English author A. A. Milne published the first volume of children's stories about the adventures of a teddy bear. So maybe one could have sat on Bondi or Coogee Beach, reading the new book *Winnie-the-Pooh* while surrounded by the whiff of poo.

It was a year that between 10 and 100 Aboriginals were massacred in Western Australia over the death of a white settler. The exact number is unknown; if the census didn't count indigenous people when they were alive, no-one was going to count them when they were dead. Meanwhile, in America, the homicide rate was reported to be 387 for the year. In 2013, the amount of people killed by guns in that country was an average of three … per hour.

1927 saw the introduction of child endowment in New South Wales – a bit late for John O'Brien and Ellen Cunningham, but never mind. Mothers would be paid 5 shillings ($16-50) per week per child up to 14 years old. This would be extended to 16 if the child was unable to earn a wage. No doubt that this became very useful in a period of high unemployment. At the same time, Sydney City Council was paying rat-catchers 12/6 ($44-) for each rat caught. So dead rats were worth more than live children. Parents probably sent their little darlings out for a pleasurable afternoon, killing rodents.

There was a big party down in Canberra when Parliament House opened. The crowd was estimated to be 30,000 – minus one Aboriginal man who came to watch but was deemed inadequately dressed and was asked to leave. Dame Nellie Melba warbled the national anthem 'God Save The King' and was heard by all. But the speechmakers, Prince Albert, Duke of York and Prime Minister Stanley Bruce were drowned out by the noise of the aerial display. And if the noise of the planes wasn't bad enough, the celebration was marred when one of the participating planes crashed. Sadly, the pilot died later in hospital. The plane crashed a short distance behind the refreshment marquee and the distinguished guests were unaware of the tragedy. The disaster could have been worse – if the plane had landed on Prince Albert, it would have changed the future of the British monarchy. Albert would later go on to become King George VI, Queen Elizabeth's father.

It's a reasonable thought that there was some imbibing of alcohol after all the official rigmarole was over, but one hopes they didn't party to the late hours. It seems NSW was going through a crisis with working out just how late you could drown your sorrows till. An earlier referendum had seen the passing of a law in 1916 that made licensed premises close at 6.00pm. As most businesses and workplaces closed at 5.00pm, this led to what was known as the 'six o'clock swill'. Workers would rush to their local and drink as much as possible in the hour before closing. No doubt, this would have affected the O'Brien side of the tree.

But hang on, said the restaurants and the hotels that served food – our customers want to have an alcoholic beverage with their dinner and most of them come in after 6.00pm. They wanted an extension to their liquor licensing hours which allowed them to serve booze until 9.00pm. The matter went to the NSW parliament who debated it for days. The prohibitionists said 'no', the morally unrestricted said 'yes'. They came to an agreement that provided a meal was served, the establishment could serve alcohol until 9.00pm. They even defined what a meal was, just in case there was any confusion – 'A meal was at least two courses which the persons partaking thereof should be seated at a table, the meal to include fish or meats, other than in sandwich form, and cooked vegetables'.

Once that brilliant definition was reached, another chap stood up and asked whether the meal should be consumed or was it enough for a licensee to say that he was prepared to serve it. Oh dear.

The breweries just stuck to appealing to the lunch crowd –

> 'The midday lunch is often the opportunity for an informal business conference – it sees the development of commercial schemes or the diplomatic sounding of the friendly opposition. On each occasions [sic] he is wise who keeps his mind active and thoughts clear by the judicious selection of his luncheon liquor. Sparkling 'K.B.' combines

the attractive qualities of a refreshing beverage with a gently stimulating action … TOOTH'S K.B. It's a true lager.'[3]

I should also point out that in this year of 1927, David Kirkpatrick was born. He would go on to be known as Slim Dusty and one of his future hit songs would not have sounded the same if he used the verbosity of his youth – 'I like to have a refreshing beverage with a gently stimulating action … with Duncan.'

A blazing gun battle in a Victorian bedroom saw the death of a notorious gangster, Joe 'Squizzy' Taylor; a Sydney ferry named *Greycliffe* was cut in half by a liner on the harbour and 40 people were killed; the Queensland government authorised the slaughter of over 500,000 koalas and twice as many possums while in Canberra, the Clerk of Federal Parliament suffered a stroke while handing a paper to the Speaker of the House of Representatives. He later died from the stroke. Ironically the paper he was delivering was a formal confirmation of the death of his predecessor. The year also saw the birth of Peter Cundall, gardener and television presenter and that's your bloomin' lot for 1927.

I am curious as to how my female ancestors would have handled 1928. An early report decreed that 'modern women who have independence through careers, sit at the wheels of motor cars and smoke on all occasions was causing distractions to men'. In London, the Women's Wear Exhibition introduced a new fashion which would have caused distraction – gold and silver skullcaps. These were worn so they would cover the ears as well as the hair. Apparently, the trend for women's hair was wearing it shorter and the idea was to achieve a 'young boyish look'. Playwright George Bernard Shaw said the new fashion was 'dressing as a real human being rather than upholstery for Victorian angels'. But elsewhere in the world, not everyone was happy. The German Post office banned skirts shorter than 8" below the knee and international confectioners complained that the 'slimming craze' was making them go broke.

It seems that the Germans were taking the 'slimming craze' to extreme levels –

---

3. *Maitland Daily Mercury,* 3rd February 1927

'In Germany, at a home in the country for slimming, the women follow the lettuce treatment which has proved most ineffectual. Dishes of fresh lettuce are laid on a table … and patients are urged to eat as much of the vegetable by itself as they possibly can, the first thing in the morning, with the primary meals and again the last thing at night.'[4]

We here in Australia had other ideas for weight loss –

'Three lots of Epsom salts baths a week, followed by a brisk rub-down with a loofah, sprinkled with eau-de-cologne, is supposed to have great slimming results.'[5]

In America, they had ideas on how to improve other aspects of yourself –

'In New York, the fruit breakfast cure is chiefly in the ascendant today for improving the complexion. No food whatever must pass the lips save fruit until the middle of the day … children may have a basin of chopped bananas with milk instead of bread … carrots may be served in various ways and perhaps the most appetising is carrot mash. Carrot salad is good and raw carrot may be grated over white soup or sauce … it gives an attractive look to the dish … Onions, too! South Sea Islanders who live on nothing but onions are said to have the most dazzling complexions of any people on the face of the map.'[6]

So, there you have it. Soak yourself in a bath of Epsom salts and scoff down a big plate of lettuce with onions and mashed carrot and you will be skinny and radiant. But why all this fuss? A glimpse of the Hollywood news in the *Sunday Mail* on October 3rd might have the answer –

---

4. *The Sun,* 8th July 1928
5. Ibid.
6. Ibid.

'For a year, the perfect Joan Crawford lived under a system of the strictest diet and reducing exercises. Producers saw that she was pounds overweight and would have to lose those pounds before she would even get a part. Toast, lamb chops, pineapple and spinach constituted her monotonous diet for months but she was successful and is now one of the fairest exponents of the boyish figure.

Practically all Hollywood contracts contain one clause relative to weight. A player must keep within a margin and if she goes beyond that limit, the company is permitted to break the contract, though in the case of a very popular star, she is given so many months to reduce. Even those who are well within the margin diet for the sake of their complexions, for producers know too well that one blemish on a leading lady's face can hold up production for days at the cost of hundreds of dollars.'

Well, really. Ninety years later, you wouldn't see young ladies starve themselves just so they can be an attractive celebrity, would you? Oh … hang on …
Anyway, once you had thinned yourself down and you looked like a boy with anaemia and had flatulence like an old carthorse, you could race down to the shops (providing you had the energy) and purchase the latest in swimwear – Speedos!
'Speedo Bathing Costumes – This is a fine knit, all-wool cashmere costume in plains shades – Vieux Rose, Saxe, Green, Navy & Black one-piece costume with skirt – Priced from 7/11 to 9/11.'
These cossies, which would be priced around $26 - $35 today - would go nicely with the terry-towelling surf cape, the rubber surf belt and oiled silk bathing cap, which were also available for purchase.
While 1928 was a big year for trying not to be big, it was a big year for aviation as well. Bert Hinkler flew solo from London to Darwin; it only took 15 days. Charles Kingsford Smith became the first to fly across the Pacific Ocean; his journey from the USA to Brisbane took eight days. Neither pilot had satellite navigation, in-flight entertainment or Frequent Flyer points. The Federal government awarded Kingsford

Smith £5000 ($335,000) for his efforts. At the same time, the NSW government gave local councils a grant of £10,000 ($670,000) to be used to pay for relief work by the jobless.

In world affairs, the jobless figure was reduced with several key regal and political appointments. Ahmet Muhtar Zogoli was proclaimed King Zog 1 of Albania, beginning a fairly unpopular reign in which he survived over 50 assassination attempts. Hirohito was confirmed as the 124th Emperor of Japan, beginning a reasonably unpopular reign in which he survived several assassination attempts and World War II. Herbert Clark Hoover was swept into power as the President of the USA, beginning a reasonably unpopular term, in which there were no assassination attempts but a man carrying dynamite was arrested when he approached him. Stanley Melbourne Bruce continued on as Prime Minister of Australia; there were no assassination attempts on him (if you don't count the fact that he was shot while serving in WWI), however his father and two of his brothers committed suicide. Oh and a horse named Statesman won the Melbourne Cup.

As 1929 flicked into life, it was clear that since the arrival of my ancestors in Australia, the quality of entertainment available had improved. Gone were the days of sitting around a candle, singing songs of the homeland. The Tivoli Theatre in Sydney was packing them in with such treats as Martin, Florence and Martin, jugglers of racquets, balls, Indian clubs and hoops; Edgar Benyon the contortionist; the Dancing Danburys and Koko San, a singer from Japan who sang in English and Yiddish. Other theatres were showing the latest 'talkies' – motion pictures in which you could hear the actors speak. People flocked to see 'Dracula', 'The Canary Murder Case', 'Wolf Song' and 'The Jazz Singer'. Many actors saw their careers die with the advent of talkies; while they looked glamorous on the screen, their speaking voices were considered unpleasant and no-one wanted to hear them, or their accent was unintelligible, and no-one could understand them.

Fox Films delivered a truck to Australia that would carry the first mobile sound picture equipment around the country. The expensive load was shipped in a vehicle that was called a REO Speedwagon. So, I can't fight this feeling that the truck could pick up the equipment and take it on the run.

Life in the Past Lane

In early June, as winter rain poured down, a crowd was gathering in Sydney's Market-street early one morning. Newspapers of the time indicate that there were several hundred people gathered by 7.30am and the line stretched into George-street. By 9.00am, there were over 500 – so what was happening? They were queued to obtain tickets for the first week's seats at the new State Theatre. The building was advertised rather ambitiously by its management as the 'greatest building in the British Empire'. People would enter the theatre and be amazed by the Grand Assembly with the two marble staircases leading to the top dress circle. Once seated in the theatre which held 3000 people, they could gaze in awe at the monstrous three-and-a-half-ton chandelier hanging from the roof – and presumably praying that it would stay there.

The theatre opened on the 7th in what the press described as 'a gay scene' and we must remember that these were more innocent times. Dignitaries included the acting premier, Ernest Buttenshaw, Governor-General Lord Stonehaven and state Governor Sir Dudley de Chair. Mr Buttenshaw was quoted as saying that when he entered the theatre, he thought he would have a great deal to say but when he saw the interior, he could find no words. This probably would have brought a round of applause. The opening night featured a 'talkie' with Al Jolson who introduced actors speaking about the building. It was followed by a film called 'The Patriot' starring Emil Jannings - who would go on to win the first ever Best Actor Oscar and then feature in pro-Nazi propaganda films. There was also orchestral music with Price Dunlavy soloing on the Wurlitzer organ and some artistic dancing.

It's just as well that Sydney had the theatre. Other forms of entertainment just weren't cutting it. The best-selling song of the year was 'Tiptoe Through the Tulips'; writer, C. Hartley Grattan penned 'literature is not an intimate concern of the Australian' and the Minister for Education advised that 'too much knowledge would result in the production of misfits'.

It was a year for the birth of many future entertainers. Brian Wenzel (actor), Ernie Carroll (TV personality and voice of Ossie the Ostrich), June Bronhill (opera singer), Reg Lindsay (country music singer) and Bob Hawke (made people laugh) all opened their eyes to the world.

Away from showbiz, there were some mumblings about immigration and the high level of unemployment. During the previous year, a poster had been on display in England –

> The Southern cross – the stars which shine over Australia; the land of opportunity. The call of the stars to British men and women. Men for the land, women for the home, employment guaranteed, good wages, plenty of opportunity.

But like a photo of a hamburger in a fast food outlet, the reality was somewhat disappointing. A Mr E. West wrote to the *Australian Worker* newspaper –

> 'Thirty shillings a week and keep sounds attractive to the prospective migrant who is unemployed in his native land, so he decides to come to this 'Land of Golden Opportunity' and partake of the milk and honey with which is it reputed to be overflowing.
>
> He arrives in Australia (where there are already many thousands of unemployed) and receives a job at 15/- to 25/- per week and keep (one must have experience or be very fortunate to receive 30/-) and thus, keeps a former employee, who has refused to be 'sweated' out of employment.
>
> The migrant's only chance of securing employment is by accepting the lower rate of pay and by doing so, he automatically gives the employer more power with which to oppress him.
>
> The migrant, having accepted the low wage, eventually realises the folly of his action with disastrous results. He becomes dissatisfied and drifts to the city to become a unit of the great unemployed masses.'

It's interesting to note that nearly 90 years later, an article written by Ben Doherty in *The Guardian* addressed an issue that South Koreans were facing –

> 'They are young, some overseas for the first time … lured to Australia with promises of fun and sun, good well-paying jobs, a chance to study or a working holiday. Instead they find themselves housed in overcrowded hovels, indentured to labour in construction, late-night cleaning or restaurants, under brutal conditions and for as little as $9-an hour.'

So not everyone has found the milk and honey or the golden opportunities, but back in 1929 one Scottish migrant thought she had. Annie McFettridge Craig, from Port Glasgow, married Herbert Kingdom, grandson of old George Kingdom. She had just arrived in time – the Federal government suspended migration to Australia around the same time that they married. And as they were my second set of grandparents, it's probably lucky for me, too.

No-one knows what is going to happen in the future but as 1930 rolled into place, some learned fellows thought they would share their predictions for the future. One of them, Roger W. Babson, a famous American statistician, had previously predicted that 1929 would be a year of prosperity. In fact, it was the year of the Black Friday stock market crash in the USA which led to the Great Depression felt around the world. So what other gems did Mr Babson share?

He started well by saying that with television, we would be able to carry on conversations across continents and oceans. He also suggested that two-deck streets would evolve, and cars would be constructed with automatic gearboxes. However, he also said that those cars would be able to move sideways as well as forward and backwards. His predictions also included: aviation would never become practical until the perfection of the helicopter then every house would have a hangar; a miracle ray would be developed which restored life to dead things that had been frozen; men's suits would be made from paper and purchased from vending machines (although to be fair, he did add that he didn't think these would be very popular) and then there is my favourite one – you would be able to purchase tins of sunlight so you could store away heat for a future use.

A French scientist claimed there would be manned flights to the moon within 15 years – he was a bit out. A professor of astronomical physics at Princeton University said that it would be another century before that happened and when it did, his spaceship would weigh 70,000 tons, carry 72 scientists and engineers, and use dozens of cannons for its propulsion – well, he shouldn't have been let out.

Lord Birkenhead, in his report entitled 'The World in 2030', also shared his thoughts. He suggested that stereoscopic television, in natural colours, would enable a Test match in Australia to be seen with perfect clearness in London. He also opined that agriculture would be superseded by chemically-made food and that human beings will be created in a laboratory. But unfortunately, he kept going – parliamentary debates would be heard by everyone and end in a national vote by all electors within 20 minutes; there would be one week's work to three weeks leisure time for everyone; there would be a practical abolition of all disease; a federation of Europe would be formed which would transcend all nationalities and aeroplanes would supersede motor cars except for shopping and picnics. Yes, I can see some difficulties in landing your Cessna in the Coles car park.

There is one thing that didn't need any predicting in 1930 and that was the Australian unemployment rate. It reached 20% and newspaper reports indicated the streets were swarming with buskers trying to earn a bob, people selling trinkets and children going door-to-door selling possessions. At night they would return to hessian shacks in parks, camp out in sand dunes or even in caves. Houses stood empty as unemployed people shared accommodation. Many suffered psychological issues while the police stated that arrests for petty theft had increased. But we weren't alone – New Zealand had introduced a flat-rate tax to cover the cost of unemployment and England's figure had doubled. There is a famous photograph of a man in the street, wearing a sandwich board that reads – 'I know 3 trades, speak 3 languages, I fought for 3 years, I have 3 children, and no work for 3 months but I only want 1 job'.

The *Newcastle Sun* of 1930 suggested that our troubles had been caused by excessive borrowing and excessive buying of necessities and luxuries from overseas. The country needed to rely more on what we made ourselves rather than importing from other countries. The Federal government then introduced a sales tax which was to be paid on all goods manufactured in Australia with exemptions granted for goods exported for sale. The local product, which everyone wanted you to buy, had just become dearer.

In news about another local product, at Nurse Austin's Private Hospital in Armidale, a child was born to Herbert Kingdom, 26-year-old Royal Australian Naval steward and Annie Craig, formerly of Scotland. She was christened Jean Nance Kingdom – yes, you're right, my mother had arrived in the world. As she was wrapped in swaddling clothes and taken home, a 5-year-old boy named John O'Brien may have been playing in the streets of Tempe, hundreds of kilometres away. He would have been quite oblivious to Jean's birth; indeed, it would take some 30 years for him to acknowledge her birthday but when he finally did, he did it for the rest of his life.

I will end the story here. My mother's days had just begun and there was a whole world for her to explore. For other members of my family, their days were continuing. It's only fitting that I have a look at what was on offer, one last day in all their lives - the *Sydney Morning Herald* for New Year's Eve, 1930, will be our guide.

E. F. Wilks and Co, Ltd, 124 Castlereagh-street, had a sale on 70 slightly-used pianos. From £2 ($134-) deposit.

Mt Cook Tourist Co. of New Zealand, 9a Bligh-street, offered a special summer tour of New Zealand. 24 days from Sydney, 17 days in New Zealand. £58- ($3886-).

Anthony Hordern and Sons, Pitt-street, had John Bull Polishing Mops for 3/6 ($11.75) and a steak-and-kidney pie lunch with mashed potato for 10d ($2.80).

Hoyts Regent Theatre presented the 'Brilliant Oriental Pantomime – The Wedding of Tee Nee Sing', with 70 stars on stage, including a 'troupe of Chinese Kiddie Acrobats'.

Penrith Speedway, 74 racing motorcycles and 20 whizzing cars, admission 2/5 ($8.10).

Johnston's Musical Instrument Store, 211 George-street, had banjo mandolins at 45/- ($150.75) and musical saws at 30/- ($100.00).

Barker College, Hornsby, day and boarding school for boys. Modern classrooms, central heating, open-air sleeping and spacious oval.

Government Savings Bank of NSW, interest on savings accounts – 4% up to £1000.00. 192 branches, 644 agencies.

Radio station 2GB. 11.00am, Women's radio service, Mrs Dorothy Jordan. Recipes, Miss Ruth Furst. Toilet hints, Mrs Jordan. Music and community singing.

Purchase fuel from your local dealer whom you know to be honest. Use Red Union in a super spirit branded in every drop – protected from the refinery to your car – guaranteed to impart to your engine a cleaner, smoother, and non-detonating action.

Price of gold in London was quoted at 85/1 ($285.03).

Willoughby Council has banned the playing of mini-golf on a Sunday.

The Australian Museum announced a growing number of visitors and its outstanding achievements during the year included the restoration of the head of a large, extinct lizard and the installation of a large model of a milk termite nest.

Spencer Nolan, dentist, 28 Oxford-street. 'Send for particulars of my method for making of teeth by post'.

And so, life rolled on.

25. Remarkable Times

My family have lived in this country for nearly 180 years. The separation from homeland was a daunting prospect for my early ancestors. Some of them chose to gamble with their lives. The dice rolled – some people won, some lost their shirt.

Life unfolded around these people, as life does. It was thrilling, it was frightening, it was good, it was bad. When we look at some of the unfortunate events and concepts that happened in this period of history, we are glad that they are no longer an event or a concept today. Yet, some of them still are. You can't learn from your mistakes if you don't fix them.

If I traced my O'Brien and Kingdom family heritage all the way back to the times of Brian Boru, I would have uncovered 2,147,483,648 ancestors – and this book would be really, really, big. But I have only gone back to the 1830s. This incorporates only 16 ancestral links. Scientists say that I possess about 6% of each of those ancestor's DNA. The family tree isn't the jigsaw puzzle – I am.

These 16 people – with surnames of O'Brien, Kingdom, Cunningham, McAuliffe, O'Grady, Carroll, Skehan, O'Shea x 2, Elliott, Doyle, Cappel, Craig, McFettridge, Freeburn and Rogerson – all had at least four siblings. That adds up to 80 people. These 80 people married (mostly) and had children ,,. who married and had children … who married and had children. I am related to the whole bloody lot of them. I hope they all never come around for Christmas lunch – I don't have enough room.

To make it even more interesting, *Traces* magazine, Vol.3, stated there had been some new research from Ancestry.co UK. It revealed that Irish people, including Irish Australians, might have as many as 14,000 living cousins. These numbers include genetic eighth cousins or closer, based on ancestors who have lived during the last 200 years.

So many people, so many lives.

But that's it, isn't it? They were lives. They sailed in ships and rode horses and built houses and lost money and saw new technology come and old monarchs go. They breathed and drank and slept and watered their gardens and kicked the dog under the table when it farted and sang songs and told stories to their children.

In this day and age, when they tell you that 'your call is very important to us' but really, you are a number and a password with eight characters, you need to know that you are alive. In 200 years, when some family genealogist researches me, I hope they look beyond the dates of my birth and death.

Because I lived, too. I lived in remarkable times … just like my family did before me.

Appendix - Unfortunate Creatures

In 1817, a ship named the *Sir William Bentley* sailed into Port Jackson carrying a motley assortment of transported convicts. One of the convicts was Robert Henry Dye, a twenty-five year old baker from Norfolk. He was 5 foot 10 inches tall and had light brown hair, blue eyes and a fair complexion. He was the recipient of a fourteen-year transportation sentence, having been convicted of passing forged bank notes in London. His future was grim and becoming grimmer – as soon as he arrived in Sydney, he was put onto another ship, the *Elizabeth Henrietta*. He was being sent to Port Dalrymple in Van Diemen's Land or as we know it today, Launceston in Tasmania.

At some stage afterwards, he was transferred to Hobart. Dye stayed out of trouble for nine months before being caught stealing four cartwheels from a Mr Peters, which he then set fire to – the wheels, not Mr Peters. For that crime, in December of 1817, he received a twelve month sentence which he would spend breaking up rocks with a gaol gang. This obviously didn't meet with his approval as six months later, he and five other men stole two government boats in an attempt to escape. They were found 'lurking about' in a cove on the Derwent River. For his trouble, Dye received 100 lashes and a three-year transportation order to Newcastle. This was the penal colony that the crims wanted to avoid – the worst of the worst were despatched there and it was known as a hellhole. But Dye's fate could have been worse:

'The lenity shown the misguided men whose daring and atrocious crime might have been made a capital felony and caused the forfeiture of their lives, we sincerely hope will operate as a warning to others.[1]

Robert Henry Dye was put on to the *Lady Nelson* with his fellow miscreants and despatched northwards. The Governor of Van Diemen's Land had sent a letter to the commandant of Newcastle with the ship. He advised him of the ship's load of cedar and prisoners with special mention of Dye and his mates. They were described as being 'pirates from Van Diemen's Land, to be kept at the settlement, wrought in double irons and to be strictly watched, as they were dangerous and desperate characters'.

Two years later a lady arrived at Port Jackson. She sailed in on a ship called the *Lord Wellington,* having earned a fourteen-year tour in New South Wales. Her name was Sarah Horton (sometimes spelled Orton) and she was five foot tall, with a fair complexion, dark hair and hazel eyes. She had initially been sentenced to hang for the crime of forging bank notes. Sarah received a reprieve from the gallows and her punishment was commuted to transportation. She appears to have left behind a husband and possibly two children, however she did have one family member with her – her daughter, Louisa, aged 6, had been allowed to accompany her. Upon arrival, Sarah was one of 40 women sent to the Female Factory at Parramatta. Fourteen of the women had at least one child with them.

By 1822, Robert Dye and Sarah Horton had both turned up in Sydney. It's possible that Robert knew Sarah in England – perhaps it was her dodgy 'tom and funny' he was handing out. In July 1822 the pair applied to be married – Sarah with apparent disregard for her husband back in England.

A year later, Dye was in trouble again but this time he had a new accomplice – his blushing bride. Their offence was having stolen goods in their possession. Dye was ordered to complete his original sentence at the penal colony of Port Macquarie, while Sarah received two years back at Parramatta. Shortly afterwards, a letter was written on their behalf

---

1. *The Hobart Town Gazette and Southern Reporter,* 23rd May 1818

to the Governor, Sir Thomas Brisbane. It requested that Sarah (and presumably Louisa) be allowed to join her husband at Port Macquarie. In the letter, Dye was described as being 'truly penitent for his past offences' and had actually been made a Constable by the commanding officer of Port Macquarie.

Sir Thomas was obviously impressed as he approved the transfer. While Sarah sat in Sydney Gaol, awaiting conveyance to Port Macquarie, she found someone else to write a letter for her. This time she petitioned the Colonial Secretary for a day release – she asked if she could be let out, in the company of a constable, to make 'some necessary purchases at the most reasonable prices'. After some 19th-century retail therapy, she sailed off to join Robert.

By 1827, Robert Henry Dye and his beloved had returned to Sydney. He had apparently found being 'truly penitent' boring and had decided to go back to being 'dangerous and desperate'. At the General Court Sessions of Sydney in April, Robert and Sarah were convicted of being in possession of stolen property again. Dye copped an eighteen-month shift on a road gang while Sarah was sent back to Parramatta for twelve months. Louisa may have gone with her or the alternatives are just as pleasant – she might have been already working or if not, she was probably sent to the Destitute Asylum.

By the time of the 1828 census, Sarah had found herself a lawful occupation and she and Louisa were listed as working in a dressmakers' establishment at Darling Harbour. Robert was still on the iron gang and that would be his career until 29 May 1830, when Robert Henry Dye was granted his Certificate of Freedom. On the certificate, his left hand is described as being tattooed with an anchor so maybe he had developed an interest in sailing. He had clearly developed an interest in business as he became the publican of the Bee Hive Inn in Cumberland-street, The Rocks, in June of 1831. Now he and Sarah could build a happy life together.

Three months after he took over the Bee Hive, a man named Richard Campbell took out an ad in the *Sydney Gazette*, warning everyone not to buy property from Robert Dye. It appears Dye was trying to sell Campbell's property by passing it off as his own. The old criminal habits had come back – that's if they ever left.

Sometime in the next two years, he acquired a schooner and called it *Farewell*. In April of 1833, a robbery on the schooner was reported and 'various sundry articles' were taken. Nine days later, a Joseph Burns or Kearns was indicted for stealing a jacket from Dye. Was he a target or did events just speak of the company he kept? Around the same time, it appears that Dye was trying to sell the Bee Hive Inn. In the classified advertisement, he does send out a warning –

> 'I request that all persons indebted to me will immediately settle the accounts to prevent further trouble.'[2]

But apparently, this only worked one way. A fortnight later, Hannibal Cordoy, the captain of Mr Dye's vessel, *Farewell*, had reason to call on the publican at his residence. He had resigned from his position and was owed some back pay. He had requested payment from Dye on several occasions only to be offered an excuse and no money. Mr Cordoy had finally lost patience and called on Dye to collect what was owed. Robert greeted him at the door and told him that – 'I have no time for conversation with fellows such as you'. Mr Cordoy was taken aback by this rudeness and respectfully requested his wages. Robert Dye moved forward and punched Cordoy in the face, telling him – 'This is the way I pay my debts now'.

Unsurprisingly, poor old Hannibal wasn't pleased by this treatment and reported the matter to the 'ducks and geese'. Robert Dye was committed to stand trial. Several weeks later, the Attorney General and Justice Dowling were forced to seize the bail Dye had put forth and order further prosecution against him as he hadn't turned up for the trial. A short while after his court non-attendance, his ownership of the *Farewell* was looking shaky. A man named Andrew Sommerville sought financial recompense from the Sheriff as Dye owed him money. Robert Dye's world was collapsing around him – what was a man to do?

Dye took off.

In January of 1834, the schooner *Farewell* was said to be in South America. The craft was in the hands of a ragged crew of escaped convicts. Was Robert Henry Dye among these men? Well, not any

---

2. *The Sydney Monitor*, 6th March 1833

more. The crew reported that Mr Dye had 'died suddenly', fourteen days after leaving Sydney. Had he had a heart attack? Had he been bludgeoned and tossed over the side? Was he actually dead? The *Hobart Town Courier* of May 16 1834 had an opinion – 'The captain of the *Farewell* (Dye) was said to have died (most probably killed) on the passage and a convict named Wright had possession of her.'

We don't know what actually happened but whatever the story was, Robert's *Farewell* was his farewell. 'Full fathom five thy father lies … those are pearls that were his eyes.'

The grieving widow, Sarah, was left with no husband and a pub to run and soon there was more sadness. On 16 June 1834, her daughter Louisa died at the age of twenty. She had spent the majority of her childhood in prison with no real education and no real chance in life. She had probably forgotten what her birth father looked like, her mother was a habitual criminal and her stepfather was a pirate and a blackguard.

Sarah must have been devastated by her losses … but she recovered quickly. Six months after Robert's apparent death, she applied to marry a mariner by the name of William Cole. He was at least ten years younger than her. Less than four weeks later, they were hitched and in a further two months, Cole took over the publican's licence at the Bee Hive.

William then disappeared for twelve months before renewing the licence again. He applied to have the licence transferred to a new pub in Prince Street. It was perched high on the rocky outcrop above Argyle Street and it was situated perfectly to quench the thirsts of travellers who battled the weary climb – for this was before the Argyle Cut was created. Cole had been making money by transporting cedar and wool from the Clarence River area and it seemed to be time to invest in some real estate. He purchased some land on a quiet track in Millers Point – this track will end up being known as Argyle Place.

It was not all beer and skittles in the Bee Hive, though. In March of 1840, a gentleman entered the pub, somewhat inebriated, and proceeded to order more drink. Two soldiers, sitting at the bar, happened to notice that the gentleman was waving a lot of money around. The chap mentioned that he was concerned about getting home in one piece and the soldiers offered to be his guides. Of course, as soon as they had him outside the pub, they bopped him on the head and took his money. The police interviewed Sarah Cole and she stated that while she recognised the culprits, she wasn't going to the barracks to identify them.

Captain Cole looked to expand his business interests. He already owned a schooner named *Sally* – which quite coincidentally, is the same name of the vessel that transported Robert Dye to Port Macquarie. In 1841, Cole bought a brig named *Clarence.* This he would use for sailing to the southern seas and the lucrative whaling grounds. In time, he would hire captains and he would stay at home more, watching over his pub and accumulating more real estate. This 'retirement' probably saved him his life.

In October of 1843, the *Sally* was caught in a storm near Seal Rock and was shipwrecked. The captain, three crewmen and a passenger were drowned. One crewman survived by grabbing onto a piece of broken mast and floating ashore. Ten months later, the *Clarence* hit a reef on Bampton's Shoal, 1,000 kilometres east of Queensland. The captain gave the order to man the lifeboats and away they rowed. One boat containing the captain and a few crew members found land. While they attended to boat maintenance and the drying of clothes, a group of curious natives walked onto the beach. The natives made a fire and kept their distance – but not for long. During the night, the crew were attacked. One sailor was speared four times and the captain received a spear through the thigh. The natives ran away and the crew prepared to set off. Twelve days later (five of them without food) they arrived at Brisbane.

Let us move forward to 1848. Sarah Cole had been ailing and passed away in November. The funeral procession left the Cole's residence in Upper Fort Street for its journey to Camperdown cemetery. Meanwhile, just up Prince Street, not far from the Bee Hive, a young woman named Ellen Kennedy (nee O'Brien) had just given birth to her fourth child. She and her husband John christened the new baby, William. Ellen had been in the country for nine years after her family arrived here as sponsored Monteagle immigrants.

As we move forward, it seems that John Kennedy abandoned the family and sailed off to California in search of gold. Whether he did this with his wife's consent is unknown. What is known is that he definitely disappeared from the scene and he plays no further part in the drama. Ellen now had four young children (the eldest was 8 in 1850) and possibly no means of support. The 'promising new life' wasn't looking so promising. Perhaps, like many new arrivals, she drowned her sorrows in alcohol. After all, there were pubs down the road. She needed a job or a kindly benefactor. Possibly the publican in the Bee Hive might have a solution – and it appeared that he did.

In June of 1853, Ellen gave birth to a daughter. The father was listed as William Cole and the child was baptised as Susannah Kennedy Cole. They all lived in Lower Fort Street. A year later, a boy, William Sydney Cole was born (little William Kennedy had died in 1854) and eighteen months later, Emily Kennedy Cole entered the world.

On Christmas Eve 1855, William Cole Senior went to see his old friend, the solicitor James Naimby Shuttleworth. Perhaps William wasn't feeling very well as he had decided to write out his last will and testament. He appointed Shuttleworth, William Perry and George Hamilton as his executors. Over a short period of time, William Cole had built up quite an estate and he wanted to make sure his affairs were in order.

Mr Shuttleworth's affairs, on the other hand, were not in order. In January 1856, Shuttleworth acted as the official starter of the sculling and yacht races on Sydney Harbour. He probably enjoyed being out on the water as he could get away from his money problems. But those problems never really go away, do they? Three months later, he was in court – which is not unusual for a solicitor, but alas he was the one in strife. He had to file for insolvency with debts of £1,818 or around $136,000 today. He offered to pay his creditors in full over a period of time, adding 6% interest on the debt. This obviously wasn't successful – in June of 1856, an auction was held and Shuttleworth's extensive law library, office fixtures and fittings and 'various sundries' were put up for sale.

Two months after the auction, William Cole passed away. The attending physician Dr McKay advised his patient had died from the effects of gout. On 21 August 1856, Cole's funeral procession left his residence at 34 Lower Fort Street and solemnly made its way to Camperdown cemetery.

For all of his money and property, William Cole had kept away from the limelight. Maybe that is because William went to the grave with a secret – one, that if revealed, would destroy his good name.

When Cole married Sarah Dye back in 1834, it seems that he might have been already married. Back in 1819, in London's Middlesex district of Stepney, a young man named Henry Thomas Cole married a girl called Elizabeth McDonald. He would have seven children with her before disappearing in the early 1830's – around the time that William Cole appeared on the Sydney scene. In the 1841 census, Elizabeth described herself as a widow. She may have believed that to be the case or she was acting under the 7-year rule. Whatever the reason, there is considerable evidence that Henry Thomas Cole and William Cole were the same man, as will be shown shortly.

Eight days after Cole's funeral, Shuttleworth and Hamilton filed for probate. William's will is a large document, depicting an Aladdin's Cave of real estate and other goodies with a wide range of recipients of the treasure. To his old friend, William Wells, publican of the Lord Nelson Hotel (a drinking establishment not far from the Bee Hive), he left 50 guineas (around $3,900) to buy a mourning ring. Another old friend was given 15 guineas to buy a suit. Then we come to the real estate. He left the Bee Hive Inn and two houses adjacent to the pub to his nephew, while his sister, a niece and another nephew were each left a house in Fort-street. A butcher's shop and eight houses in various locations were left to Sarah Horton's sister. He left seven houses (including 34 Lower Fort Street and a row of six dwellings in Argyle Street called Cole's Buildings) to his children. He left another Argyle Street property known as Osborne House and all his other worldly possessions to James Naimby Shuttleworth. Ellen Kennedy received the right to reside with her children in Lower Fort Street. She was to provide for the children until they were 21, from the rental proceeds of Cole's Buildings.

In April of 1857, Shuttleworth's finances were a shambles again and an auction was held to try and recoup some money. It looks like he was overextended in the debt department – 30 acres of land at Pennant Hills, 15 acres at Cook's River (under mortgage), 10 acres of North Shore water frontage (under mortgage) and a staggering 940 acres (under mortgage) at Artarmon was put up for sale. He also had to auction off his legacy from William Cole – Osborne House. This residence was no tumbledown shack – in the early 1850s, it had been occupied by (and probably got its name from) Baronet Sir Samuel

Osborne-Gibbes, former West Indian plantation owner and Provincial Grand Master of the Freemasons of NSW. Sir Samuel was also the uncle of Colonel John Gibbes, the Collector of Customs for the Colony of New South Wales. Shuttleworth was about to lose Osborne House, his other real estate, his boat, furniture, linen, plates and those ever-present 'sundry items'.

On the day of the auction, there was plenty of interest in the properties – but no buyers. The whole shebang, nearly 1,000 acres of choice Sydney real estate, was withdrawn, as the reserve price wasn't met. The reserve price was £2,400 – about $180,000 in today's money. You can only imagine what that price would be today. Two years later, James Naimby Shuttleworth passed away at the age of 42, leaving a wife and three children … and debts. Five months after his passing, an auction was held to sell his law books and an oil painting. They had run out of sundries to flog off. The bottom of the barrel was being scraped.

The 1861 Gipps Ward Assessment book shows that Ellen Kennedy was still living in Lower Fort Street while the rest of Cole's properties were being rented out – 9 Argyle Place (Osborne House) had a tenant who was none other than Mr Henry Parkes. But everything was not as rosy as it seemed. On 26 June of 1861, a classified appeared in the *Sydney Morning Herald*. Richardson and Wrench were under instructions from the mortgagee – the Bee Hive Inn, Cole's Buildings in Argyle-street and the houses in Lower Fort-street were to be sold. The bank had foreclosed on the mortgages. William Cole's two nephews managed to buy some of the properties but a man named Billyard snapped up the rest. The only house that wasn't sold was the one that Ellen and the children were living in. Had they kept the wolf from the door?

A little later, in the 1863 Assessment book, Richardson and Wrench are listed as the owners of the house but there was a different tenant. Ellen Kennedy had apparently been kicked out. What had happened to her? A newspaper article on 26 September 1865, told the story of her demise, after the long battle with just about everything in this world:

'DEATH IN THE STREETS – A woman, known by the names of Ellen Kennedy, Cole and O'Brian [sic], was found in Druitt-street, on Monday morning, suffering from sickness and destitution. The unfortunate creature was removed by the police to the Infirmary, but she expired either on the way or immediately on her admission. An inquest was held before the City Coroner, and the evidence proved that the deceased was a confirmed drunkard, and a woman of immoral life. A son of the deceased stated that her last husband had left her £20 a month and that she had squandered the money in drink, and had reduced herself to wretchedness and beggary. In accordance with the medical evidence, which was fully borne out by that of other witnesses, the jury found that "Deceased, aged 40 years, died from exhaustion brought on by intemperance, exposure and neglect".'[3]

Was it just coincidence that she was found in Druitt Street? That is where the O'Brien family lived after their arrival some 26 years earlier. In her condition, was she searching for some connection with earlier happier times?

In 1867, eleven years after William Cole's death, the NSW Colonial Secretary received a letter from San Francisco, California. A man named John Silas Cole had written, asking for a search of the NSW court records in an endeavour to find a will. He wrote that the will would have been made out by Captain William Henry Thomas Cole, publican of the Bee Hive Inn at The Rocks in Sydney. John Silas Cole stated that once he was a sailor and he had visited Captain Cole at the inn in 1852. He also stated that the captain had been away from his family for some thirty-three years and that he (John Silas) believed that William Cole was his father. Sadly for J.S. Cole, his father's money was all gone by 1867. John Silas Cole appears to have died in San Francisco in 1907. Ironically, research has shown that he also appeared to have had two wives in two different countries.

---

3. *Clarence and Richmond Examiner & New England Advertiser,* 26th September 1865

In 1869, Elizabeth Cole who was John Silas's mother and apparently William's wife, died in the Stepney Union workhouse. She was buried in Little Ilford cemetery in London. It was a pauper's plot – her number is 77992 and she was buried with twelve other people on the day. I've only seen one page of the Interment Register – there were probably more.

In May of 2013, I visited Millers Point and The Rocks to see what remained. The Bee Hive Inn is gone – the street it was on, Prince Street, was buried under the Bradfield Highway. Cole's Buildings still stand, spruced-up and looking nice on the outside, with views over Walsh Bay and bearing million-dollar price tags. Osborne House still stands and has undergone heritage restoration. These buildings have stood for over 150 years – the people they housed are now memories, their lives are stories in a book. I stood in the street where people talked, children played and lives were led. The sound of autumn leaves being blown along the ground is the only noise … but perhaps if you listen closely, very closely … the faint whispering of ghosts can be heard in the wind.

Michael O'Brien

Acknowledgement & Notes

This is not meant to be a scholarly work. I am not a historian. There may be mistakes within and if there are, it is all my fault. Where possible, I have used the original spelling and phraseology from the past eg George-street for George Street. People's surnames have altered over the years, too: the Kingdom family name in this book is referred to as Kingdon sometimes, and Mary O'Sullivan is often listed as Sullivan in historical documents. And do not get me started on the surname of Sorahan. Bloody nightmare.

Researching your family tree is like sitting down to complete a jigsaw puzzle only to find that most of the pieces have been picked up by your baby and scattered all over the house. You will need to open every door, lift every rug and peer into every dark space to find the pieces. It might take you years to find all the pieces and you might not find them all. The pieces you do find will make up a framework of the people that made you what you are. But it's not enough just to have reams of paper with names and dates of births and deaths. Things happened in between those dates – these people were real. What were their lives like?

My ancestors lived in Australia, England, Ireland, Scotland and the USA. In my search for the roots of the family tree, I have 'met' some distant relations that I didn't know I had. But families are like a box of assorted chocolates – you can find hard nuts amongst those softies. Thanks to all those who supplied information, a jolly good story or just a cup of coffee.

The Internet is a sea of information and a cesspool of disinformation. Ancestry.com is a marvellous site and has been very helpful, if you stick to the facts and brush aside certain family member trees that have been created by well-minded people who have no real idea of what they are doing. One person had listed my great-grandmother giving birth to four children – after she died. This is even too much for the *Jerry Springer Show*.

Thanks to the National Library of Australia for creating 'Trove'. I don't know whose idea it was, but I hope you've been knighted.

This book has been written over a number of years. I am sorry that my parents didn't get to see it – they would have enjoyed the idiosyncrasies. And to all those friends who asked – 'How's your book going?' – thanks for asking and keeping me motivated.

SELECT BIBLIOGRAPHY AND SOURCES

Australian Dictionary of Biography
Birmingham, John, *Leviathan,* Vintage, 2000
Curzon, Peter and McCracken, Kevin, *An Australian Perspective of the 1918-19 Influenza Pandemic,* NSW Public Health Bulletin, 2006
Darwin, Charles, *The Voyage of the Beagle,* London, 1839
Dennis, Peter and Grey, Jeffrey and Morris, Ewan and Prior, Robin, *The Oxford Companion to Military History,* Oxford University Press, Melbourne, 1995
Dunn, Judith, *The Parramatta Cemeteries – All Saints and Wesleyan,* Parramatta Historical Society, 2007
Ferry, John, *Colonial Armidale,* University of Queensland Press, 1999
Hoskins, Ian, *Sydney Harbour – A History,* University of NSW Press, 2009
Kohl, Johann Georg, *The British Isles and Their Inhabitants,* Chapman and Hall, London, 1844
Lydon, James, *The Makings of Ireland,* Routledge, London, 1998
Metz, Leon Claire, *Dallas Stoudenmire: El Paso Marshal,* University of Oklahoma Press, 1979
Walter, J. and MacLeod, M., *The Citizen's Bargain: A Documentary History of Australian Views Since 1890,* University of NSW Press

NEWSPAPERS (via Trove)

The Argus
Barrier Miner
Clarence and Richmond Examiner & New England Advertiser
The Hobart Town Gazette and Southern Reporter
Maitland Daily Mercury
Maitland Mercury and Hunter River General Advertiser
The Mercury
The Sun
Sydney Gazette & new South Wales Advertiser
Sydney Monitor
Sydney Morning Herald
Sunday Times

WEBSITES

Ancestry.com
Sydney Town Hall

GOVERNMENT RECORDS

Affidavit to Commissioner of Insolvent Estates, NSW State Archives
House of Representatives Official Hansard
Service Records, Australian War Memorial
Transcripts of Ships Records, State Archives
War Records, National Archives of Australia, and the Red Cross.

www.ingramcontent.com/pod-product-compliance
Lightning Source LLC
Chambersburg PA
CBHW071945110426
42744CB00030B/291